D1345720

ENGLISH CIVIL JUSTICE AFTER THE WOOLF AND JACKSON REFORMS

John Sorabji examines the theoretical underpinnings of the Woolf and Jackson Reforms to the English and Welsh civil justice system. He discusses how the Woolf Reforms attempted, and failed, to effect a revolutionary change to the theory of justice that informed how the system operated. He elucidates the nature of those reforms which, through introducing proportionality via an explicit overriding objective into the Civil Procedure Rules, downgraded the court's historical commitment to achieving substantive justice or justice on the merits. In doing so, Woolf's new theory is compared with one developed by Bentham, while also exploring why a similarly fundamental reform carried out in the 1870s succeeded where Woolf's failed. Finally, he proposes an approach that could be taken by the courts following implementation of the Jackson Reforms to ensure that they succeed in their aim of reducing litigation cost through properly implementing Woolf's new theory of justice.

JOHN SORABJI is a practising barrister and also the current legal secretary to the Master of the Rolls, to whom he provides advice on a wide range of subjects, and specifically the English civil justice system's development. Since 2012 he has taught University College London's LL.M. course on Principles of Civil Justice.

ENGLISH CIVIL JUSTICE AFTER THE WOOLF AND JACKSON REFORMS: A CRITICAL ANALYSIS

JOHN SORABJI

CAMBRIDGE
UNIVERSITY PRESS

CAMBRIDGE
UNIVERSITY PRESS

University Printing House, Cambridge CB2 8BS, United Kingdom

Cambridge University Press is part of the University of Cambridge.

It furthers the University's mission by disseminating knowledge in the pursuit of
education, learning and research at the highest international levels of excellence.

www.cambridge.org
Information on this title: www.cambridge.org/9781107051669

© John Sorabji 2014

First published 2014

Printed in the United Kingdom by Clays, St Ives plc

A catalogue record for this publication is available from the British Library

Library of Congress Cataloguing in Publication data
Sorabji, John, 1972– author.
English civil justice after the Woolf and Jackson reforms : a critical analysis / John Sorabji.
pages cm
ISBN 978-1-107-05166-9 (Hardback)
1. Civil procedure–Great Britain. 2. Woolf, Harry, Sir, 1933– 3. Jackson, Rupert M.
4. Justice, Administration of–Great Britain–History. 5. Constitutional law–Great Britain.
6. Law reform–Great Britain. I. Title.
KD7325.S67 2014
347.42′05–dc23 2013040711

ISBN 978-1-107-05166-9 Hardback

For
Clare and Helena

CONTENTS

FOREWORD

Until the final decades of the last century, civil procedure in this jurisdiction had been almost wholly ignored by legal academics as a serious topic in its own right, and it had been treated by the legal profession as being no more than a boring and unimportant, but unfortunately necessary, adjunct to litigation. Even now, civil procedure is still regarded as very much of an also-ran in the worlds of legal academics and legal practitioners. This is thoroughly unfortunate, because it represents a serious detriment to the legal process, and therefore to the rule of law. On thinking about it, anyone who has practised in the civil courts of this country would acknowledge how vital procedure is to the dispensation of justice – both in itself and taken together with substantive law. Procedural rules and decisions routinely influence, and not infrequently actually determine, the outcome of a dispute; and procedural law can no more be detached from substantive law than style can be divorced from content in a novel.

For that reason alone, a high-quality book on the subject of civil procedure is to be welcomed with enthusiasm by every civil legal academic and practitioner in England and Wales. However, there are other reasons for applauding John Sorabji's book.

First, it is being published at a highly opportune time, when significant alterations in our civil procedure are under way. The Woolf Reforms, introduced some twelve years ago, have had time to bed down, and the Jackson Reforms are about to come on stream. As is explained in this book, although these are generally treated as two separate sets of reforms, they should in fact be treated as closely connected proposals, not least because many of the Jackson Reforms were put forward to cure the shortcomings of the Woolf Reforms. It is invaluable for practitioners and judges to have a book which points out and analyses the deficiencies in the conception and implementation of the Woolf Reforms which, as John Sorabji explains, were 'not an unalloyed success', in that, while they introduced a new theory of justice, they were unable to secure its implementation. It is especially timely to be publishing this book just as the Jackson Reforms are starting to be implemented.

Secondly, this book contains a very useful and important history of past attempts at reform. Unless we understand the history of an institution or system, we will never properly understand the institution or system itself. Furthermore, the experiences of previous attempts to change the rules of court are instructive, if sometimes in a rather depressing sense, to those seeking to introduce or implement further changes.

Thirdly, this book includes an analysis of the purpose of civil proceedings; in particular, this involves identifying and discussing Jeremy Bentham's utilitarian approach, and the change from what John Sorabji calls substantive justice to what he calls proportionate justice. Such an analysis is again vital to an understanding of the whole topic of civil procedure and any changes being made to the court rules. More particularly, by contrasting the intended change of approach embodied in the Woolf proposals with the effect of recent decisions of the Court of Appeal, this book gives much food for thought for advocates and judges involved in cases on procedural issues in coming years.

Fourthly, for those many judges (including the writer of this foreword) who have been referred on an incalculable number of times to CPR rule 1, there is a valuable, original, critical and considered analysis of the overriding objective, and, in particular, of proportionality, and the implications of those concepts.

Fifthly, the book contains very useful guidance on what the Jackson Reforms are intended to achieve and how they may operate, rightly emphasising the 'heavy duty' on the judiciary 'to implement the reforms properly'. It is an important and difficult time to be a judge in the civil courts of England and Wales. The introduction of the Jackson Reforms certainly render the role more important. While the reforms may make the role more difficult for a period, I believe that they will also make it more interesting and rewarding, and, in the longer run, easier.

I can think of nobody with better credentials than John Sorabji to write this important book. He not only has, and for some time has had, a foot firmly in both the academic and the practical camps: he works both at University College London and at the Royal Courts of Justice. But, in addition, his work in both places is and has been largely concerned with civil procedure. Unlike most academics, he has much first-hand experience of civil procedure: having qualified as a barrister, he has advised successive Lord Chief Justices and Masters of the Rolls, and other senior judges on civil procedure (and other legal and constitutional matters), and advised, contributed to, and attended meetings of, the Civil Procedure Rules Committee and the Civil Justice Council, and was one of the main contributors to the *Report on Super-Injunctions* in 2011. As a graduate and fellow at UCL (appropriate for someone who writes about Jeremy Bentham), his experience as a lecturer and teacher in civil procedure, who wrote his doctoral thesis on the topic, John Sorabji also has an academic insight into the topic, a qualification which can be claimed by very few, if any, practitioners.

In short, then, this is a book which I would unhesitatingly recommend to all those concerned with civil litigation, whether as an academic or in practice.

Lord Neuberger of Abbotsbury
September 2013

~

Introduction: civil justice in 2013

Thou shalt not ration justice.[1]

The Woolf Report represented a strong administrative initiative to provide
for a rationed and rational system of judicial resolution of disputes.[2]

This book examines reforms to the English and Welsh civil justice system
carried out following Lord Woolf's Access to Justice Review (1994–96)
(the Woolf Reforms)[3] and Sir Rupert Jackson's Costs Review (2009)
(the Jackson Reforms).[4] It specifically examines the way in which they
have both attempted to reduce litigation cost and delay so that the courts
are better able to carry out their constitutional function of vindicating
and enforcing rights and thereby securing the rule of law.[5] It does so
because both reforms adopted a novel approach to their task; one
that had not been attempted since reforms carried out in the 1870s.
Historically, the civil justice system has been committed to, and reformed

---

[1] L. Hand cited in G. Hazard, 'Rationing Justice' VIII (1965) *The Journal of Law and Economics* 1 at 1.

[2] S. Issacharoff, *Civil Procedure* (3rd edn) (Foundation Press, 2012) at 196.

[3] H. Woolf, *Access to Justice: Interim Report to the Lord Chancellor on the Civil Justice System in England and Wales* (hereinafter H. Woolf (1995)) (HMSO, 1995); H. Woolf, *Access to Justice: Final Report to the Lord Chancellor on the Civil Justice System in England and Wales* (hereinafter H. Woolf (1996)) (HMSO, 1996); H. Woolf, *Access to Justice: Draft Civil Proceedings Rules* (HMSO, 1996).

[4] R. Jackson, *Review of Civil Litigation Costs: Preliminary Report* (May 2009, Vols. I and II) (hereinafter R. Jackson (May 2009)); R. Jackson, *Review of Civil Litigation Costs: Final Report* (The Stationery Office, December 2009) (hereinafter R. Jackson (December 2009)); A. Clarke, 'The Woolf Reforms: A Singular Event or an Ongoing Process?', in D. Dwyer (ed.), *The Civil Procedure Rules Ten Years On* (Oxford University Press, 2009) at 49: '[The Jackson Review] will be a review that is entirely consistent with the approach Woolf advocated in his two reports. It will be so because it will look for answers to the problems of cost consistent with the new approach to litigation Woolf's reforms introduced. That is to say, whatever conclusions it reaches will be ones that are consistent with the overriding objective and the commitment to proportionality to which it gives expression.'

[5] N. Andrews, *Principles of Civil Procedure* (Sweet & Maxwell, 1994) at 21–34ff.

1

consistently with, a specific legal philosophy or theory of justice.[6] That philosophy is one that has embodied a single substantive policy aim, which has variously been referred to as the achievement of justice in the individual case; substantial or real justice; complete justice; a correct decision; rectitude of decision; justice on the merits;[7] or substantive justice.[8] Choice of terminology has changed over time. During the nineteenth century, the two common means of capturing the idea were to refer to the court's role as being to arrive at a decision on the merits or to do complete justice. The twentieth century preferred to refer to courts doing substantive justice or justice on the merits. Despite these terminological differences, the idea they expressed was the same: justice was achieved when an individual claim or dispute concluded with a court judgment that was 'substantively accurate'.[9] A substantively accurate decision was one arrived at through the correct application of true fact to right law, such that when properly acted on it vindicated or enforced legal or equitable rights or obligations. In this book, the term substantive justice is used to express this theory of justice, except where the historical context requires a contemporary term to be used.

The revolutionary change that the Woolf and Jackson Reforms brought about was to reject this traditional theory of justice.[10] Rather than maintain a commitment to that historic approach, rights were to be vindicated through the application of a new theory of justice, similar to one developed by Bentham in the nineteenth century, as well as to one developed by Zuckerman over the last twenty years.[11] This new theory is committed to what has been described as proportionate

---

[6] J. Jolowicz, 'The Woolf Reforms', in Jolowicz, *On Civil Procedure* (Cambridge University Press, 2000) at 387.

[7] See for instance, *Knight* v. *Knight* (1734) 3 P. WMS 331, 334; *Alderson* v. *Temple* (1785) 4 Burr. 2235, 2239; 98 ER 165, 167; *Smith* v. *Baker* (1864) 2 H & M 498; 71 ER 557; *Bruff* v. *Cobbold* (1871–72) LR 7 Ch. App. 217, 219; *Indyka* v. *Indyka* [1967] 1 AC 33 at 66; *Davis* v. *Eli Lilly & Co* [1987] 1 All ER 801 at 804; 149. J. Bentham, 'Rationale of Judicial Evidence', in *The Works of Jeremy Bentham* (ed. Bowring) (Edinburgh, 1843) Vol. VI at 203–4; A. Zuckerman, 'Dismissal for Delay – The Emergence of a New Philosophy of Procedure' 17 *CJQ* (1998) 223, 225; J. Jolowicz, 'Adversarial and Inquisitorial Models of Civil Procedure' 52 (2003) *International Comparative Law Quarterly* 281, 286.

[8] H. Woolf (1995) at 114; H. Genn, *Judging Civil Justice* (Cambridge University Press, 2010) at 14–16.

[9] M. Damaska, *The Faces of Justice and State Authority* (Yale University Press, 1986) at 148; L. Solum, 'Procedural Justice' 78 (2004) *Southern California Law Review* 181, 184–5.

[10] J. Sorabji, 'The Road to New Street Station: fact, fiction and the overriding objective' [2012] *EBLR* 1–77.

[11] See Chapter 2.

justice.[12] Within it, substantive justice is no longer the substantive policy aim. It is one aim amongst others, those being the pursuit of economy, efficiency, expedition, equality and proportionality. Each of these policy aims is intended to support the achievement of a wider public policy aim: the need to ensure that the limited resource allocation by the State to the justice system could be distributed fairly amongst all those who need to call on the State to vindicate and secure the effective enforcement of their rights.[13] Rather than focus on securing individualised justice as the historical approach had, the new theory focused on securing a form of distributive justice.[14] The ultimate consequence of this is that, in contrast to the position that prevailed prior to 1999 when the Woolf Reforms took effect, individuals who seek rights-vindication do so through a 'a rationed and rational system of judicial resolution of disputes'.[15] A limit is now placed on the amount of resources individuals and the State can properly expend on securing substantive justice in any particular case. The limit operates in two ways. In some cases it requires the court to refuse to allow a claim to proceed to judgment. It thus denies substantive justice in its entirety. In other cases – the majority – it restricts the amount of time and money that is spent on litigation. As such, it reduces the court's ability to achieve substantive justice. By limiting, for instance, the nature and extent of evidence placed before the court, the quality of decision-making is necessarily reduced. In both cases, rather than to secure substantive justice, the system is only able to secure proportionate justice.

---

[12] A. Clarke, *The Future of the CPR* (District Judges' Annual Conference, Warwick, 25 June 2009) at [15], 'The CPR simply provide a formal means by which the court as part of its case management role can encourage and facilitate proper settlement. Secondly, by encouraging the greater use of ADR court resources are released to other cases. It increases access to justice for those whose cases cannot settle through assisting those who wish to settle to do so. In this it is entirely consistent with the aim of achieving proportionate justice for all.' Available at <http://www.judiciary.gov.uk/Resources/JCO/Documents/Speeches/mr-dcj-conference-25062009.pdf>; Sorabji, 'The Road to New Street Station' at 89.

[13] H. Woolf (1996) at 24, to 'preserve access to justice for all users of the system it is necessary to ensure that individual users do not use more of the system's resources than their case requires. This means that the court must consider the effect of their choice on other users of the system', as explained by D. Neuberger, 'A New Approach to Justice: From Woolf to Jackson', in G. Meggitt (ed.), *Civil Justice Reform – What has it achieved?* (Sweet & Maxwell, 2010); Sorabji, 'The Road to New Street Station' at 88; J. Dyson, *The Application of the Amendments to the Civil Procedure Rules* (18th Lecture in the Implementation Programme) (22 March 2013) at [18]: 'We have a managed system. That system must be managed for the needs of all litigants.'

[14] S. Fleischacker, *A Short History of Distributive Justice* (Harvard University Press, 2005).

[15] Issacharoff, ibid., at 196.

This limit is necessary because it is the means by which the justice system can properly vindicate rights for the majority of citizens. Rationing does not undermine the provision of justice. It is a necessary condition for it to be effected properly by the State.

In order to explore the nature and effect of this revolutionary change, this book is divided into three substantive parts. Part I explores historical and theoretical issues. Chapter 1 examines the nature and purpose of the civil justice system, the manner in which reform has been attempted in the past and the Woolf and Jackson Reforms' revolutionary nature. Chapter 2 looks at a previous, and eventually successful set of revolutionary reforms, those that took place in the nineteenth century. It does so in order to tease out three important points: that the theory of justice that governed the system's operation from the 1870s was itself the contingent product of revolutionary reform; that it took over fifty years for reform to succeed; and that the theory the reforms implemented sowed the seeds for the problem the Woolf Reforms identified as lying at the heart of excess litigation cost and delay: the subversion of the rules of court from their aim of achieving substantive justice. Chapter 3 is concerned with an examination of Bentham's theory of justice, which is an applied aspect of his broader utilitarian philosophy. This theory was never put into practice. It is examined because the theory the Woolf and Jackson Reforms introduced in many ways is a variation of it. Part II explores the revolutionary nature of the Woolf and Jackson Reforms. It examines how they go beyond the traditional nineteenth-century theory of justice discussed in Chapter 2 and how it adopts the same structure as Bentham's theory. It does so by discussing the centrepiece of the new theory of justice, the introduction of an overarching purposive provision – an explicit overriding objective – into the rules of court. Chapter 4 examines how this provision has been misinterpreted as no more than an expression of the traditional theory of justice. Chapters 5 and 6 provide an exegesis of its proper interpretation. The final part of the book turns to the question of implementation. It is one thing to articulate a new theory of justice; it is another to ensure that it is put into effect. In the nineteenth century it took over fifty years to effect a reform of a similar kind to that which the Woolf Reforms have attempted. Successful implementation takes considerable time and effort. It requires the courts to explain the nature of the new theory, to do so consistently, and to give practical guidance in respect of how it is to operate in practice. If they do not, change does not take place. Following the Woolf Reforms implementation in 1999, the courts failed to take this approach.

If the new theory is to be implemented properly following the introduction of the Jackson Reforms in 2013, the nineteenth-century approach to implementation will need to be adopted. If not, the rationed system of justice the new theory was, and is, intended to introduce will not operate effectively, and the problems that the Woolf Reforms identified, and the Jackson Reforms also sought to remedy, will remain unabated.

Before turning to these issues, two caveats need to be made. This book concentrates on justice in the English and Welsh High Court and Court of Appeal. Justice in the County Courts is not considered. This is for no reason other than that the exposition of the nineteenth-century theory of justice took place within the pre-1873 superior courts of record and then post-1873 through the operation of the Rules of the Supreme Court. It is not suggested that justice in the County Courts was not carried out consistently with the traditional theory of justice. It undoubtedly was. The second caveat concerns the specific procedural reforms recommended by, and then introduced as a consequence of the Woolf and Jackson Reforms. These reforms, such as the reform of discovery, the introduction of case and then costs management and docketing, are considered only in so far as they relate to the operation of the new theory of justice. The book does not provide a detailed critique of individual procedural reforms. It focuses instead on the theory that informed those reforms and how they are to be applied in practice. The Woolf and Jackson Reforms' ultimate success will hinge on the courts' ability to apply case and costs management effectively. That in turn will only be possible if the courts, lawyers and litigants properly understand the purpose for which such management is to be carried out. It is one thing to introduce a managed, a rationed system of justice. The real question is how it is to be managed, how justice is to be rationed and to what purpose. As such, it is 'necessary to start by identifying the enterprise that litigation management involves and what it aims to achieve'.[16] By examining the new theory of justice this book seeks to identify the nature of that enterprise.

---

[16] A. Zuckerman, 'The Challenge of Effective Civil Justice Reform: Effective Court Management of Litigation' 1(1) (2009) *City University of Hong Kong Law Review* 49 at 53.

PART I

Theories of justice

The crisis in civil justice

Every now and again some forlorn and law-wrecked suitors cry aloud about the cost, the delay, the bewildering confusion of our legal system. . . The chief grounds of complaint against the existing system are (1) its cost, (2) its delay, (3) its want of finality.[1]

Civil litigation is in a state of crisis.[2]

1.1 Introduction

This book is about the English and Welsh civil justice system, the institutions, rules and procedures through which substantive civil rights are adjudicated, vindicated and enforced.[3] It assesses its purpose and how that has changed as a consequence of the Woolf and Jackson Reforms.[4] In order to place those reforms in context, this chapter does a number of things. It outlines the justice system's purpose; the problems of litigation complexity, cost and delay that have historically undermined its ability to achieve that purpose, and the reforms that have tried, and continually failed, to cure them; and finally, the Woolf and Jackson Reforms and the claim that they are revolutionary in nature.

1.2 The justice system's purpose

The civil justice system forms part of the judicial branch of the State. It comprises the following:

---

[1] T. Snow, 'The Reform of Legal Administration: An Unauthorised Programme' 8 (1892) *Law Quarterly Review* 129, 129.
[2] C. Glasser, 'Solving the Litigation Crisis' 1 (1994) *The Litigator* 14.
[3] Hereinafter English and England.
[4] H. Woolf (1995) at 211; H. Woolf (1996); R. Jackson (May 2009); R. Jackson (December 2009).

- the County Courts,[5] High Court, Court of Appeal (Civil Division) and the Supreme Court of the United Kingdom;
- the judges appointed to serve in them;
- the procedural or adjective law operative therein;
- civil legal aid, where available;[6] and
- effective enforcement mechanisms.

The civil justice system exists in order to enable individuals, businesses, and local and central government to vindicate and, where necessary, enforce their civil legal rights and obligations, whether those rights are private or public.[7] It exists to ensure that the mere assertions of the civil law are 'translated into binding determinations'.[8] Equally, it provides the basis for individuals to resolve disputes concerning their civil legal rights and obligations consensually through any of various informal and formal means of alternative dispute resolution procedure, as well as the means to enforce consensual resolution.[9] In this way, the system provides a secure framework through which social and economic activity takes place, property rights, civil rights and liberties are secured and government is rendered subject to the due process of law. In delivering justice in this manner, the civil justice system provides a public good by giving life to the rule of law.[10] It does so notwithstanding the fact that the vast majority of civil disputes are settled consensually.[11] It may be true that very few disputes are resolved following litigants having their day in court, but the existence of a readily accessible and effective civil

---

[5] Although see the Crime & Courts Act 2013, s. 17 which, when it comes into force, will merge the County Courts into a single County Court.

[6] See Legal Aid, Sentencing and Punishment of Offenders Act 2012.

[7] *Attorney General* v. *Times Newspapers Ltd* [1974] AC 273, 307; *Bremer Vulkan Schiffbau and Maschinenfabrik* v. *South India Shipping Corp Ltd* [1981] 1 All ER 289, 295.

[8] N. Andrews, *English Civil Procedure* (Oxford University Press, 2003) at 15.

[9] H. Genn, *Judging Civil Justice* (Cambridge University Press, 2010); N. Andrews, *The Three Paths of Justice* (Springer, 2012).

[10] J. Jacob, *The Fabric of English Civil Justice* (Stevens & Co., 1987) at 66, the civil justice system 'provides the effective safeguard against arbitrary, capricious or unprincipled invasion or denial of the legal rights of any person, and it takes on the character of a protective shield to prevent any person being deprived of or suffering any loss of his rights except by due process of law'; Genn, *Judging Civil Justice* at 1–12.

[11] F. Sander, 'Varieties of Dispute Processing' 70 (1976) *Federal Rules Decisions* 111; L. Hoffmann, 'Changing Perspectives on Civil Litigation' 56 (1993) *Modern Law Review* 297; C. Menkel-Meadow et al., *Dispute Resolution: Beyond the Adversarial Model* (Aspen Publishers, 2011).

justice system forms the necessary condition on which consensual settlement rests.[12]

The question then arises how the civil justice system provides the public good of securing the rule of law. There is, of course, any number of ways in which the system could be constructed and operated so as to do justice. No two civil justice systems are entirely alike. They differ in court structure, judicial personnel and administrative processes. Some, like the Anglo-American systems, adopt an adversarial or accusatorial process, others an inquisitorial one.[13] Irrespective of such differences, any civil justice system if it is to secure the public benefit that arises from the effective vindication of civil rights, will have to do two things. It will have to be capable of producing substantively correct results and a fair process. If it is to enable litigants to receive 'what is legally due to them', it will have to be capable of determining right fact, including providing the means by which probative evidence is gathered and tested, and applying it to right law to produce, in so far as that is possible, a correct or accurate decision.[14] It will need to do so through the application of a fair process. Such a process will not only have to be capable of producing substantively correct results, it will itself have to be substantively just. As such, it will, for instance, have to be properly accessible to all those who need to use it. Its rules will have to be clear, reasonably straightforward, cost-effective. It will need to be sufficiently efficient such that both adjudication and enforcement are achieved at a time when they are of practical value: where necessary, financial support for the impecunious should be available. Its processes will also have to be open to public scrutiny and applied fairly by an impartial and independent judiciary. Court processes that are too slow, too expensive, inherently unfair, applied in an unequal, arbitrary or biased manner to individual litigants or classes of litigant, or that are not open to public scrutiny, will in and of themselves tend to undermine both public confidence in the system and

---

[12] D. Neuberger, *Equity, ADR, Arbitration and the Law: different dimensions of justice* (4th Annual Keating Lecture, 19 May 2010) <http://www.judiciary.gov.uk/Resources/JCO/Documents/Speeches/mr-keating-lecture-19052010.pdf>.

[13] For a discussion, see Damaska, *The Faces of Justice and State Authority*.

[14] A. Zuckerman, 'Justice in Crisis: Comparative Dimensions of Civil Procedure', in A. Zuckerman (ed.), *Civil Justice in Crisis: Comparative Perspectives of Civil Procedure* (Oxford University Press, 1999) at 3ff; A. Zuckerman, 'Quality and Economy in Civil Procedure: The Case for Commuting Correct Judgments for Timely Judgments' 14 (1994) *Oxford Journal of Legal Studies* 353, 354

the rule of law, but equally will do so through undermining the justice system's ability to secure substantively accurate decisions. Fair process and just result go hand in hand.

1.3   The problem of complexity, cost and delay

The English civil justice system since the 1980s has been subject to the criticism that it is unable to deliver justice; that it is in 'a state of crisis'[15] caused by excessive litigation cost and delay.[16] Such cost and delay renders access to the justice system the preserve of the wealthy few. It undermines the system's ability to secure justice for all members of society. Equally, it undermines its ability to do so for those who can afford to access it. Unreasonable delay denudes evidence of its probative value, thus increasing the possibility of adjudicative error.[17] It can also lead to an inequality of arms between litigants, frustrating attempts to secure both a substantively just process as well as the achievement of a substantively just result.

1.3.1   A short history of failed reform

Complaints concerning litigation's cost and delays are not, however, simply a feature of the last thirty years. They have been a commonplace since the Middle Ages. They formed part of the background to Magna Carta (1215).[18] They recurred in the thirteenth and fourteenth centuries.[19] Further sporadic reform was then attempted until the beginning of

---

[15] Glasser, 'Solving the Litigation Crisis' at 14. Such criticisms and crises are not unique to England, but are a common feature of all other civil justice systems: see Zuckerman (ed.), *Civil Justice in Crisis*.

[16] As noted by R. Pound, 'The Causes of Popular Dissatisfaction with the Administration of Justice' 40 (1906) *American Law Review* at 729: '(d)issatisfaction with the administration of justice is as old as law'.

[17] A. Zuckerman, *Zuckerman on Civil Procedure: Principles of Practice* (2nd edn) (Thomson, 2006) at 11.

[18] A. Clarke, 'The Woolf Reforms: A Singular Event or an Ongoing Process?', in D. Dwyer (ed.), *The Civil Procedure Rules 10 Years On* (Oxford University Press, 2009); Magna Carta (1215) Chapters 17 and 40; W. McKechnie, *Magna Carta* (2nd edn) (Maclehose & Sons, 1912) at 262ff and 395ff; S. Milsom, *Historical Foundations of the Common Law* (Butterworths, 1981) at 35.

[19] E. Jenks, 'Edward I, the English Justinian', in *Select Essays in Anglo-American Legal History* (Little, Brown & Company, 1907, 1992 reprint) Vol. I at 148; Commands in Delay of Justice Act 1328 (2 Edw. III c.8).

the nineteenth century,[20] when a series of reforming Commissions were appointed from the 1820s to the 1870s.[21] The Commissions all had the same aim: to make recommendations to 'render proceedings shorter, cheaper and more certain' so that the justice system was better able to achieve substantive justice.[22] To achieve their aim, they effected a number of incremental structural and procedural reforms. For instance, they generated the restructuring of the county courts; a minor increase in the number of judges; changes to judicial salaries and court funding; and reforms intended to simplify civil procedure.[23] The various Commissions failed to achieve their collective aim. Complexity, cost and delay remained endemic. In order to finally tackle the problems, in 1867, the Judicature Commission was appointed. It had a wider remit than the previous Commissions. It was required to consider fundamental reform. The incremental approach had been tried and had failed. A more radical approach that called into question the justice system's fundamental structure and approach was required, and was recommended. The

[20] E.g., *Short Apology for the Common Law, with Proposals for Removing the Expence and Delay of Equity Proceedings* (1731) cited in W. Holdsworth, 'Blackstone's Treatment of Equity' 43 (1929) *Harvard Law Review* 1, 2; The Report by the Commissioners into the Practice of the Court of Chancery (No. 143) (1826) at 7 and 35ff; E. Sunderland, 'Expert Control of Legal Procedure through Rules of Court' 13 (1927) *American Bar Association Journal* 2, 2; J. Getzler, 'Chancery Reform and Law Reform' 22 (2004) *Law & History Review* 601, 606; M. Lobban, 'Preparing for Fusion: Reforming the Nineteenth-Century Court of Chancery, Part I' 22 (2004) *Law & History Review* 389, 409ff.

[21] Unattributed articles, 'A Plea for New Legal Procedure' (11) *Law Review & Quarterly Journal of British and Foreign Jurisprudence*, November 1849–February 1850, 233 and 'Special Pleading Reform' (12) *Law Review & Quarterly Journal of British and Foreign Jurisprudence*, May–August 1850, 27; E. Sunderland, 'The English Struggle for Procedural Reform' 29 (1925) *Harvard Law Review* 725, 728ff; H. Holland, 'Jeremy Bentham' 10 (1950) *Cambridge Law Journal* 3, 22; W. Odgers, 'Changes in Procedure and in the Law of Evidence', in *A Century of Law Reform* (Macmillan & Co, 1901).

[22] C. Bowen, 'Progress in the Administration of Justice during the Victorian Period', in ibid. at 516ff; H. Street, *Justice in the Welfare State* (Stevens & Sons, 1968) at 5; J. Jolowicz, '"General Ideas" and the reform of civil procedure' [1983] *Legal Studies* 295, 296; Second Report of the Common Law Commissioners into the Practice and Proceedings of the Superior Courts of Common Law (House of Commons, 1830) Appendix B 46 and 56–57.

[23] E.g., The Uniformity of Process Act 1832; The Court of Chancery Act 1841; The County Courts (England) Act 1846; The Court of Chancery Act 1850; The Chancery Amendment Acts 1850; The Court of Chancery Act 1851; The Common Law Procedure Act 1852; The Court of Chancery Act 1852; The Chancery Amendment Acts 1852; The Common Law Courts Act 1852; The Common Law Amendment Act 1852; The Common Law Amendment Act 1854; The Common Law Procedure Act 1854; The Chancery Amendment Acts 1858; The Chancery Amendment Acts 1860; The Chancery Rules and Orders Act 1860; The Common Law Amendment Act 1860.

Commission, unlike its predecessors, each of which aimed to introduce reforms that worked within the existing parameters of the justice system –i.e. its court structure, the nature of procedure – identified those parameters as the source of the centuries-old problem. Previous reform had failed because it accepted those parameters when, in fact, they were the cause of the problems and consequently the cause of the failure of each of the reforms introduced from 1820 to 1870.

The main problem the Judicature Commission identified as under-pinning the nineteenth-century's crisis in civil justice was the existence of separate civil justice systems.[24] English civil justice since its early medieval origins, had been essentially binary in nature. Common law rights and obligations were the province of the common law courts, particularly the Courts of Common Pleas, of King's or Queen's Bench and of Exchequer. Equitable rights, obligations and remedies were the province of the equity courts, particularly the High Court of Chancery.[25] Previous reform had accepted the binary nature of the system as a given. Reform operated, and failed, within the framework it provided. The Judicature Commission drew what might have been thought to be the obvious conclusion and rejected the status quo. The binary system had to go. Its proposed solution was both structural and procedural. Structurally, it recommended that all England's civil courts should be merged and that a new single, superior court should have the jurisdiction of all its statutory predecessors.[26] Its recommendations, in nearly all respects, were enacted in the Judicature Acts 1873–75. Procedurally, it recommended the creation of either new procedural rules or a new code of procedure for the new Supreme Court.[27] The latter option was implemented, and the new procedural code, the Rules of the Supreme Court (or RSC), formed part of the

---

[24] The First Report of the Royal Commission to inquire into the Operation and Consti-tution of the High Court of Chancery, Courts of Common Law, Central Criminal Court, High Court of Admiralty, and other Courts in England, and into the Operation and Effect of the Present Separation and Division of Jurisdiction between the Courts (No. 4130; 1868–69) (The First Judicature Report) at 5–9.

[25] For an outline, see Milsom, *Historical Foundations of the Common Law*.

[26] The First Judicature Report at 5–7, 9 and 25; The Second Report of the Royal Commis-sion to inquire into the Operation and Constitution of the High Court of Chancery, Courts of Common Law, Central Criminal Court, High Court of Admiralty, and other Courts in England, and into the Operation and Effect of the Present Separation and Division of Jurisdiction between the Courts (C 631; 1872) (The Second Judicature Report); Judicature Act 1873, ss. 3 and 24.

[27] The First Judicature Report at 6–10; Judicature Act 1873 ss. 3, 5 and 6.

Judicature Act 1873.[28] It was vastly simpler than previous rules of court. It incorporated the most efficient and effective procedural devices of the common law and equity systems while also incorporating new and improved mechanisms of its own, e.g. a simplified pleading process, a summary judgment process, reform of the means to obtain witness evidence, greater judicial discretion regarding litigation process, and time limits to appeal.[29] It would, importantly, have a clear aim. Rather than operate in the manner previous common law procedure had, it would operate according to the terms of the theory of justice that previously governed equity proceedings. It would operate so as, in the terms of the time, to achieve complete justice, i.e. substantive justice.[30] Finally, it was believed, the problems of 'the intolerable evil'[31] of complexity, cost and delay would be cured.[32]

Within twenty years the intolerable evils had reasserted themselves.[33] The courts might have embraced the new theory of justice, but in the process of doing so the RSC had itself become increasingly complex, succumbed to delay and produced a 20 per cent increase in litigation cost.[34] Fundamental reform had failed. As the nineteenth century passed

---

[28] The RSC was initially a Schedule to the Judicature Act 1873. It was reissued four times: Schedule 1 of the Supreme Court of Judicature Act 1875; SI unnumbered of 1883; SI 2145 of 1962; SI 1776 of 1965, and amended on an annual basis. County Courts remained separate from the High Court and were governed procedurally by the County Court Rules (CCR) (SI 1687/1981), made pursuant to County Court Act 1975 s. 75 and its statutory predecessors during the period after 1873 and up to 1999.

[29] The First Judicature Report at 10–24; F. W. Maitland, *Equity: a course of lectures* (Cambridge, 1909, 2011 reprint) at 16; the new rules contained in the RSC were 'supposed to combine all the best features of the two old systems, the system of the common law, and the system of equity'.

[30] See Chapter 2.

[31] H. Lurton, 'The Operation of the Reformed Equity Procedure in England' 26 (1912) *Harvard Law Review* 99, 99–101.

[32] 141 (1875) *Edinburgh Review* 179, 179–80, cited in A. Manchester, *Modern Legal History* (Butterworths, 1980) at 149: 'The Judicature Act crowns the edifice of legal improvement, which has been slowly built up since the beginning of the century.'

[33] Snow, 'The Reform of Legal Administration: An Unauthorised Programme' 129: 'Every now and again some forlorn and law-wrecked suitors cry aloud about the cost, the delay, the bewildering confusion of our legal system... The chief grounds of complaint against the existing system are (1) its cost, (2) its delay, (3) its want of finality'; H. Humphrey, 'The Judges' Report on Practice from a Chancery Point of View' 8 (1892) *Law Quarterly Review* 289, 289.

[34] 1851 Report at 30; Holdsworth (1921–23); Bowen LJ cited in *Aon Risk Services Australia Ltd* v. *Australian National University* [2009] HCA 27 at [21]; C. Bowen, 'The Law Courts under the Judicature Acts' 2 (1886) *Law Quarterly Review* 1, 8; S. Rosenbaum, 'Studies in English Civil Procedure II: The Rule-Making Authority VI' 63 (1915) *University of Pennsylvania Law Review* 273, 291.

and the twentieth began, civil justice remained in crisis. That it did following reforms that promised to put an end to the problems made it all the more galling. As Humphrey put it:

> There has never been a time when the law has not been abused for its delay and its costliness. Of late years the complaint against it has increased, all the more so because the belief prevailed that by the Judicature Acts the old evils had been swept away and a better state of things introduced.[35]

In order to rectify the problems inherited from the 1870 reforms, the first four decades of the twentieth century concentrated primarily on structural reform.[36] In 1908, the Gorell Committee examined the relationship between the High and County Courts.[37] In 1913 and 1922, the St Aldwyn and the Swift Committees examined delays in the High Court.[38] Ten years later the Hanworth and Peel Commissions were appointed. The former was specifically required to make recommendations to secure 'greater expedition in the dispatch of business, or greater economy in the administration of justice'.[39] Its central findings were that the post-1870 court structure was inadequate and the RSC had become too complex.[40] Once more, structural and procedural reform was recommended, which it was hoped would ensure the justice system could finally secure substantive justice whilst minimising cost and delay.[41] The latter Commission was required to focus its work on improving the High Court, King's Bench Division's efficiency.[42]

---

[35] Humphrey, 'The Judges' Report on Practice from a Chancery Point of View'.

[36] Jolowicz, '"General Ideas" and procedural reform', in Jolowicz, *On Civil Procedure* at 355–9.

[37] The Report of the County Courts Committee 1909.

[38] Royal Commission on Delay in the King's Bench Division (Cmd 6761, 1913; Cmd 7177, 1914); The Committee on County Court Procedure.

[39] Royal Commission on the Business of the Courts Committee (Cmd 4265, 1933; Cmd 4471, 1933; Cmd 5066, 1936). See its 1st Interim Report (Cmd 4265, 1933) at 3.

[40] A complaint that would be reiterated in 1953 in the 2nd Interim Evershed Report (Cmd 8176, 1953) at 705, when the then *Annual Practice* was 3,800 pages; again in 1999 by Lord Woolf MR in H. Woolf (1995) at 211; H. Woolf (1996) at 272; and, in 2010, by Lord Neuberger MR in D. Neuberger, 'A New Approach to Civil Justice: from Woolf to Jackson', in *Civil Justice Reform – What has it achieved?* (G. Meggitt ed.) (Sweet & Maxwell, 2010) 11, 17.

[41] W. Odgers in ibid. at 9–10, 15–16, 20–1.

[42] Report of the Royal Commission on the Despatch of Business at Common Law (Cmd 5065, 1936), esp. 11–12, 33ff, 79, 103–6; W. Odgers, *The Principles of Pleading and Practice in Civil Actions in the High Court of Justice* (Stevens & Sons, 1912) at 67–71.

Neither the Hanworth nor Peel Commissions managed to cure the problem that, as the latter put it in a piece of decided understatement, had been the subject of complaint 'for at least a generation'.[43] Just as their predecessors failed to produce lasting improvement, they, too, failed. With the conclusion of the Second World War, the reform process recommenced. In 1947, Sir Raymond Evershed (later Lord Evershed MR) was appointed to chair a Committee to conduct the most wide-ranging review of the justice system's operation since the Judicature Commission.[44] For the first time since its creation in 1873, the justice system as a whole was to be subject to scrutiny. The Committee was to assess whether and how the civil justice system could be reformed, structurally or as far as procedure was concerned, by 'legislation or otherwise, for the purpose of reducing the cost of litigation and securing greater efficiency and expedition in the despatch of business'.[45] In carrying out this examination, the Committee, in its own piece of sublime understatement, noted that delay and cost were difficult problems to remedy. It particularly noted how excess litigation cost 'was a very difficult question' and one that put justice out of the 'average litigant['s]' reach.[46] It went on to comment how it was 'remarkable to observe . . . in reading the Reports of earlier Committees, that notwithstanding the many changes which have occurred . . ., the difficulties encountered in arranging for the efficient despatch of business and the remedies have varied little'.[47] The problems of complexity, cost and delay were endemic. Far-reaching reform was thus necessary.[48]

Six years, three Interim Reports and a Final Report later, genuinely far-reaching reform, bar one exception, was not recommended.[49] Unlike its Victorian predecessor, the Evershed Committee avoided fundamental questions or issues of principle. Whether the commitment to an adversarial process should be abandoned in favour of an inquisitorial approach

---

[43] Cmd 5065, 1936 at 109.

[44] The Committee on Supreme Court Practice and Procedure (First, Second and Third Interim Reports, Cmd 7764, 1949; Cmd 8176, 1951; Cmd 8167, 1951, respectively) and The Final Report (Cmd 8878, 1953).

[45] Cmd 7764, 1949 at 4.   [46] Cmd 8878, 1953 at 11.   [47] Cmd 7764, 1949 at 19.

[48] Ibid. at 5.

[49] Cmd 8878, 1953 at 319–42; C. Clark, 'The Evershed Report and Civil Procedural Reform' 29 (1954) *New York University Law Review* 1046; C. H. van Rhee, 'English Civil Procedure and the Civil Procedure Rules (1998)' in C. H. van Rhee (ed.), *European Traditions in Civil Procedure* (Intersentia, 2005) at 152ff.

was, for instance, dismissed out of hand.[50] Whether the two branches of the legal profession should be fused in order to reduce litigation cost was taken to be outside the ambit of the terms of reference and side-stepped safely.[51] Notwithstanding the fact that the indemnity rule was arguably a source of 'extravagant' litigation cost, it was to remain as it was.[52] Its recommendations remained firmly in the tradition of its twentieth-century predecessors and were met with a mixture of disappointment and relief.[53] Structural and procedural reform was recommended.[54] The centrepiece of the Committee's recommendations was, however, neither structural nor strictly procedural: it was cultural. The Committee, as the Woolf Review would do over fifty years later,[55] called for a 'new approach' to litigation to take hold. This was to cure the problem of cost and delay.[56] Unfortunately, the new approach was nothing more than the old approach. Its focal point was the proposal that a more robust approach to the control of litigation had to be taken by the courts, albeit no power was provided for them actively to manage litigation. Party-controlled case management was to be carried out through a more robust use of existing procedural rules.[57] Lawyers, and litigants, were to bring about effective reform. Faith in a new robust party-management of proceedings was, unsurprisingly, misplaced.[58] Lawyers' working practices did not change and Evershed's new approach to litigation was 'a dead letter'.[59]

The Evershed Committee and its reports, despite their best intentions, and their desire to introduce a new approach to civil justice, ultimately produced more of the same: no real change.[60] It continued to place its faith in the belief that all that was truly needed to ensure the justice system was better able to do substantive justice as economically and efficiently as possible was to ensure that litigants and their lawyers managed litigation to that purpose. Unlike the Judicature Commission,

---

[50] Cmd 8878, 1953 at 12.   [51] Ibid. at 11–13, and see 314–18.

[52] Ibid. at 337.

[53] L. Gower, 'The Cost of Litigation: Reflections on the Evershed Report' 19 (1954) *Modern Law Review*.

[54] D. Llewelyn Davies, 'The English New Procedure' [1933] *Yale Law Journal* 377; J. Jacob, 'The Rules of the Supreme Court (Revision) 1965', *The Legal Executive* (1966) at 167, cited in van Rhee (ed.), *European Traditions in Civil Procedure* at 154–7.

[55] Cmd 8878, 1953 at 9–10, 319.   [56] Ibid. at 9.

[57] Ibid. at 70–7; Diamond, 'The Summons for Directions', 44; M. Zander, 'What can be Done about Cost and Delay in Civil Litigation?' 31 (1997) *Israel Law Review* 703, 706.

[58] Diamond, 'The Summons for Directions' at 51.

[59] Ibid. at 44.   [60] Cmd 8878, 1953 at 319ff.

it did not approach reform on the basis that all previous reform had failed because it had shared a common, even if unspoken, assumption. It did not question, as that Commission had, the justice system's framework and recommend a change in the theory of justice according to which the system operated. It simply approached reform on the same basis as its immediate predecessors: reform was to be considered within established parameters, which for the twentieth century were those set by the Judicature Commission and the Judicature Acts. Established parameters produced traditional reform recommendations, which in turn produced no lasting improvement. The crisis first considered in the 1820s continued.

Further reform followed in the 1960s and 1970s via the Winn Committee[61] (1968) and Cantley Committee[62] (1979). Both of these Committees focused on delay in the disposal of personal injury actions.[63] Both reports again looked at procedural reform. As might have been expected in the light of past experience, neither Winn nor Cantley produced any significant or permanent improvements. Following a further discrete review into the operation of the High Court's Chancery Division in 1981, significant reform was once again considered at the turn of the 1980s with the appointment of the Civil Justice Review (1988).[64] This was to be the most far-reaching review since that conducted by the Evershed Committee. Its task, as it had been of all past reformers, was to:

> ... improve the machinery of civil justice in England and Wales by means of reforms in jurisdiction, procedure and court administration and in particular to reduce delay, cost and complexity.[65]

Structural and procedural reform remained the order of the day. To that end, it made ninety-one reform recommendations, including the abolition of the County Court jurisdiction's upper limit in order to ease pressure on the High Court; an increase in the small claims limit (or as it was then called, the general trial jurisdiction of County Court

---

[61] Report of the Committee on Personal Injury Litigation (Cmd 369, 1968).

[62] Report of the Personal Injuries Litigation Procedure Working Party (Cmd 7476, 1979).

[63] The Report of the Royal Commission on Assizes and Quarter Sessions (Cmd 4153, 1969) (the Beeching Review) also considered some issues concerning the operation of the civil justice system in the context of a wider review of Assizes and Quarter Sessions.

[64] The Report of the Review Body of the Chancery Division of the High Court (Cmd 8205, 1981).

[65] The Report of the Review Body on Civil Justice (Cmd 394, 1988) at 1 and 2; National Consumer Council, *Ordinary Justice, Legal Services and the Courts in England and Wales: A Consumer View* (HMSO, 1989) at 258ff; R. Thomas, 'Civil Justice Review – Treating Litigants as Consumers' *CJQ* 9 (1990) 51.

registrars); the introduction, subject to some exceptions, of a County Court power to grant injunctive relief; the introduction, for the first time, of a move away from the strict adversarial approach to civil litigation that had hitherto pertained, through the introduction of a 'cards on the table' approach to litigation by parties[66] and active court-controlled case management, which if implemented, would, for the first time, replace party-controlled case management; standard directions in all courts; and the introduction of a common core set of procedural rules for the County and High Courts.[67] The vast majority of its proposals were implemented through the Courts and Legal Services Act 1990. The exhortation to adopt a 'cards on the table' approach to litigation, where parties shared information prior to trial, was introduced in 1992.[68] Active case management and a core set of rules would have to wait. At the time the Civil Justice Review's recommendations were introduced it was said that they marked 'a great leap forward, designed to improve the administration of civil justice which in turn improves the access to justice for those that need it';[69] one that was no less than

> a landmark in the on-going history of English civil procedure. Indeed, it may be claimed that the changes effected ... are more profound and extensive than any made since the Judicature Acts of 1873 and 1875.[70]

Initially, the reforms yielded a degree of improvement. It only took a short while, however, before it was all too readily apparent that the problems of complexity, cost and delay remained as acute as ever. Just as their many predecessors had done before them, the Civil Justice Review reforms failed to produce any real improvement.[71] Within four years of being lauded as a great leap forward, three further reports would be published recommending fundamental reform to the system: the Heilbron–Hodge Report in 1993;[72] the Interim and Final Access to Justice Reports in 1995 and 1996 (the Woolf Reports);[73] and the

---

[66] A recommendation foreshadowed by the Winn Report (Cmd 369, 1968): see M. Zander, 'What can be Done about Cost and Delay in Civil Litigation?' at 707.
[67] Cmd 394, 1988 at 154–62.   [68] Practice Direction [1992] 1 All ER 385.
[69] J. Jacob (ed.), *Supreme Court Practice Vol. I* (Sweet & Maxwell, 1993) at vii.
[70] Jacob ibid.
[71] Ibid. at 8; N. Andrews, 'The Adversarial Principle: Fairness and Efficiency: Reflections on the Recommendations of the Woolf Report', in A. Zuckerman and R. Cranston (eds), *Reform of Civil Procedure: Essays on 'Access to Justice'* (Clarendon Press, 1995).
[72] H. Heilbron and H. Hodge, *Civil Justice on Trial – A Case for Change*, Joint Report of The Bar Council and Law Society (1993).
[73] H. Woolf (1995); H. Woolf (1996).

Middleton Report in 1997.[74] As the twentieth century approached its end, for England – as for the rest of the world – the problems of litigation complexity, cost and delay continued unabated.[75] The civil justice system remained, in Glasser's famous phrase, in a 'state of crisis';[76] a crisis that would not, as he suggested, simply be cured by one more two-year study of civil litigation.[77]

1.3.2   Internal and external questions

Two centuries of reform had left England's civil justice system, by the early 1990s, in an increasingly unsatisfactory condition. Complexity, cost and delay were as intractable a triumvirate as they had ever been.[78] To a significant degree this was inevitable; a certain degree of reform in the light of changing needs and circumstances will always be necessary. If the Judicature Acts had rendered the justice system perfect, they would have done so in terms of the needs of society at the time. Society is not static. Structures inevitably become outdated as it evolves. Where this occurs, as it had in the late eighteenth and early nineteenth centuries, pre-existing structures that become unable to cope with the changing nature and volume of litigation will have to change.[79] The same is true of procedure, which may stand in need of reform in order to deal with changing circumstance or because it becomes inefficient or ineffective over time through misuse or abuse. Such reforms are not just inevitable; they are inescapably time-limited in so far as their benefits are concerned. They have in-built obsolescence. They succeed, where they do succeed,

---

[74] P. Middleton, *Report to the Lord Chancellor* (HMSO, 1997).

[75] For a discussion of the worldwide crisis, see Zuckerman (ed.), *Civil Justice in Crisis*; and see, for instance, Review of the Civil Justice System in Northern Ireland (Northern Ireland Court Service, 2000); Effective and Affordable Justice – Report of the Civil Justice Reform Group Working Party (British Columbia Review Task Force, 2006); Civil Justice Reform Project: Summary of Findings & Recommendations (Attorney General's Office, Ontario, Canada); Civil Justice Reform Final Report (Chief Justice's Working Party on Civil Justice Reform, Hong Kong Special Administrative Region, People's Republic of China, 2004); Scottish Civil Courts Review: A Consultation Paper (Scottish Civil Courts Review, 2007); Civil Justice Review Report (Victorian Law Commission Report, Victoria, Australia, 2008).

[76] Glasser, 'Solving the Litigation Crisis' at 14.   [77] Ibid. at 21.

[78] M. Zander, 'Why Woolf's Reforms Should be Rejected', in Zuckerman and Cranston (eds), *Reform of Civil Procedure.*

[79] Lobban, 'Preparing for Fusion: Reforming the Nineteenth-Century Court of Chancery, Part I'; M. Lobban, 'Preparing for Fusion: Reforming the Nineteenth-Century Court of Chancery, Part II' 22 (2004) *Law & History Review* 565, 566ff; Cmd 4265, 1933 at 10ff; Cmd 5065, 1936 at 58ff.

because they make the system fit for the times and, where necessary, eliminating less-than-optimal practices. Times change, faulty practices return and further perennial reform is needed. Every justice system cannot but be subject to such regular reform; it is inescapable.

There was, however, a second reason why the problems of complexity, cost and delay were still endemic during the twentieth century. Reform had been approached on a false basis. If the justice system were a scientific one, two centuries of continued resistance to reform would have led some practitioners to raise the question whether it had reached the point that Ptolemaic astronomy had reached by the fifteenth century. By that time it had ceased to provide an explanation for newly discovered astronomical phenomena through the normal application of its established general principles.[80] In his analysis of scientific systems that had reached this stage, Kuhn describes how, where it becomes apparent over time that any

> normal problem, ... [which] ought to be solvable by known rules and procedures, resists the reiterated onslaught of the ablest members of the group within whose competence it falls ... [and] normal science repeatedly goes astray... [then] ... the profession can no longer evade anomalies that subvert the existing tradition of scientific practice ... [It is then that] ... extraordinary investigations [begin] that lead the profession at last to a new set of commitments, a new basis for the practice of science.[81]

Ptolemaic astronomy's failure to answer normal problems by known rules led to the emergence of Copernicus' extraordinary investigation of its fundamental principles. He did not seek an answer to astronomy's problems by an application of its known rules. He did not attempt a traditional form of reform. He proposed that its problems would only be resolved through a study of the paradigm's basic structural assumptions, by engaging in an extraordinary investigation that famously gave rise to the rejection of the Ptolemaic system's central premise, the belief in the stationary Earth, in favour of heliocentrism. It brought about the replacement of one set of assumptions and fundamental principles underpinning the science with new ones.[82] A new scientific paradigm was born, and thereafter, normal science could resume, underpinned by the new principles. Kuhn's insight was the recognition, by those such as Copernicus, that where normal science was no longer able to solve

---

[80] T. Kuhn, *The Structure of Scientific Revolutions* (3rd edn) (University of Chicago Press, 1996) at 68ff.
[81] Ibid. at 5–6 and 84.   [82] Ibid. at 6, 12ff and 82ff.

scientific problems there was a need to search for and implement a new form of science with new assumptions and aims. Normal science had to be recognised as being incapable of resolving problems that it ought to have been expected to resolve through the application of its accepted assumptions, principles and practices. Once such recognition arose, the first step could then be taken towards the conduct of an extraordinary investigation. Once that step had been taken, the journey towards a full-blooded scientific revolution or paradigm shift had begun.[83]

In order to draw out the distinction between normal science and extraordinary investigations, a further distinction needs to be drawn between two different types of question reformers can ask: internal and external. Internal questions arise within an established framework. They assume a problem arises within the framework; they are the hallmark of normal science. External questions arise in respect of the established framework; they are the hallmark of extraordinary investigations, as they challenge its underlying assumptions.[84] There are two types of internal and external questions: those that correctly and those that incorrectly identify the source of the problem. In the first instance, the proposed reform could cure a problem, albeit that is not guaranteed. If the problem is an internal one and is identified as such, the proposed solution may or may not work. If it is an external one, however, and is wrongly identified as an internal one, and vice versa, the proposed solution cannot possibly work. It cannot work because the problem has been misidentified. Problems of complexity, cost and delay could arise as internal ones. They would thus be capable, in principle, of being cured by internal solutions. If the problem of complexity simply stemmed from the way in which procedural rules had been drafted, then the answer would be to revise the rules. An internal question would need to be asked. If, however, the source of the problem lay in the framework itself, asking internal questions could produce no real solution. The problem would be intractable. If the problems of excess complexity, cost and delay were caused by problems arising within the terms of the established framework and were properly identifiable as internal questions or issues, there was no reason in principle, setting to one side perennial reform, why either the Judicature Commission or one of its successors, as exercises in normal science, could not have supplied a complete answer. If they were problems that

[83] Ibid. at 67–9.
[84] R. Carnap, 'Empiricism, Semantics and Ontology', in R. Carnap, *Meaning and Necessity* (2nd edn) (University of Chicago Press, 1956) at 205ff.

arose from the established framework, asking internal questions would render reform's failure inevitable.

Throughout the twentieth century there was no acknowledgement that the fact that civil justice reform was 'the subject that refuses to go away' might have been due to the fact that it focused on internal questions and did so because it treated complexity, cost and delay as problems of normal science.[85] Reform's continuing failure ought to have suggested that, at the least, some external questions needed to be asked, even if they were ultimately shown to be unnecessary. In Kuhn's terms, civil justice reform during the twentieth century was an object lesson in how to evade the intractable problems of normal science in a failed paradigm by failing to embark on a necessary extraordinary investigation that challenged the system's framework. The Ptolemaic system in the fifteenth century, faced with its many intractable problems, had a choice: either accept that they were incapable of resolution through normal means or that they could only be resolved or, more accurately, dissolved, through examining and reforming the system's basic principles. Genuine reformers embraced the second of the two. Given civil justice reform's repeated failures over the course of the twentieth century, brought into sharp relief by the failure of the Civil Justice Review's failed great leap forward, the time had surely come for it to face the same choice. Did it ask the same internal questions once more or did it engage in an extraordinary investigation?[86] The Woolf Reforms could have taken the tried and tested approach and simply focused on examining the justice system to ascertain which aspects of its structure, procedure and their operation were responsible for the continuing problems of complexity, cost and delay. They could have concluded that the problems were capable of resolution but that the Civil Justice Review, for all its breadth, had not gone far enough in this traditional pattern of reform and that all that was needed was 'one more push' and success would be achieved. However, just as the Judicature Commission, by questioning the structural framework and the approach to how the procedural rules should operate, had gone beyond the mere internal and looked at external questions, so did the Woolf Review. It took the second approach, and embarked on a true revolution in civil justice.[87]

---

[85] Cmd 4471, 1933 at 2; Cmd 5065, 1936 at 8–11 and 81; Cmd 8878, 1953 at 9; Cmd 7476, 1979 at 7; Cmd 8205, 1981 at 1 and 40.

[86] M. Zander, *The State of Justice* (Sweet & Maxwell, 2000) at 27.

[87] N. Andrews, *English Civil Procedure: Three Aspects of the Long Revolution* (Conference paper, Centro di studi e ricerche di diritto comparator e straniero, Rome 2001) at 1.

It did so through placing the fundamental aspect of the justice system's framework – its aim of securing substantive justice – under critical scrutiny. By doing so, and through the reforms the Review ultimately recommended, it effected a revolution in civil justice, which as Lord Falconer LC described it in 2005 in his foreword to the second edition of the Civil Procedure Rules, was a 'paradigm shift' in civil justice.[88] An external question produced a change in the framework of justice.

1.4 The Woolf and Jackson Reforms: revolutionary or not?

The first step towards an extraordinary investigation was not however taken by the Woolf Review, but by the authors of the 1993 Heilbron–Hodge Report.[89] They noted that following the Civil Justice Review's implementation, the problems of cost and delay remained as acute as ever; that despite almost constant scrutiny and reform over the previous century, the civil justice system stubbornly remained one where delay and unnecessary expense were endemic. Its rules were still hidebound, technical and inflexible. This prompted them to advocate, as had their predecessors, the need for a complete change in litigation culture.[90] In doing so, their recommendations contained many traditional aspects of reform. They reiterated, for instance, albeit in wider terms than the Civil Justice Review's call for it, the case for a single procedural code for the County and High Courts. They called for a standardised procedure for all types of action, with individual modifications for specialist areas and more robust sanctions for failure to properly progress claims.[91] They also echoed the Civil Justice Review's unimplemented call for more effective court control of litigation to reduce the 'unacceptable and otherwise avoidable delay as well as unnecessary expense', which arose as a result of party-control of litigation.[92] If they had stopped at these and similar traditional reform measures, the call for a complete change in litigation culture would have been nothing more than yet another reworking of the previous and numerous calls for a new

---

[88] C. Falconer, Foreword to the 2nd edn Civil Procedure Rules (HMSO, 2005) at vi.

[89] Heilbron and Hodge, *Civil Justice on Trial – A Case for Change* (Heilbron–Hodge Report).

[90] Ibid. at 6–7.   [91] Ibid., Appendix 1 at [9–12], [26–7], [33], [66–8].

[92] Ibid. at 5 and Appendix 1 at [25].

approach to civil justice. It would have been as much an exercise in normal science as the Evershed Committee's call for a new approach to litigation had been. They did not stop there, however: they took a first half-step toward extraordinary reform. In advocating 'further fundamental reform and modernisation' they proposed, as the Woolf Reforms would later acknowledge, a 'radical reappraisal of the approach to litigation'.[93] They alluded, for the first time, to the possibility that the civil justice system's aim should change; they went beyond the purely internal questions of normal science. They did so by suggesting that the justice system's aim should change to one that encouraged the early settlement of litigation. They thus suggested that the system's aim should no longer simply be vindicating rights through securing substantive justice.[94]

Looked at in isolation, the suggestion that the promotion of settlement should play such a central role in the civil justice system is a radical departure from the traditional approach to reform. It is because the promotion of settlement requires at the very least a modification, if not a rejection, of the aim of securing substantive justice. A system committed to promoting settlement is one which must try to give effect to more than one substantive value; in this case, substantive justice and consensual settlement in the absence of substantive justice.[95] The success or failure of such a system as a necessary corollary cannot therefore be gauged by its ability to secure the former. That is no longer its sole aim. In the context of the Heilbron–Hodge Report as a whole, it is clear, however, that the authors saw the encouragement of early settlement as an adjunct to the traditional approach to reform rather than a departure from it. Encouraging early settlement was not to take priority. Substantive justice's achievement was to remain the justice system's overarching aim. The encouragement of consensual settlement was ultimately, then, not to be a departure from normal science. Events, however, overtook the Heilbron–Hodge Report. Nine months after its publication, Lord Woolf was commissioned to conduct a formal review of the civil justice system.[96] It had nevertheless raised the possibility that the justice system's aim might be subject to fundamental change.

---

[93] Ibid. at 1; H. Woolf (1995) at 5 and 29.   [94] Heilbron–Hodge Report at 6–7 and 72ff.
[95] Damaska, *The Faces of Justice and State Authority* at 148.
[96] H. Woolf (1995), Introduction.

1.4.1   Woolf's revolution

The Heilbron–Hodge Report raised the possibility of an extraordinary investigation. For the first time during the course of the twentieth century, it posed an external question concerning the justice system's aim. If the Woolf Review were to go further and actually result in a Copernican revolution, a number of things would have to occur, according to Kuhn.[97]

First, there would have to be a sustained period during which the existing paradigm's explanatory efficacy declined and where it was unable, through the application of normal methods, to reverse that decline. This had clearly occurred during the twentieth century, as each reform committee failed to cure the ills of complexity, cost and delay. Despite regular reform attempts, the justice system could not be brought to a state where these problems no longer posed a problem for its ability to achieve substantive justice economically and efficiently. The Woolf Review recognised the terminal nature of this period of sustained inefficacy.[98] Having identified the problem as one that was more than a mere anomaly, 'a new candidate for a paradigm' had to emerge.[99] Such a candidate would have to be more than a radical application of the type of reform which had been carried out by civil justice reformers over the past two hundred years. Such reform, as Kuhn put it, would have to reconstruct

> the field from new fundamentals ... [so that] when the transition [from the old system to the new was] complete, the profession will have changed its view of the field, its methods and its goals.[100]

The Woolf Review acknowledged that such a radical restructuring was necessary.[101] It was necessary in order to create a justice system capable of meeting the 'needs of the public in the twenty first century'.[102] It did so through endorsing the underlying theme of the Heilbron–Hodge Report.[103] This restructuring was to be accomplished in two ways. First, the justice system was to abandon its commitment to several aspects of

---

[97] Kuhn, *The Structure of Scientific Revolutions* at 66ff.; J. Sorabji, 'The Road to New Street Station: fact, fiction and the overriding objective' [2012] *EBLR* 1–77, 89.

[98] H. Woolf (1995) at 8–12, 164 and 175.

[99] Kuhn, *The Structure of Scientific Revolutions* at 84.   [100] Ibid. at 85.

[101] H. Woolf (1995) at 19.

[102] H. Woolf (1996) at 12; Neuberger, 'A New Approach to Civil Justice', 13.

[103] H. Woolf (1995) at 5; Heilbron and Hodge Report at 6(i)–(iii); Woolf, in Zuckerman & Cranston (eds), *Reform of Civil Procedure* at vii.

party autonomy; aspects of the adversarial nature of the system were thus to be done away with. Rather than leaving responsibility for the progress of litigation in the hands of litigants and their lawyers, it was to be handed to the court. The lesson of the repeated failure of the summons for directions had finally been learnt. Court-controlled case management was to be introduced. The court was to direct the civil process.[104] Secondly, and more importantly, a new culture or approach to litigation was to be effected by the introduction of a device long known to Anglo-American civil justice: an explicit overriding objective in the rules of court that would express the underlying aim and philosophy of the justice system. This was to set out the manner in which the court was to manage litigation. It was to do so by setting out the justice system's new aim, one that replaced its previous commitment to securing substantive justice. The nature of this aim forms the focus of the remainder of this book.[105] This was the new paradigm.

The emergence of a new paradigm is never, however, the end of the story. As Kuhn noted, in any scientific revolution there is a third and final stage during which the battle for its acceptance takes place. During that stage, a number of things have to occur if the battle is to be won. It must be understood that there is a new paradigm. It is all too easy for a new paradigm to be interpreted consistently with the parameters and according to the assumptions of the old. If that occurs, the paradigm shift will not take place and the problems it seeks to cure will continue and remain intractable. Ensuring that a new paradigm is properly understood and applied is, as Kuhn was all too well aware, something that cannot be achieved in a short period of time. Truly radical reform is unlikely to be fully appreciated or applied consistently in the short term. It takes time to take root and establish itself. Proper understanding and implementation is not the work of an hour, but of a significant period of concerted effort.[106] The Woolf Review's ultimate success, then, rests on it being understood to have proposed a new paradigm and for that to then be properly understood and implemented. If this occurs, then it ought not to succumb to the fate of its numerous predecessors.

---

[104] R. Turner, '"Actively": The Word that Changed the Civil Courts', in Dwyer (ed.), *The Civil Procedure Rules Ten Years On.*

[105] H. Woolf (1995) at 4–5, 7–26; H. Woolf (1996) at 1–12; *Aldi Stores Ltd* v. *WSP London Ltd* [2008] 1 WLR 748 at [28]–[30].

[106] R. Turner cited in M. Zander, 'The Government's Plans on Civil Justice' 61 (1998) *Modern Law Review* 382, 388.

This is not to say that normal reform of the type outlined earlier will not even then need to take place on an ongoing basis. It would, as Lord Woolf acknowledged.[107] However, it would need to do so within the bounds of the new framework.

Any sustained or terminal failure, either to properly understand or implement the Woolf Reforms would, however, as Zander predicted, see them suffer the same fate as previous reform attempts; they would do so even though they represented an attempt to bring about a revolution in civil justice.[108] Past experience ought perhaps to lead to a pessimistic conclusion of the type submitted by Thomas, later Lord Denman CJ, to the Common Law Commissioners in 1829. He concluded that: 'The fate of former attempts at a systematic reformation of the English Law, must be owned to be discouraging. They have been numerous, and all failures.'[109] Experience since 1829 would no doubt reinforce his view if he were asked to offer an opinion on whether the Woolf Reforms would, in the long term, succeed. He would perhaps point out that while Copernicus' revolution succeeded, not all revolutions succeed, or do so completely.[110] The force of this is readily apparent from the fact that nine years after the Woolf Reforms were implemented, problems remained concerning the understanding and implementation of their nature by academics, practitioners and the courts: problems that, amongst others, prompted the appointment of Sir Rupert Jackson to conduct the first post-Woolf civil justice review. Part of that review's function was to consider what reforms were needed to secure the proper implementation of the changes the Woolf Reforms had introduced, to ensure that the change in philosophy was understood and implemented properly.

---

[107] H. Woolf, 'A New Approach to Civil Justice', in *Law Lectures for Practitioners 1996* (*Hong Kong Long Journal* special edn) (Sweet & Maxwell Asia, 1996) at 2.

[108] Zander, 'Why Woolf's Reforms Should be Rejected', in Zuckerman and Cranston (eds), *Reform of Civil Procedure*; J. Leubsdorf, 'The Myth of Civil Procedure Reform', in Zuckerman (ed.), *Civil Justice in Crisis* at 53; M. Zander, *The State of Justice* (Sweet & Maxwell, 2000) at 27; M. Zander, 'Judging Civil Justice' 159 (2009) *New Law Journal* (7630) 367; M. Zander, 'Zander on Woolf', in ibid.; M. Zander, 'The Woolf Reforms: What's the Verdict?' in Dwyer (ed.), *Civil Procedure Rules Ten Years.*

[109] First Report of the Common Law Commissioners into the Practice and Proceedings of the Superior Courts of Common Law (House of Commons) (1829) at 639 cited in A. Clarke, *The Supercase – Problems and Solutions: Reflections on BCCI and Equitable Life* (29 March 2007) at 8. <http://www.judiciary.gov.uk/Resources/JCO/Documents/Speeches/kpmg_speech.pdf>.

[110] N. Andrews, 'A New Civil Procedural Code for England: Party-Control "Going, Going, Gone"' 19 (2000) *CJQ* 37.

It therefore formed part of the process by which a proper understanding and acceptance of the radical nature of the Woolf Reforms was to be effected.

1.5   Conclusion

This chapter has provided an overview of the historically intractable problems of complexity, cost and delay that have faced the civil justice system and undermined its ability to secure substantive justice. That those problems have been intractable is readily borne out by the sheer number of attempts to reform the system over the past two hundred years. It has explained how, if the civil justice system were a scientific one, it would, in the face of such long-term problems, have yielded to calls for fundamental reform. Such fundamental reform would have taken the form of a scientific revolution in the form outlined by Kuhn, and most famously evidenced by the replacement of Ptolemaic astronomy with Copernican astronomy. Such scientific revolutions are predicated on challenges to the fundamental assumptions of the scientific paradigm, and extraordinary investigations that consider the validity of the framework within which normal science take place.

No twentieth-century civil justice review questioned the civil justice system's framework, or its underlying principles or assumptions. From the Judicature Reforms in the 1870s, all reform was conducted as an exercise in normal science. The Woolf Review broke with that historical approach. Following a suggestion made in the Heilbron–Hodge Report, it considered both internal and external questions: they questioned the justice system's underlying framework, and specifically its aim. The outcome of that extraordinary investigation was the rejection of the theory of justice that had underpinned the civil justice system since the 1870s. In the following chapter, the last time English civil justice reform departed from normal science is examined. It is examined because it was a paradigm shift that succeeded, and as a consequence, set the framework within which twentieth-century reform took place. That reform, effected by the Judicature Commission, finally ensured that the civil justice system as a whole was committed to the theory of justice the Woolf Review rejected. As an extraordinary investigation it succeeded and presents lessons to be learnt today for those who seek to implement the terms of the extraordinary investigation carried out by both Woolf and Jackson.

2

Substantive justice and the RSC

the object of the Courts is to decide the rights of parties, and not to punish them for mistakes they make in the conduct of their cases by deciding otherwise than in accordance with their rights. . .[1]

to do justice between the parties. . . is to bring out the result that the litigant succeeds according to the goodness of his cause and not according to the blunders of his adversary.[2]

2.1 Introduction

All civil justice systems are committed, to varying degrees, to determining civil disputes through ascertaining true fact and applying it to right law in order to secure an accurate decision.[3] In that way they arrive at substantive justice.[4] From its origins in the medieval Curia, England's civil justice system was no different. The evolution of the common law, with its forms of action, its pleading process, which narrowed the matters in dispute down to a single issue of either law or fact that could then be determined by either judge or jury,[5] of the jury trial itself, of witness cross-examination,

---

[1] *Cropper* v. *Smith* (1884) 26 ChD 700 at 710–711.

[2] *Collins* v. *The Vestry of Paddington* (1879–80) LR 5 QBD 368 at 380.

[3] C. H. van Rhee and A. Uzelac, 'The Pursuit of Truth in Contemporary Civil Procedure Revival of Accuracy or a New Balance in Favour of Effectiveness', in C. H. van Rhee and A. Uzelac, *Truth and Efficiency in Civil Litigation* (Intersentia, 2012) at 3: 'In the pursuit of justice, truth always plays a prominent role.'

[4] This is not to say that other goals and aims are not pursued. Economy, efficiency, finality of litigation, the protection of certain confidential relationships, each of which in certain circumstances and to varying degrees can be either supportive or antagonistic to the court reaching an accurate decision, can be and are all validly pursued. Accuracy can be given another meaning: procedural accuracy, i.e. where procedural requirements must be and are complied with fully. Throughout this book, unless otherwise indicated, accuracy does not refer to procedural accuracy but to substantive accuracy, i.e. a decision reached through applying true fact to right law.

[5] *First Report of Her Majesty's Commissioners into the Process, Practice and System of Pleading in the Superior Courts of Common Law* (HMSO, 1851) (the 1851 Report) at 12:

all attested to its commitment to securing substantive justice. The same can be said for the development of a more inquisitorial form of procedure, documentary discovery and appellate review in equity.[6] Civil justice before both the common law courts and the Court of Chancery sought to achieve substantive justice in each claim prosecuted before them. By the beginning of the nineteenth century, however, the problem both faced was that they could not deliver substantive justice for the majority of society. Processes ostensibly developed to secure substantive justice were too complex, technical, slow and expensive. In too many cases they produced the perverse result that it was frustrated on procedural grounds. The common law courts may have purported to decide cases on their 'real merits',[7] the Chancery Court to secure 'substantial justice between the parties',[8] but the reality too often fell short. The common law courts were, it was said, 'sadly hampered in the year 1800 by cumbrous procedure and pedantic technicalities which caused the suitors expense, delay, vexation and disgust. It took years for a merchant to recover a debt due to him.'[9] The Court of Chancery was no better: '[for] all its distinction and excellence, [it] was practically closed to the poor. The middle classes were alarmed at its very name, for it swallowed up smaller fortunes with its delays, its fees, its interminable paper process.'[10] Chancery's delays were so bad that at one stage litigants had to wait up to four years

'[The aim of pleadings is]... to ascertain what are the matters really in controversy between the parties, so as to avoid all discussion and enquiry on those things which are not so, – thus simplifying the matter for the decision of the Judge and jury, and saving the parties unnecessary trouble and expense ... parties are (thus) not taken by surprise, they know precisely what is in dispute, and the expense is saved which would otherwise be incurred in coming prepared to prove matters not intended to be controverted.'

[6] J. Langbein, 'The Demise of Trial in American Civil Procedure: How it happened, is it convergence with European Civil Procedure', in van Rhee and Uzelac, *Truth and Efficiency in Civil Litigation* at 119ff.

[7] J. Stephen, *Pleading in Civil Actions* (3rd edn) (Saunders & Benning, 1835) at 271; J. Tubbs, *The Common Law Mind: Medieval and Early Modern Conceptions* (Johns Hopkins University Press, 2000) at 23.

[8] *First Report of the Common Law Commissioners into the Practice and Proceedings of the Superior Courts of Common Law* (House of Commons, 1829) (the 1829 Report) at 465; J. Story, *Commentaries on Equity Jurisprudence as Administered in England and America* (4th edn) (Little, Brown & Co, 1886) at 41ff; F. Tudsbery, 'Equity and the Common Law' (1913) 29 *Law Quarterly Review* 154, 159; G. Adams, 'The Origin of English Equity' 16 (1916) *Columbia Law Review* 87, 89.

[9] W. Odgers, 'Changes in Procedure and in the Law of Evidence', in *A Century of Law Reform* (Macmillan & Co, 1901) at 212.

[10] Bowen, 'Progress in the Administration of Justice during the Victorian Period', in *A Century of Law Reform* at 527ff.

between hearings[11] and George Spence, author of a leading Chancery text of the time, complained that, 'No man, as things now stand, can enter into a Chancery suit with any reasonable hope of being alive at its termination, if he has a determined adversary.'[12] For far too many the courts were simply unable to secure substantive justice and vindicate rights, either at all or at reasonable cost and in reasonable time.

The nineteenth-century reforms outlined in the previous chapter and which culminated in the 1873–75 Judicature Acts were intended to cure the problems and ensure that substantive justice was not undermined by excess cost, delay or complexity.[13] They did so through a mix of, in Kuhn's terms, reform as normal science and extraordinary investigation. The majority of the reforms, focused on rendering the system and procedural rules more efficient and effective, were exercises in the former, as they worked within the parameters set by the justice system's overarching framework. The reconstruction of the courts in 1873 and the change to how the new High Court and Court of Appeal created that year would secure substantive justice went beyond normal science. The RSC's introduction was part of the latter exercise, as it marked the final rejection of the common law's formalist interpretation of what it meant to secure substantive justice and, conversely, the final acceptance of equity's complete justice interpretation of it. As such, it marked the establishment of the framework, the theory of justice, which the Woolf Reforms would overturn. This chapter initially considers the common law and equity approaches to substantive justice. It then examines the

---

[11] J. Jacob, 'Civil Procedure since 1800', in *The Reform of Civil Procedural Law and Other Essays in Civil Procedure* (Sweet & Maxwell, 1982) at 202.

[12] Cited in T. O'Main, 'Traditional Equity and Contemporary Procedure (2003) 78 *Washington Law Review* 429 at 448; see further G. Spence, *The Equitable Jurisdiction of the Court of Chancery* (Stevens & Norton, 1846).

[13] The 1829 Report at 7. The Commissioners noted that to 'render proceedings shorter, cheaper and more certain is the great object to be proposed in recommending any alteration in the established course of practice... In executing the duty imposed upon us, we shall endeavour in each part of the subject under examination, to point out the shortest and least expensive course, consistent with the safe administration of justice to both the litigant parties;' *Second Report of the Common Law Commissioners into the Practice and Proceedings of the Superior Courts of Common Law* (House of Commons, 1830) (the 1830 Report) at 29; *Third Report of the Common Law Commissioners into the Practice and Proceedings of the Superior Courts of Common Law* (House of Commons, 1831) at 37–8; *Fifth Report of the Common Law Commissioners into the Practice and Proceedings of the Superior Courts of Common Law* (House of Commons, 1833) at 7; *First Report of Her Majesty's Commissioners into the Process, Practice and System of Pleading in the Superior Courts of Common Law* (HMSO, 1851) at 2–6.

way in which the latter's approach was adopted by the RSC. Finally, it looks at the central problem that the RSC's commitment to equity's approach to securing substantive justice created.

2.2 The common law and equity: formalism and complete justice

The common law adopted a formalist approach to securing substantive justice. It was a highly technical approach and one of 'iron rules', all of which had to be fully complied with by litigants if disputes were to be determined accurately.[14] Any failure to comply with the formal rules would result in a claim failing, not, as might be expected, on procedural grounds, but on its substantive merits. The common law adopted this approach for one specific, historical, reason: its failure, due to its development as a writ-based formulary system, to draw a proper distinction between substantive and procedural law.[15] Under the common law they were one and the same.[16] This had a number of important consequences. The most significant of those was that it transformed procedure from being the means by which the court could identify and apply true fact to right law into an end in itself.[17] Procedure, if it could be called that given its admixture with what we now know as substantive law, was the law that had to be applied to true fact. As a consequence of this, in order to achieve an accurate decision and secure substantive justice, the common law required three things to be done.

First, a plaintiff had to select the right procedural basis for his claim. He had to choose the right form of action and obtain the relevant writ from the Royal Chancery.[18] By the early nineteenth century this was no

---

[14] F. Maitland, cited in D. Subrin, 'How Equity Conquered Common Law: The Federal Rules Of Civil Procedure in Historical Perspective' 135 (1986–87) *University of Pennsylvania Law Review* 909 at 918.

[15] F. Pollock and F. Maitland, *The History of English Law*, Vol. II (2nd edn) (Cambridge University Press, 1898) at 559ff; J. Getzler, 'Patterns of Fusion', in P. Birks (ed.), *The Classification of Obligations* (Oxford University Press, 1997) at 173.

[16] J. Jolowicz, 'The Dilemmas of Civil Litigation' 18(2) (Spring 1983) *Israel Law Review* 161, 163.

[17] J. Gordley, 'The Common Law in the Twentieth Century: Some Unfinished Business' 88 (2000) *California Law Review* 1815, 1818: 'Until the nineteenth century, the judges were not simply asking themselves whether a result was fair or sensible but also whether it should be reached under the forms of action recognized at common law.'

[18] R. Caenegem, *The Birth of the English Common Law* (2nd edn) (Cambridge University Press, 1988); F. Maitland, *The Forms of Action at Common Law* (Cambridge University Press, 1909, repr. 1962).

easy task; a fact emphasised by the 154 pages the leading practitioners' guide of the time dedicated to explaining the different means by which claims could be issued.[19] Choice of the correct writ was essential, because it provided the legal basis on which the court had jurisdiction to deal with the claim and, if justified, grant the remedy sought. If a litigant failed to choose the correct form of action, the court could not secure an accurate decision because it could not apply the right law.[20] If, for instance, a claim were one that should have been brought as a claim for trover, it would fail if brought as a claim for trespass.[21] Accuracy in identifying the form of action was thus a prerequisite of achieving an accurate decision.[22] As Hepburn put it:

> If the wrong action was adopted, the error was fatal to the whole proceedings, however clear the facts of the controversy might have been brought before the court. The plaintiff may have served his adversary in due time, and may have given as full information as to the material facts of the case as could be given in any other action, he may have proceeded openly and fairly in all matters, there may have been no question as to the substantial justice of his claim, but all this would not avail if his action was not technically the proper one. He must pay the costs and go out of court. If he chose, he could begin again, but under like conditions. At his peril he must select the appropriate formula.[23]

---

[19] W. Tidd, *Tidd's Practice* (7th edn) (H. Bryer, 1821) at 104ff.

[20] The court derived its authority to decide claims at law from writ, which set out the nature and extent of each individual form of action. It had no *vires* to go beyond the authority given to it by the writ, hence it had no choice but to deal with the proceedings according to the terms of the law chosen by the plaintiff. The 1829 Report at 80: 'In former times then, the original writs not only answered their direct purpose of enforcing the defendant's appearance, but they also served to show the King's permission to sue, to found the jurisdiction of the Court, and to increase the Royal revenue. In addition to those uses too, they had the incidental effect of defining the form and scope, and limiting the number of the legal remedies; for, as the suit could not commence except by original writ, and as that instrument always set forth the cause of complaint, to which it became necessary afterwards to adhere, the consequence was, that no action lay, except in a case where a writ would be granted out of Chancery, nor in any form but such as that writ prescribed;' E. Albertsworth, 'The Theory of Pleadings in Code States' 10 (1921–22) *California Law Review* 221, 223, put it: '... the judge ..., drawing his authority to try the case from the words of the original writ, issued by the chancellor, had no authority to allow amendments...'

[21] *Ward* v. *Macauley* (1791) 4 Term Rep 489, 100 ER 1135.

[22] F. Tudsbery, 'Equity and the Common Law' 29 (1913) *Law Quarterly Review* 154, 157: '... if the form was not strictly complied with, the law would not interfere to assist a litigant, even in the redress of an intolerable hardship.'

[23] Hepburn, cited in A. Reppy, *Introduction to Civil Procedure Actions and Pleading at Common Law* (Dennis & Co, 1954) at 95–6.

Secondly, if the correct form of action was chosen, the law then had to be applied correctly. Each form of action had its own distinct procedure, any deviation from which was again not merely a procedural error; it was a misapplication of substantive law. If there was any deviation in the pleadings from the wording required by the terms of the form of action[24] or between the allegations pleaded and those proved at trial,[25] or if the pleadings were not taken in the required order, or there were drafting errors in the pleadings, the claim would again fail.[26] Substantive justice could not be achieved because right law had not been applied properly. Only after there had been absolute compliance with the procedure prescribed by the specific form of action, would the court be in the position to consider the narrow factual or legal issue in dispute between the parties.[27]

The failure to separate procedural and substantive law might at first sight appear to treat formal, procedural compliance as more important than the substantive merits of any claim. The common law might, as Sunderland described its rules concerning joinder of parties, appear to be committed to 'procedural despotism'[28] rather than substantive justice. Equally, its 'pedantically strict'[29] approach to rule-compliance might make it appear to have transformed mere procedural rules into

---

[24] *Colt* v. *The Bishop of Coventry* (1792) Hob. Rep 164, ER 1247 *per* Hobart CJ, 'The law requires in every plea two things, – the one, that it be in matter sufficient; the other, that it be deduced and expressed according to the forms of law; and if either the one of the other of these be wanting, it is the cause of demurrer'; Tidd, *Tidd's Practice* at 455; the 1829 Report at 73.

[25] The 1830 Report at 35: 'At the trial of the cause, a material variance between the allegation in the pleading and the state of the facts proved, is a fatal objection, and decides the suit in favour of the objecting party; and a variance is often considered in this technical sense, as material, though to common sense it may appear to be trifling, and though it may be wholly irrelevant to the merits of the case.'

[26] Tidd, *Tidd's Practice* at 455; Stephen, *Pleading in Civil Actions* at 426; J. Chitty, *Precedents in Pleading* (2nd edn) (W. Benning & Co., 1847) at 2–4.

[27] *Robinson* v. *Rayley* 1 Burr. 316, 319; 97 ER 330, 331; W. Blackstone, *Commentaries on the Laws of England*, Vol. III (Chicago University Press, 1979 repr.) at 310–16; Tidd, *Tidd's Practice* at 460; the 1829 Report at 11ff; Stephen, *Pleading in Civil Actions* at 55, 124–30; the 1851 Report at 12; E. Daniell, *The Practice of the High Court of Chancery* (3rd edn, ed. Headlam) (Stevens & Norton, 1857) Vol. I at 230–1; Pollock and Maitland, *The History of English Law* at 609; C. Wells, 'The Origin of the Petty Jury' 27 (1911) *Law Quarterly Review* 347, 347–9; Reppy, *Introduction to Civil Procedure Actions and Pleading at Common Law* at 659.

[28] E. Sunderland, 'Joinder of Actions' 18 (1919–20) *Michigan Law Review* 571 at 573ff.

[29] Odgers, 'Changes in Procedure and in the Law of Evidence' at 212.

'instruments of injustice'.[30] In one sense this was true. It was easy for claims to fail on the basis of technical, procedural points rather than on the basis of the substantive merits.[31] The obvious consequence of this was that proceedings became ever-more protracted and expensive as litigants took what would now be viewed as procedural points. In another important sense, though, it was not true. Due to the common law's failure to draw a distinction between procedural and substantive law whether a claim failed through the application of true fact to right law, or because the plaintiff chose the wrong form of action or made a pleading error, it had failed as much for substantive reasons as it had for procedural reasons.[32] While the common law held to the medieval position that failed to distinguish these two forms of law, it could not but view accuracy and substantive justice in terms of procedural, formal purity. This can be illustrated by reference to Magna Carta. Its famous demand that 'no man of what estate or condition that he be, shall be put out of land or tenement, nor taken, nor imprisoned, nor disinherited, nor put to death, without being brought in answer by due process of law',[33] is taken today as the first significant demand for the right to fair trial. At the time it was first issued and then subsequently reissued, it was not simply a demand for a fair trial prior to the imposition of lawful punishment or the lawful dispossession of land. It was not simply a demand for procedural due process. Due to the failure to separate out the two forms of law, the demand for due process was as much a demand for the proper application of substantive law as it was for the proper application of procedural law. In such a system, in order to achieve an accurate decision, only a pedantically strict approach to process obligations would do. That the common law took such a precise approach to procedure – to due process – might today look as if it made procedure the master when it should be the servant of justice, but in its context, master and servant were one and the same. Its obsession with procedural purity, far from

---

[30] Unattributed Review Article, 'The Severance of Law and Equity' 8 (May 1848–August 1848) *Law Review & Quarterly Journal of British and Foreign Jurisprudence* 62 at 64.

[31] The 1829 Report at 74, 78–80, 121, 488–93, 500–10 and 531–39; the 1830 Report at 9; the 1851 Report at 2.

[32] As Jolowicz noted, under the common law it made no real sense to talk of judgments on the substantive merits. Such language only becomes meaningful where a proper distinction is drawn between substance and procedure. As a necessary corollary it made no real sense to talk of procedural objections or claims failing on procedural grounds: see Jolowicz, 'The Dilemmas of Civil Litigation' 161 at 167.

[33] 28 Edw. 3, c. 3, Chapter 29.

being evidence of it adopting an approach that valued procedural form more highly than the substantive merits of a claim was, in fact, evidence of the high value it placed on determining cases on their merits. Technicalities did not get 'in the way of the real merits'.[34] They were the means by which the common law determined cases on their real merits and secured substantive justice.

Equity did not, however, adopt common law formalism as its means of securing substantive justice. It took a markedly different approach, both structurally and procedurally. Equity was administered in a single superior court, the Court of Chancery, by a single judge, the Lord Chancellor, without a jury. Its pre-trial and trial process was, in contrast to the common law, quasi-inquisitorial and discontinuous.[35] The former because it placed a number of procedural devices in the hands of the court, which enabled it to take steps to pursue the truth; quasi-inquisitorial rather than inquisitorial because the process was one that did not enable the Chancery Court to initiate proceedings as a properly inquisitorial process would.[36] The latter because the trial process specifically took place over several hearings, rather than as a single event that jury trial necessitated at common law. Most significantly, in so far as its procedure was concerned, it differed in two fundamental ways from the common law.

First, there was never any question of substantive and procedural law being fused in equity. This was because its jurisdiction, in order to enable equity to remedy defects in the common law,[37] arose from a general delegation of authority to the Lord Chancellor under the prerogative of grace, rather than through a specific delegation to the common law courts by way of the writ containing the form of action.[38] Substantive

---

[34] A. Zuckerman, *Civil Procedure* (1st edn) (Butterworths, 2003) at 28.

[35] P. Vinogradoff, 'Reason and Conscience in Sixteenth-Century Jurisprudence' 24 (1908) *Law Quarterly Review* 373; H. Coing, 'English Equity and the *Denunciatio Evangelica* of the Canon Law' 71 (1955) *Law Quarterly Review* 223; T. Haskett, 'The Medieval Court of Chancery' 14 (1996) *Law & History Review* 245.

[36] A. Kessler, 'Our Inquisitorial Tradition: Equity Procedure, Due Process, and the Search for an Alternative to the Adversarial' 90 (2005) *Cornell Law Review* 1181 at 1184, n. 16.

[37] *Maud wife of William de Hotot* v. *Joan wife of Alan de Chartres* EELR III 235; *Robert Forester of Bayworth* v. *Thomas son of John Bayon & Others* EELR IV 329 at 330; *Clemence de Menyl* v. *Nicholas de Menyl* EELR I 6; J. Mitford (Lord Redesdale), *A Treatise on Pleadings in Suits in the Court of Chancery by English Bill* (5th edn, ed. Smith) (Stevens & Norton, 1847) at 6–7; Odgers, 'Changes in Procedure and in the Law of Evidence' at 207; M. Avery, 'An Evaluation of the Effectiveness of the Court of Chancery under the Lancastrian Kings' 86 (1970) *Law Quarterly Review* 84.

[38] Story, *Commentaries on Equity Jurisprudence as Administered in England and America* at 42; Spence, *The Equitable Jurisdiction of the Court of Chancery* at 337 and 407.

and procedural equity were always entirely distinct from each other.[39] There was, consequently, no equivalent to the common law form of action in equity, which could define and limit its jurisdiction. Claims in equity were begun by petition, which simply needed to set out the alleged facts and the remedy sought.[40] While there was a standard form that petitions were expected to follow, this never hardened into a template that permitted no deviation or variation. It was a standard as a guide only, even if in practice parties hardly ever deviated from it.[41] Where the common law was rigid and unyielding in its approach, equity was flexible and discretion-based, both in respect of initiating process and more generally.[42] This was further facilitated by the fact that equity procedure was, unlike the common law's, trans-substantive, i.e. the same procedure applied irrespective of the substantive law in issue in the claim. These differences between common law and equity had an obvious consequence. There was no prospect of a claim in equity failing because the wrong procedural form had been chosen.[43] More broadly, it meant that unlike at common law, procedural compliance was not a factor that equity had to consider when assessing the substantive merits of a case. As under the RSC and today, equity simply needed to consider the application of true fact to right substantive law. Procedure remained a means to an end, rather than an end in itself. Substantive justice was a function of substantive rather than procedural accuracy.

The separation of procedure and law in equity meant that equity did not necessarily have to adopt a common law formalist approach to achieving substantive justice. However, it was the second difference

---

[39] There was, for instance, always a clear distinction between Chancery procedure, substantive equity such as the law of trusts, and equitable remedies, such as injunctive relief or specific performance: Spence, *The Equitable Jurisdiction of the Court of Chancery* at 430ff, 644, 668 and 677ff; M. Lobban, 'Preparing for Fusion: Reforming the Nineteenth-Century Court of Chancery, Part II' 22 (2004) *Law & History Review* 565, 587.

[40] For a starkly simple early example, see Year Book, 9 Edward IV vi 26 in Avery, 'An Evaluation of the Effectiveness of the Court of Chancery under the Lancastrian Kings' at 85–6, where the petition simply stated, 'Set me on a way how I shall spece in my right for I dir not gon home for doute of my life.'

[41] Daniell, *The Practice of the High Court of Chancery* at 338 and 412ff; Mitford, *A Treatise on Pleadings in Suits in the Court of Chancery by English Bill* at 33ff.

[42] Subrin, 'How Equity Conquered Common Law: The Federal Rules Of Civil Procedure in Historical Perspective' at 918ff.

[43] W. Holdsworth, *A History of English Law* (7th edn) (Sweet & Maxwell, 1966) Vol. IX at 343–4: '... in equity ... there was much more uniformity in the manner of beginning proceedings, and no risk that the selection at the outset of the wrong form would cause failure.'

between common law and equity that positively influenced how it would pursue accuracy in order to realise that aim. That difference stemmed from its development out of a form of canon law procedure, which required the Chancery Court to act as a Court of Conscience and thereby secure the reformation of sin through correcting a litigant's corrupt conscience.[44] To achieve this it placed a positive duty on the court not to act unconscionably.[45] While equity over the course of time would transform an ecclesiastical concept of conscience into a civil one, it maintained its commitment to ensuring that it would, in the words of Lord Nottingham LC, 'never ... confirm an award against conscience'.[46] The question then is, how did it ensure that it never confirmed an award in a party's favour when that was unmerited? It did so through ensuring that it would pursue, as Lord Talbot LC described it in *Knight* v. *Knight*, 'complete justice'.[47] This meant that equity not only had to determine claims on their substantive merits as between the immediate parties to the litigation, but also as between all those individuals who had an interest in it, whether they had an actual or potential equitable interest in the subject matter of the claim. Lord Redesdale gave the clearest explanation of the expansive nature of the commitment when he stated that it was, 'the constant aim of a court of equity to do complete justice by deciding upon and settling the rights of all persons interested in the subject of the suit, to make performance of the order of the court perfectly safe to those who are compelled to obey it, and to prevent litigation.'[48] It not only required equity to go beyond the interests of the immediate parties, it also required it to ensure that the judgment reached was absolutely accurate. Only if its judgments were perfectly safe could it

---

[44] Bacon LC, cited in Getzler, 'Patterns of Fusion' at 184.

[45] Year Book 9 Edward IV, 14 No. 9 in Spence, *The Equitable Jurisdiction of the Court of Chancery* Vol. I at 375; *The Earl of Oxford's case* (1615) 1 Rep Ch 1, 6; 21 ER 485, 486; Coing, 'English Equity and the *Denunciatio Evangelica* of the Canon Law' at 225–7; J. Langbein, 'Fact Finding in the English Court of Chancery: A Rebuttal' 83 (1973–74) *Yale Law Journal* 1620, 1628; D. Klinck, 'Lord Nottingham and the Conscience of Equity' 67(1) (2006) *Journal of the History of Ideas* 123.

[46] *Bulstrode* v. *Baker* (1675) in D. Yale, *Lord Nottingham's Chancery Cases* (Selden Society, 1961) Vol. I at 213; *Lawrence* v. *Berney* (1677) cited in ibid. Vol. II at 584. By this time conscience had come to mean civil conscience rather than morality, *per* Nottingham LC in *Cook* v. *Fountain* (1676) 3 Swanns 585, 36 ER 984.

[47] (1734) 3 P. Wms. 331, 334; 24 ER 1088, 1089; Holdsworth, *A History of English Law* at 373.

[48] Mitford, *A Treatise on Pleadings in Suits in the Court of Chancery by English Bill* at 190; Daniell, *The Practice of the High Court of Chancery* at 201ff.

be sure that it had done nothing unconscionable, that it had properly required the law to be enforced and enforced against the right parties in the correct way. Such an approach was one that could not but leave no stone unturned in the pursuit of accuracy, and would do so irrespective of the time it took or the cost that engendered. It was the *ne plus ultra* version of substantive justice.[49] This had three important consequences for equity, and ultimately, the common law's and the RSC's development, which were: the development of procedural devices distinct from those available at common law; a strong commitment to rectifying error in decision-making; and a strict approach to rule-compliance married to a liberal approach to relief from adverse consequences for non-compliance.

Equity developed a number of procedural devices that were absent from common law process, each of which promoted accurate decision-making. It introduced in virtue of its canon law origins, for instance, the means by which litigants could obtain documentary evidence from their opponents. More significantly, it did so because documentary discovery – or as it is now called, disclosure – was understood to be a paramount means to ensure that equity could act as a Court of Conscience. It was the means by which, as Lord Bowen would later describe it, a litigant could 'scrape the conscience' of his opponent by securing all relevant and probative documentary evidence.[50] Taken together with equity's other innovation, the interrogatory, through which a litigant could secure witness evidence under formal examination, equity introduced the two most important means by which parties could procure relevant evidence of fact, and thereby promote accuracy in decision-making.[51] Equity then complemented these accuracy-enhancing measures with an equally

---

[49] *Dudley* v. *Dudley* (1705) Prec. Ch. 241 at 244; 24 Eng. Rep. 118; 1826 Chancery Report at 6–7 and 26; *First Report of Her Majesty's Commissioners into the Process, Practice and System of Pleading in the Court of Chancery* (HMSO, 1852) (the 1852 Report) at 3–4, 16 and 116; *Second Report of Her Majesty's Commissioners into the Process, Practice and System of Pleading in the Superior Courts of Common Law* (HMSO, 1853) at 35–45; Daniell, *The Practice of the High Court of Chancery* at 201 and 376; Spence, *The Equitable Jurisdiction of the Court of Chancery* at 128 and 206–7; Mitford, *A Treatise on Pleadings in Suits in the Court of Chancery by English Bill* at 4 and 13; Story, *Commentaries on Equity Jurisprudence as Administered in England and America* at 1–5; C. Langdell, 'A Brief Survey of Equity Jurisdiction (I)' 1 (1887–88) *Harvard Law Review* 55.

[50] *The Report by the Commissioners into the Practice of the Court of Chancery* (No. 143) (1826) (the 1826 Chancery Report) at 7; C. Bowen, cited in J. Jacob, *The Fabric of English Civil Justice* (Stevens & Co., 1987) at 93; Klinck, 'Lord Nottingham and the Conscience of Equity' at 129.

[51] The 1826 Chancery Report at 7; E. Bray, *The Principles & Practice of Discovery* (Reeves & Turner, 1885) at 1; Pollock and Maitland, *The History of English Law* at 667; J. Wigmore,

strong rectification mechanism. Errors can always occur. Where complete justice, correct in every way, is the aim, a low-to-minimal threshold for error can be tolerated. As a consequence of this, equity introduced an extensive appellate process by way of, potentially, multiple reviews or rehearings *de novo*,[52] of both interlocutory and final decisions, as a means to rectify judicial error.[53] Consistent with its commitment to achieving complete justice as a means to ensuring that it acted consistently with conscience, equity's appellate process was not, as today, subject to reasonable time limits. A commitment to finality of litigation, which justifies the imposition of procedural time limits on any right of appeal, was incompatible with a commitment to complete justice. Decisions had to be perfectly safe. As such, wrong decisions could not be left to stand, even if that meant reopening a decision on appeal, as in one case, twenty years after the initial decision had been given.[54] Conscience and complete justice required it. Inevitably, these, and equity's other procedural mechanisms, which arose from and operated consistently with its commitment to securing complete justice rendered its process both expensive and time-consuming; such consequences were inevitable in the circumstances, given the degree to which it pursued justice. Under equity, truth could not but be loved too well or obtained at too high a price.

Equity did not simply develop and promote the use of procedural mechanisms that would enable it to secure complete justice; it also took a distinctive approach to rule-compliance. Originally, and unsurprisingly in stark contrast to the common law, equity was governed by no fixed rules of procedure. It was simply regulated by broad 'principles of Equity and conscience'.[55] This situation did not last as equity matured.[56] Broad

---

Evidence (Chadbourn Revision, 1976), Vol. VI at 488–92; Haskett, 'The Medieval Court of Chancery' at 265.

[52] *Slingsby* v. *Hale* (1669) 1 Ca. in Cha. 122, 22 ER 723; Mitford, *A Treatise on Pleadings in Suits in the Court of Chancery by English Bill* at 101–5. *De novo* rehearings could be either before the original court or before a superior jurisdiction: Daniell, *The Practice of the High Court of Chancery*, Vol. II at 1113, 1121–3; *Moss* v. *Baldock* (1842) 1 Ph. 118, 41 ER 576; *Angell* v. *Davis* (1839) 4 My & Cr 363, 41 ER 140; *Stewart* v. *Forbes* (1849) 1 Mac. & Gor. 137, 41 ER 1215.

[53] Mitford, *A Treatise on Pleadings in Suits in the Court of Chancery by English Bill* at 101–6.

[54] Ibid. at 106; Daniell, *The Practice of the High Court of Chancery*, Vol. II at 1111–12; *Brown* v. *Sawyer* (1841) 3 Beav. 598 at 599; 49 Eng. Rep. 235 at 236.

[55] Spence, *The Equitable Jurisdiction of the Court of Chancery* Vol. I at 367–8 and 710.

[56] *Gee* v. *Pritchard* (1818) 2 Swans 403 at 428; Spence, *The Equitable Jurisdiction of the Court of Chancery* at 409; Vinogradoff, 'Reason and Conscience in Sixteenth-Century Jurisprudence' at 375–84; Coing, 'English Equity and the *Denunciatio Evangelica* of the Canon Law' at 233ff.

principle gave way to as highly technical and complex a system of rules, subject to fixed principles, as pertained at common law.[57] In addition to this, as it matured, equity adopted as strict an approach to rule-compliance as the common law. It did so not because such an approach was inevitable, as it was at common law due to the nature of the forms of action, but rather, because such an approach was understood to be the optimum means to ensure that the Chancery Court was able to achieve complete justice. While a strict approach at common law to the pleading process, for example, was necessary in order to secure the application of right law in assessing the merits of a claim, in equity it was necessary to ensure that all the necessary parties were joined to the proceedings, that all relevant issues were properly defined and then subjected to proper scrutiny and investigation.[58] Strict compliance was the servant of justice. Any errors in the pleading process would tend to undermine proper identification of the issues or relevant parties, which could then lead to claims being decided in the absence of relevant points being raised or relevant parties' interests being considered. If an error meant evidence was not obtained, again rights could not be properly determined. Procedural error could, as a consequence, undermine the Chancery Court's ability to reach the correct decision. Strict rule-compliance was therefore needed, not as at common law to ensure right law was applied, but to ensure that all relevant factual and legal matters were before the court so that it could achieve complete justice. Equity's adoption of technical rules and a formalist approach to compliance with them was thus a necessary means to an end, rather than, as at common law, an end in itself.

Equity's development of as technically complex a form of procedure as the common law, married with a strict approach to rule-compliance, was not without its obvious problems. Complex rules tend to increase the error rate. A strict approach to compliance incentivises parties to take procedural points, in the hope that they will obtain a procedural advantage. Complexity and strict formalism gave rise to the inevitable consequence that such procedural points were raised as readily as they were at common law, with the attendant cost and delay that that engendered.[59]

---

[57] (1818) 2 Swans 403 at 428.

[58] J. Adams, *The Doctrine of Equity being a Commentary on the Law as Administered by the Court of Chancery* (T. & J.W. Johnson & Co., 1850) at 301.

[59] The 1826 Chancery Report 12–15; A. Birrell, 'Changes in Equity, Procedure and Principles' in *A Century of Law Reform* at 191–2.

At common law there was nothing intrinsically wrong with this, given its failure to separate out substantive and procedural law: procedural advantage was substantive advantage. Equity could not, however, have adopted the same approach. If it had, complete justice would have been frustrated in too many cases and the Chancery Court would have failed to act as a Court of Conscience.[60] In order to ensure that its strict approach to rule compliance did not frustrate its aim of doing complete justice, it complemented it with a liberal approach to curing procedural error or rectifying process. It adopted an approach that, as Stillington LC put it in terms that could never have been heard at common law, ensured that parties would 'not be prejudiced by mispleader, or for default of form, but according to the verity of the matter; we have to judge according to conscience'.[61] To cure procedural defects, parties could apply to the court to remedy the issue. Such orders would be granted whenever it was 'necessary to enable [the court] fully to decide upon the rights of all the parties'.[62] Equity's liberal approach to relief from the consequences of procedural error can be illustrated by reference to three nineteenth-century authorities.

The first of those authorities was *Attorney-General* v. *Cooper*.[63] The issue in that case was whether, in modern terms, a claim should be struck out following an improper amendment, or whether a further amendment should be permitted to cure that defect. At common law the claim would have been struck out. In equity, however, the amendment was allowed. In considering the question, Cottenham LC first noted that there was no authority in equity for striking out a claim consequent on such an error. As he put it:

> Why an irregularity in the progress of the cause should be a ground for destroying a suit altogether it is difficult to imagine; and no authority was cited in support of such a proposition.[64]

He then went on to state that he was required to consider

> ... whether there is ground for the application made ... It cannot be justly said that all the [applicants] have to establish in support of such an

---

[60] Daniell, *The Practice of the High Court of Chancery* Vol. I at 376ff.

[61] Year Book 9 Edward IV, 14 No. 9; Spence, *The Equitable Jurisdiction of the Court of Chancery* Vol. I at 374; Avery, 'An Evaluation of the Effectiveness of the Court of Chancery under the Lancastrian Kings' at 91.

[62] Mitford, *A Treatise on Pleadings in Suits in the Court of Chancery by English Bill* at 1.

[63] 3 M & C 258, 40 ER 923.   [64] Ibid. 260, 924.

application is that the Defendants will not be prejudiced by such an alteration; they must show that justice will not be done, or that the suit cannot be conveniently prosecuted unless the alteration is made.[65]

Could justice be done absent the remedial amendment? Could the court – given equity's overall commitment to it – achieve complete justice if the amendment was not granted? If it could not, the amendment had to be granted, subject to the defendant not being prejudiced. If it could, then the error was such that rectification was unnecessary, as justice could be done without it. The guiding principle governing the court's discretion was clear: the need to ensure that justice was done on its merits. The claim could not fail simply on procedural grounds.

A similar approach was taken in *Ferrand* v. *The Mayor, Alderman and Burgesses of Bradford*.[66] In that case, the issue turned on the question of relief from the consequences of a failure to comply with a procedural time limit. Failure to comply with the time limit had resulted in the claim being struck out due to the operation of a specific rule of court. Turner LJ held that the automatic sanction should be lifted in order to enable the court to ensure the claim was determined on its substantive merits rather than on procedural grounds. As he put it:

> I have no doubt of the power of the Court to dispense with these General Orders when the circumstances and the justice of the case require . . .[67]

Not only could the court, as in *Attorney-General* v. *Cooper*, grant relief from procedural error, its duty to secure decisions on their substantive merits was sufficient authority to enable it to set aside general rules of court where necessary. In modern terms, the Chancery Court could disapply procedural rules where abiding by them would frustrate its overriding objective of doing complete justice. This ability to set aside the consequences of general rules in order to ensure that justice could be done was further elaborated in *Smith* v. *Barker*. In that case, Page Wood VC held that the court could dispense with one of the general orders governing evidence.[68] Echoing Turner LJ's approach in *Ferrand*, he held that:

> The General Order was not framed for the purpose of preventing the Court from doing justice; and whenever it is satisfied that substantial justice requires any of its own regulations to be waived, or any slip

---

[65] Ibid. 261, 924.   [66] 8 De G M & G 93, 44 ER 324.   [67] Ibid. at 95, 325.
[68] (1864) 2 H & M 498, 71 ER 557.

remedied (I say nothing of any matter depending upon statutory powers or regulated strictly by Act of Parliament), the Court will interfere for that purpose.[69]

Subject to Parliamentary or statutory intervention, the Chancery Court could, relying on its inherent jurisdiction, take such steps as necessary to enable it to decide cases on their substantive merits. This and the previous two decisions illustrate the extent of equity's commitment to securing complete justice; amendments were permitted if a refusal would frustrate its achievement. Sanctions for non-compliance with court rules and the adverse consequences of procedural error could be set aside where, to do otherwise, would render it unattainable. Rules of court, or rather, their effect, could equally be set aside where that was required.[70] The sole guiding principle was that complete justice had to be done; procedure was to operate consistently with that aim in order to ensure that that end was achieved. Just as that commitment overrode other considerations, such as the length of time proceedings took in order to ensure that all relevant parties and evidence was before the court, the costs attendant on such process, or the need to secure finality of litigation, it could override the consequences of failure to comply with procedural obligations. In this it was as absolutist, on its terms, in its pursuit of an accurate decision and through it substantive justice, as the common law was on its terms.

2.3   From the common law and equity to the RSC

The common law and equity took two very different approaches to securing substantive justice. The Judicature Act reforms are generally understood to have rejected both of them.[71] Zuckerman, for instance, has consistently argued that prior to the 1873 reforms the

> courts saw it as their main task to secure adherence with process requirements ... (and as a consequence litigants) would not be able to obtain a

---

[69] Ibid. 499–500, 557–8.

[70] Adams, *The Doctrine of Equity* at 312 and 402ff; Mitford, *A Treatise on Pleadings in Suits in the Court of Chancery by English Bill* at 67–100 and 177ff; *England* v. *Curling* 8 Beav. 129.

[71] A. Zuckerman, *Court Adjudication of Civil Disputes: A Public Service Needs to be Delivered with Proportionate Resources, within a Reasonable Time and at Reasonable Cost*, at 5 <http://www.aija.org.au/ac06/Zuckerman.pdf>; A. Zuckerman, 'The Revised CPR 3.9: a coded message demanding articulation' 32 (2013) *CJQ* 123 at 126.

judgment on the merits unless all the procedural forms were completely and precisely followed.[72]

The RSC's introduction as part of those reforms, he suggests, marked the utter rejection of the formalist fetish he describes with an equally strong fetish for a radically new commitment: 'the principle of doing justice on the merits', i.e. substantive justice.[73] In Kuhn's terms, he presents the RSC's introduction as a paradigm shift. Accounts such as this are broadly accurate in their presentation of the RSC, the procedural rules it contained and the manner in which they operated, as a break from the past. Where they go badly wrong, however, is the claim that the RSC represented a complete break with the past. The reality is more nuanced. Its introduction evidenced a considerable degree of continuity with the past.

The difficulty with the complete-break-with-the-past account arises in two ways. Most obviously, it fails to take proper account of the nature of the common law's and equity's guiding principles. It assumes that for the common law formalism was an end in itself. It equally assumes that for equity an approach that to a large degree mirrored the common law's absolutist approach to rule-compliance meant that it, too, was primarily concerned with compliance as an end in itself. Such assumptions are, however, unsustainable. As discussed earlier, the common law's love of formalism was the only proper means by which it could produce an accurate decision. Given its failure to separate substantive and procedural law, procedural formalism was the means by which it obtained, in Zuckerman's terms, justice on the merits. Formalism was a means to an end. Equally, equity did not approach rule-compliance as an end in itself. It took a strict approach to compliance, which it married with a liberal approach to relief from procedural error, in order to ensure that it, too, arrived at accurate decisions. Its complete justice was also committed to achieving justice on the merits. As such, the adoption of that principle following the 1873 reforms as the justice system's fundamental principle marks, on one level, a point of fundamental continuity with, rather than a break from, the past. The idea that in 1873 the courts suddenly started to see their role as securing justice on the merits rather than securing absolute formalist rule compliance is thus wrong, because at common

---

[72] A. Zuckerman, *Zuckerman on Civil Procedure: Principles of Practice* (2nd edn) (Thomson, 2006) at 25–7.
[73] Ibid. at 27.

law any procedural judgment was one on the substantive merits, while at
equity formal compliance was never treated in an absolutist fashion,
given the liberal approach to relief from the adverse consequences of
non-compliance and rectification of procedural error.

There is a second reason why the 1873 reforms mark a point of
continuity with the past; a reason that again the complete-break-with-
the-past account fails to appreciate. From the 1820s to 1873 there was a
decisive shift away from the common law's formalist approach to securing substantive justice towards equity's complete justice approach; a shift
that was finalised by the introduction of the RSC post-1873. This continuity arose through two fundamental changes in the common law: its
separation of procedural from substantive law; and its adoption of
equity's approach to rule-compliance. The procedural paradigm shift
that occurred in 1873 was not one that saw the justice system adopt
justice on the merits, substantive justice, as its overriding objective
following the straightforward rejection of a formalist approach to justice.
It was one that saw the justice system, after a long struggle to free the
common law from its formalist approach to securing substantive justice,
adopt equity's approach as the guiding principle applicable to all disputes. These points can be illustrated by reference to the separation of
form and substance in the common law during the nineteenth century
and the common law procedural reforms from 1850 to 1870.

2.3.1   Separating substantive and procedural law

In a review of aspects of nineteenth-century reform, Sunderland noted
the historical difficulty lawyers had in distinguishing between rights and
remedies, and between substantive law and the means by which it was
secured and vindicated, procedural law. He summed up the difficulty in
this way:

> The rules respecting rights and obligations define the goal of professional
> endeavor, while the rules relating to remedial processes are only means
> toward that end. . . But the history of procedure has been a long and discour-
> aging demonstration that nothing is harder for the legal mind to understand
> than this difference. Means and end are always being confused. . .[74]

By the end of the eighteenth century, that confusion had been recognised.
Blackstone had, for instance, drawn the distinction between the two

---

[74] E. Sunderland, 'Joinder of Actions' 18 (1919–20) *Michigan Law Review* 571 at 571.

forms of law in his *Commentaries*.[75] Courts and lawyers were also beginning to think of the two as separate,[76] while from the 1820s common law reformers started to consider the merits of effecting such a separation. From that time there was a growing appreciation that the procedure prescribed by the common law forms of action, rather than enabling the courts to determine disputes on their substantive merits, was doing the opposite. There was a growing realisation of the difference that existed between procedural and substantive law and that the failure to draw that distinction properly was leading to claims failing for reasons of form, not substance. Evidence to the First Common Law Commission, for instance, stressed the need for procedural reform, which would divest common law procedure of all its 'technical and capricious difficulties' so that the courts could decide cases on their substantive merits.[77] Reform was needed in order to 'to prevent justice being defeated by form, and to secure decisions on the merits'.[78] Again, it was stressed, 'mere error in form [should not be treated] as a failure on the merits'.[79] Form and substance had to be separated. By the middle of the nineteenth century, such views were being acted on and implemented by statutory reform.[80]

Initially, the reform process focused on simplifying procedure in order to reduce the potential for procedural error. The most striking example of this was the introduction of a single form of originating process to replace the previous multiplicity of original writs through which common law actions were commenced. The new process was, foreshadowing later developments, modelled on the same process used in equity. In this way procedural complexity, and the attendant litigation cost and delay that generated was reduced, as was the scope for claims to fail on formal grounds.[81] Procedural simplification was taken a step

---

[75] For a discussion see O'Main, 'Traditional Equity and Contemporary Procedure' at 459ff.

[76] T. Plucknett, *A Concise History of the Common Law* (5th edn) (Little, Brown & Co., Liberty Fund reproduction 2010) at 381.

[77] The 1829 Report at 214–15; the 1830 Report, Appendix B at 56.

[78] Ibid. 46 and 56–7 *per* Best CJ.

[79] The 1830 Report at 17 and 33; *Third Report of the Common Law Commissioners into the Practice and Proceedings of the Superior Courts of Common Law* (House of Commons, 1831) (the 1831 Report) at 7–8 and 3–22; *First Report of Her Majesty's Commissioners into the Process, Practice and System of Pleading in the Superior Courts of Common Law* (HMSO, 1851) (the 1851 Report) at 9ff; Common Law Procedure Act 1852, ss. 34–41.

[80] Common Law Amendment Acts 1852, 1854 and 1860.

[81] The 1829 Report at 9, 60, 82ff, 121, 487–92, 500–10; the 1830 Report at 9 and 60; Uniformity of Process Act 1832, s. 1; Common Law Procedure Act (CLPA) 1852, ss. 1–3 and Schedule A.

further in 1834, when new, simpler rules of court were introduced: the Hilary Term Rules. The intention, as with the introduction of a uniform originating process, was to reduce the complexity of the pleading process, and to introduce a less formalistic approach to rule-compliance. These reforms failed. They were, in fact, entirely counterproductive; procedure became *more* formalist. More technical points were taken and more claims were struck out for procedural non-compliance than ever before. As Pollock noted, rather than ensure more claims were determined on their substantive merits, the new rules gave rise to an 'outbreak of new technicalities'.[82] The reason why the new rules failed to achieve their objective is readily comprehensible. Like all court rules, they were implemented consistently with the prevailing culture. That culture, absent formal separation of procedural and substantive law, was one that had no choice but to treat procedural points as substantive points and vice versa. All that the new rules did was introduce a simplified form of fused procedural and substantive law. They did nothing to alter its underlying nature. Consequently, while reformers may have intended the new rules to enable the court to decide cases on their substantive merits rather than on formal grounds, absent the separation of procedure and substantive, it had no choice but to carry on treating procedure in the same way as it had prior to their introduction. The new rules had simply changed how the game was played. The basis on which the winner was decided remained the same. As such, as Coleridge CJ put it, looking back on the failure of the Hilary Term Rules: 'the merits of cases [continued to take] second place to the forms of procedure'.[83]

The Hilary Term Rules' failure to effect successful reform was inevitable because the prevailing litigation culture remained unreformed.[84] If later reforms were not to fail in the same way, they would have to undo the effects of the Provisions of Oxford and the second Statute of Westminster, which had effectively established the common law's fusion of substantive and procedural law through setting in stone the forms of action.[85] Recognising that form got in the way of the merits was not enough. Procedure would have to be separated from substantive law.

---

[82] Cited in F. Holdsworth, 'The New Rules of Pleading of the Hilary Term' 1834(1) (1921–23) *Cambridge Law Journal* 261, 271; the 1830 Report at 30; W. Whittier, 'Notice Pleading' 31 (1918) *Harvard Law Review* 501.

[83] Cited in J. Baker, *An Introduction to English Legal History* (4th edn) (Butterworths, 2002) at 89–90.

[84] The 1829 Report at 639.

[85] The Provisions of Oxford 1258; The Statute of Westminster 1285 (13 Edw. I, St. 1).

An initial suggestion to separate the two, through abolishing the forms of action, was rejected in 1831 on the grounds they helped secure substantive justice.[86] The watershed moment came with the Second Common Law Commission in 1851. It acknowledged the truth in the distinction Blackstone had drawn nearly a century previously, that there was a fundamental distinction between a cause of action, which was a matter of substantive law, and the form of action, which was a matter of procedure. It then went on to draw the conclusion that the common law's failure to draw this distinction not only no longer served no useful purpose, even if historically it had, but that it artificially increased litigation cost and delay.[87] Most significantly, the Commission concluded that it undermined the court's ability to achieve accurate decisions. Rather than promote substantive justice, it frustrated its achievement. As the Commission described it, it was

> manifest ... that as the question, whether there is a cause of action or not must depend upon the facts and not upon the form adopted, the decision of a cause on the merits is not helped by means of these forms of action.[88]

Abolition of the forms of action was accordingly recommended in order to enable the common law courts to focus on adjudicating on parties' 'substantive right(s)' rather than on 'captious objections [that were] quite immaterial to the merits of the case and of no prejudice to the opposite party'.[89] Reform was not fully implemented, however. The forms of action were not abolished. Their role in the litigation process was, however, substantially etiolated. It would no longer be necessary to refer to them in the originating process, the writ of summons: the forms were to live on in name only.[90] The first substantial step towards separation had taken place. It had been taken in order to better enable the courts secure substantive justice, without having to consider procedure as an issue relevant to the substantive merits. Unsurprisingly though, simply setting aside any requirement to refer to the forms of action in the originating writ did not entirely achieve the Reform Commission's objective. Claims still failed on procedural grounds because the wrong form of action had been chosen.[91]

---

[86] The 1830 Report, Appendix A at 5, 10ff and 27ff; the 1831 Report at 6.
[87] The 1851 Report at 1–3, 32–4.   [88] Ibid. at 33.   [89] Ibid. at 21–2.
[90] Ibid. at 34; Common Law Procedure Act 1852, ss. 2–3.
[91] See, for instance, *Bracegirdle* v. *Hinks* (1854) 9 Ex 361, discussed in J. Jolowicz, '"General Ideas" and the Reform of Civil Procedure' [1983] *Legal Studies* 295 at 299.

In the years prior to the 1873 reforms, two significant changes had thus occurred. First, there was a growing realisation that substantive justice was being frustrated by the common law's obsession with formal rule-compliance. It had begun to be understood that procedural accuracy was not an intrinsic aspect of determining claims on the substantive merits. The realisation that Zuckerman attributes to the 1873 reforms had started to take place in the 1830s and was well established by 1850, even if it was not by then fully implemented. Secondly, there was an appreciation that the over-importance accorded to procedure stemmed from the forms of action through the conflation of procedural form and cause of action. As a consequence of these two points, attempts were made to revise the common law procedural rules to reduce the possibility that formal objections could arise and, more importantly, that procedural and substantive law were separated from each other. Common law reform had moved towards an understanding that in order to achieve substantive justice, procedure's role and importance had to be reduced. If the complete-break-with-the-past account of the 1873 reforms were correct, neither of these aspects of the pre-1873 reforms could have taken place. That they did, and that they were completed by the 1873 reforms, shows that the reforms were, in fact, the final stage in a four-decade long reform process that had a consistent aim. That aim was ensuring that the justice system adopted an approach to securing substantive justice that was taken from equity.[92]

2.3.2   Reform in the shadow of complete justice

In 1852, the Second Common Law Commission took a radical step. As Jolowicz described it, for the first time such a committee concluded that reform should be carried out consistently with a 'positive objective' or a 'general idea'.[93] The idea was that, rather than simply make discrete recommendations aimed at reducing litigation cost and delay through simplifying procedural rules, reform should be carried out in order to enable the common law courts to achieve complete justice.[94] As the 1852 Report explained, 'every court ought to possess within itself the means of

---

[92] CLPA 1852, ss. 2–4 and 41; RSC (1873) Ord. 1–3 and 18; RSC (1873) Ord. 1; RSC (1875) Ord. 3 r. 2; cf. RSC (1873) Ord. 22; Jolowicz, '"General Ideas" and the Reform of Civil Procedure' at 300; Jolowicz, *The Dilemmas of Civil Litigation* 164.

[93] Jolowicz, '"General Ideas" and the Reform of Civil Procedure', 297.

[94] Ibid; the 1852 Report at 34ff.

administering complete justice within the scope of its jurisdiction'.[95] Civil justice reform would, from that point until the Woolf Reforms, be carried out pursuant to general idea, and the theory of justice taken from equity that underpinned it.[96] The Common Law Commission manifested this objective in a variety of ways. It relied on it: to question the continued existence of the civil jury;[97] and to recommend that every common law court should have at its disposal all legal, and equitable, procedural mechanisms and substantive remedies.[98] Equally, the adoption of the commitment to complete justice implicitly underpinned the Commission's call for the separation of procedural and substantive law. Equity, in its own long-established pursuit of complete justice, separated the two. If the common law courts were to achieve the same end, then they, too, would have to draw the same distinction between the two forms of law, which as noted earlier the Commission recommended.[99] There was, however, one particular aspect of the complete justice-inspired reforms recommended by the Commission that specifically bears on the question of continuity between the post-1873 justice system and its common law predecessor: the approach taken to questions concerning amending civil process. The common law historically had little to no power to permit pleadings to be amended, whereas equity, in order to secure complete justice, took a liberal approach to amendment. The RSC post-1873 would take equity's approach, as had the common law from 1850.

The increasing awareness that matters of form were undermining the common law courts' ability to achieve substantive justice initially led to a recommendation in 1831 by the First Common Law Commission that a general power to amend pleadings should be introduced.[100] This recommendation was not, however, taken forward. Even if it had been, the Hilary Term Rules' fate suggests that any such power would, at that time, have been interpreted and applied narrowly; the prevailing culture

---

[95] Ibid. at 35, said in the context of discussing providing the common law courts with the power to order discovery.

[96] Jolowicz, '"General Ideas" and the Reform of Civil Procedure'.

[97] The 1852 Report at 4ff.

[98] E.g., the common law courts should have the power to order discovery, to grant injunctive relief or order specific performance. The 1852 Report at 23 and 38; Common Law Procedure Act 1854, ss. 50, 68–70, 78–9 and 83–5; J. Langbein, *Fact Finding in the English Court of Chancery: A Rebuttal* 83 (1973–74) *Yale Law Journal* 1620, 1630; C. Allen, *The Law of Evidence in Victorian England* (Cambridge University Press, 1997).

[99] Jolowicz, '"General Ideas" and the Reform of Civil Procedure', 300.

[100] The 1831 Report at 13–22.

defines how new rules will be used in practice.[101] If matters had gone no
further than this, Zuckerman's suggestion that the RSC's introduction
marked a complete break with the past might find some support.
The Second Common Law Commission's adoption, in 1851, of complete
justice as a reforming idea meant, however, that the question of
amendment, central to equity's commitment to that approach, was
revisited. The Commission made two significant recommendations. It
proposed that a power should be introduced to enable writs to be
amended to allow the joinder of new parties: claims were not to fail on
grounds of misjoinder or non-joinder.[102] This mirrored equity. Secondly,
it noted how reforms to the pleading rules, aimed at simplifying procedure, had been applied strictly, consistently with the common law courts'
formalist approach. As such, they continued to provide a perverse incen-
tive to parties to take procedural points, which were still resulting in
claims being defeated on grounds that were now properly being seen as
technical rather than merits-based.[103] The Commission understood that
culture mattered, that new rules would be applied consistently with the
system's overarching aim or, as now, its overriding objective. To change
the culture and the way in which rules were interpreted and applied did
not just require a change to the rules themselves: it required a change in
the overarching aim of the system. The Commission's proposals
regarding the introduction of an amendment power did not just change
the rules, they represented a shift in aim from the common law's
formalist understanding of what it meant to secure substantive justice
to equity's complete justice approach to securing it. Having recommended the abolition of the forms of action, thus laying the basis for
the proper separation of form and substance, the Commission went on to
make an equally radical proposal. It recommended that a power should
be introduced into common law procedure, akin to that which already
existed in equity, to enable pleadings to be amended and, more significantly, to enable the court to forgive procedural non-compliance.[104] The
common law courts were not just to become courts capable of delivering
complete justice in the sense that they had both the common law and
equity's remedies at their disposal. They were to become so because they
also had equity's procedural mechanisms to ensure it was, in practice,
achievable. Perhaps most significantly, the new amendment power was

---

[101] Baker, *An Introduction to English Legal History* at 82.
[102] The 1851 Report at 9–10; CLPA 1852, ss. 34–8.   [103] The 1851 Report at 11–21.
[104] Ibid. at 54.

to be used to enable the court to reach judgments on their substantive merits. It was to be used in as liberal a way. These recommendations were enacted through section 222 of the Common Law Procedure Act 1852, which explicitly stated that:

> It shall be lawful for the Superior Courts of Common Law, and every Judge thereof, and any Judge sitting at Nisi Prius, at all Times to amend all Defects and Errors in any Proceeding in Civil Causes, whether there is anything in Writing to amend by or not, and whether the Defect or Error be that of the Party applying to amend, or not; and all such Amendments may be made with or without Costs, and upon such Terms as to the Court or Judge may seem fit; and all such Amendments as may be necessary for the Purpose of determining in the existing Suit the real Question in controversy between the Parties shall be so made.

The new provision was introduced explicitly to ensure that, unlike previously, the courts had full power to 'enable them to prevent the Failure of Justice by reason of Mistakes and Objections of Form'.[105]

The Second Common Law Commission's proposals and the reforms they engendered were a major step forward. They did not, however, solve all the problems that faced the common law courts. The forms of action were not abolished. They were retained, albeit, as noted earlier, in an etiolated state. As a consequence of this, the formalist approach to securing substantive justice was not fully swept away. Claims still failed for technical, formal, reasons.[106] Excess cost and delay also remained inherent to the system, as a consequence of the remaining role that formalism played. The Commission had, however, taken the first crucial step in the justice system's development. By adopting the view that the common law courts should, like equity, aim at achieving complete justice, it redefined the common law courts' aim. Procedural formalism, although it was not entirely eradicated in practice following the reforms due to the shadow the forms of action still cast, was no longer the courts' express aim. Post-1852, both common law and equity, which itself underwent reforms to better enable it to achieve its aim,[107] were committed to doing complete justice. More importantly, from a practical perspective, the common law, through the introduction of a broad power to cure procedural defects and amend process, was now in the same position as

---

[105] CLPA 1852, preamble to s. 222.   [106] *Bracegirdle* v. *Hinks* (1854) 9 Ex 361.
[107] The Court of Chancery Act 1850; The Court of Chancery Act 1851; The Court of Chancery Act 1852; The Chancery Amendment Acts 1850; The Chancery Amendment Acts 1852; The Chancery Amendment Acts 1858; The Chancery Amendment Acts 1860; The Chancery Rules and Orders Act 1860.

equity. It had the procedural means to implement its new commitment to complete justice, and thereby ensure that claims were determined on their merits rather than on formal grounds.

By the latter half of the nineteenth century, then, reform had achieved a number of significant advances. The common law had moved from starting to acknowledge that there was a distinction between form and substance, between determining claims on procedural grounds and on their substantive merits properly understood, towards an adoption of equity's version of what it meant to secure substantive justice as its guiding principle. Consistently with that, it had diminished the role the forms of action played, having acknowledged the distinction between a form of action and a cause of action. Finally, it had introduced procedural reforms which both diminished procedural complexity, thereby reducing the scope for procedural skirmishing and the prospect that claims would fail on procedural grounds, and more importantly, introduced an equity-based general power to cure procedural error so that claims could be determined on their substantive merits. It was an evolutionary approach that had moved the common law a long way from its early nineteenth-century love of formalism towards the approach taken in equity. It was an approach that the Judicature Commission would endorse and adopt. What for Zuckerman was a radical break with the past, was in reality the final stage in a paradigm shift that had started to take place in the 1830s and had begun in earnest in the 1850s. It was a paradigm shift that saw the common law and then the RSC adopt substantive justice, as equity understood it.[108]

2.4   1873 and the RSC: the triumph of complete justice

The nineteenth-century reform process is often, and correctly, presented as the triumph of equity over the common law.[109] From 1873, it was the common lawyers who did equity,[110] just as the equity lawyers continued to do. The transformation was secured by the 1873 reforms recasting

---

[108] Jolowicz, '"General Ideas" and the Reform of Civil Procedure', 299.

[109] M. Damaska, *The Faces of Justice and State Authority* (Yale University Press, 1986) at 118; S. Subrin, 'How Equity Conquered the Common Law: The Federal Rules of Civil Procedure in Historical Perspective' 135 (1986–87) *University of Pennsylvania Law Review* 909; D. Laycock, 'The Triumph of Equity' 56 (1993) *Law & Contemporary Problems* 53 esp. at 64ff for a summary; O'Main, 'Traditional Equity and Contemporary Procedure'.

[110] *Hill* v. *Parsons* [1971] 3 All ER 1345 at 1356.

the justice system in equity's image. This was achieved in a number of ways. First, the reforms completed the abolition of the common law's formulary system, which had been commenced in the 1850s. Building on those reforms, the RSC would not even require plaintiffs to specify the 'precise ground of complaint, or the precise remedy or relief to which the plaintiff considers himself entitled'.[111] The separation of substantive law and procedure had been put beyond doubt, as Lush LJ acknowledged in *Poyser* v. *Minors*:

> the mode of proceeding by which a legal right is enforced, [was] distinguished from the law which gives or defines the right, and which by means of the proceeding the court is to administer the machinery as distinguished from its product.[112]

This reform finally enabled equity's approach to procedure to become universal. It was to be truly trans-substantive. A single common process would apply to all claims, bar the prerogative writs that lived on as an exception to the new general rule, just as equity had used a single form of process. The new equity-based procedure would also, unlike the previous position at common law, enable the court to fully determine all possible issues between all interested parties rather than reduce the dispute to a single issue. In order for this to happen, equity's approach to joinder of issues and parties also prevailed, and did so after it was acknowledged by the Judicature Commissioners to be a means to secure complete justice.[113] Its approach to evidence gathering as a means to secure accurate fact-finding also prevailed, as the RSC followed the 1850 common law reforms in adopting equity's liberal approach to witness evidence and discovery.[114] It was an approach that, when explained by the Court of Appeal in *Compagnie Financière du Pacifique* v. *Peruvian Guano Company*, shortly after the RSC came into force, ensured that all litigants had at their disposal the means to secure a more than sufficient

---

[111] RSC (1875) Ord. 3 r. 2; cf. RSC (1873) Ord. 22.

[112] (1881) LR 7 QBD 329 at 333.

[113] *The First Report of the Royal Commission to Inquire into the Operation and Constitution of the High Court of Chancery, Courts of Common Law, Central Criminal Court, High Court of Admiralty, and other Courts in England, and into the Operation and Effect of the Present Separation and Division of Jurisdiction between the Courts* (No. 4130; 1868–69) (the 1868 Report) at 6–12: 'any person not originally a party to the suit, but who may have such an interest in the subject matter thereof as to make his presence necessary or expedient to enable the Court to do complete justice, should be summoned to attend the further proceedings and be bound thereby...'; The Judicature Act 1873, s. 24(7).

[114] Allen, *The Law of Evidence in Victorian England*.

evidence base on which the court could arrive at factually accurate decisions.[115] As such, it was an approach to evidence gathering entirely consonant with that required by complete justice, which, as the Chancery Commissioners had explained some fifty-five years earlier, required 'full discovery' to be given so that the court could be sure that its decision was properly made, even if it often did so irrespective of considerations of cost and delay.[116] Equity's approach to the nature of procedure was not the only area where it won out over common law process. Its approach to trial and appellate process was also largely adopted by the 1870 reforms. The common law jury, while not abolished, was diminished: it became the exception rather than the rule. The presumption under the RSC was that, as in equity, the judge should be both the tribunal of fact and law.[117] Appeals took place on the same basis as they had at equity rather than at common law, i.e. by way of rehearing; an approach specifically noted to enable the court to arrive at a 'decision upon the merits'[118] and, as the Judicature Commissioners went on to say, 'do complete justice between the parties'.[119] The one feature of the common law jury trial that remained unaltered by the reforms was the nature of the trial process. The RSC adopted the common law's rather than equity's trial process; albeit there was no reason in principle why equity's quasi-inquisitorial trial process could not have been adopted. Apart from that one small victory, the 1870 reforms were, as whole, ones that completed the paradigm shift begun in the 1850s. There were no longer two distinctive forms of procedure, one at law and another in equity. There was post-1870, in the form of the RSC, 'a reformed equity procedure'.[120]

---

[115] (1882) 11 QBD 55.

[116] The 1826 Report at 12: 'It is essential for the purposes of justice, that sufficient time should in all cases be allowed. The nature and object of equitable jurisdiction particularly require this. No decree could be satisfactorily made, embracing the various points in a causes, and binding the rights of all parties interested, under any course of proceeding, in which the plaintiff had not the opportunity of compelling full discovery from the defendant; or in which all parties had not ample time to bring forward, upon the pleadings, their respective views of the case, in a full and perfect manner.'

[117] Common Law Procedure Act 1854, s. 1; Administration of Justice (Miscellaneous Provisions) Act 1933, s. 6; Senior Courts Act 1981, s. 69; *Ward* v. *James* [1966] 1 QB 273.

[118] The 1868 Report at 24.

[119] Ibid. at 25. As such, it was an approach which, as under equity, prioritised the achievement of accuracy over considerations of cost and delay, as it rendered all issues and decisions, including interlocutory ones, taken at first instance capable of reopening and rehearing on appeal.

[120] H. Lurton, 'The Operation of the Reformed Equity Procedure in England' 26 (1912) *Harvard Law Review* 99 at 99.

To further ensure the new equity-based system could more readily secure substantive justice than either of its predecessors the rules of court – the RSC itself – were drafted in a simpler, less technically complex manner than either of its predecessors. A simpler procedure offered fewer opportunities for technical error and procedural skirmishing. It reduced the possibility of unnecessary cost and delay being generated as a consequence of such procedural wrangling. The simpler approach to the procedural rules manifested itself in a number of ways, such as the introduction of fact-pleading, and the requirement that pleadings eschew technical in favour of simple, straightforward language on pain of an adverse cost award for those who failed to do so.[121] Pleadings were also to be confined to what would now be known as the particulars of claim, defence and reply. This reduction in the number of stages to the pleading process again offered fewer opportunities for procedural default and technical objections, whilst reducing litigation cost and delay. They were only to go beyond the reply stage where further clarification was necessary to enable the court to determine the 'real question or controversy between the parties'.[122] Simplification served to reduce the prospect that claims would be defeated on technical grounds. It was not to go so far as to come into conflict with the need to secure substantive justice. Where it did, the latter took precedence just as it had under equity.

Past experience of reform made it clear that merely adopting a simplified structure or set of procedural rules was not sufficient. Structural and procedural simplification had been tried in the past and had failed. The Hilary Term Rules' failure had already demonstrated how a set of liberalising reforms could be undone by a failure to reform the prevailing attitude and approach to litigation. That failure had in turn been followed by that of the 1850 common law reforms, which saw the first attempt to adopt equity's complete justice approach come to nothing. Liberal reforms in an illiberal environment simply resulted in the continuation of the illiberal status quo. If the history of nineteenth-century reform demonstrated anything, it was that for reform to succeed, it needed more than changes to the court structure or the rules of court. It needed a change in attitude, a cultural change. The 1873 reforms

---

[121] The requirement that parties set out no more than the material facts on which they rely and do so 'clearly and intelligibly'; see W. Odgers, *The Principles of Pleading and Practice in Civil Actions in the High Court of Justice* (Stevens & Sons, 1912) at 74, 82ff; the 1868 Report at 11; RSC (1873) Ord. 2 r. 2.

[122] The 1868 Report at 11; RSC (1875) Ord. 24.

went further than their predecessors by effecting that cultural change. They did so by ensuring that equity's approach to amendment and its liberal approach to relief from procedural error were applied in practice. Complete justice did not simply influence structural and procedural reforms. It was applied in practice and applied so well that by 1907 Collins MR could say in *Re Coles and Ravenshear*, in a way that echoed the principle which underpinned Cottenham LC's dictum in *Attorney-General v. Cooper*,[123] Turner LJ's in *Ferrand v. The Mayor, Alderman and Burgesses of Bradford*,[124] and Page Wood VC's in *Smith v. Barker*,[125] that:

> the relation of rules of practice to the work of justice is intended to be that of handmaid rather than mistress, and the Court ought not to be so far bound and tied by rules, which are after all only intended as general rules of procedure, as to be compelled to do what will cause injustice in the particular case.[126]

He could because a series of Court of Appeal decisions shortly after the RSC's introduction ensured that the Judicature Commissioners' commitment to embedding equity's complete justice approach into the system was carried out in practice. They ensured that it became the RSC's implicit overarching principle or overriding objective. Those decisions centred on the application of two specific rules, the effect of which ensured that 'doing justice on the merits [was] more important than enforcing compliance with the rules or court orders'.[127] They ensured that, as under equity, the predominant consideration was not to secure compliance with the rules for the sake of compliance, but to ensure that claims progressed to a decision on the substantive merits, i.e. substantive justice. Compliance was important, but a liberal approach to relief from the consequences of non-compliance, for instance, was more important still. As Fry LJ explained it, by reference to the power to permit parties to amend their pleadings, the whole policy underpinning the Judicature Act and the RSC was one that required the real issues to be put before, and hence then determined on their substantive merits by, the court.[128] Everything was to be done to enable the court to be in the best position

---

[123] 3 M & C 258, 40 ER 923. [124] 8 De G M & G 93, 44 ER 324.
[125] (1864) 2 H & M 498, 71 ER 557.
[126] [1907] 1 KB 1 at 4; see also, *Ward v. The Mayor and Town Council of Sheffield* (1887) 19 QBD 22.
[127] Zuckerman, *Zuckerman on Civil Procedure: Principles of Practice* at 26.
[128] *Kurtz v. Spence* [1887] LR 36 ChD 770 at 776; RSC (1965) Ord. 19 r. 1; Ord. 24 r. 16.1.

possible to accurately determine a claim. The two rules in question were RSC (1875) Ord. 27 r. 1, the power to amend pleadings, and Ord. 59, the power to grant relief from the consequences of procedural default. The former, as had been recommended by the Judicature Commissioners,[129] straightforwardly replicated section 222 of the Common Law Procedure Act 1852 and provided that:

> The Court or a Judge may, at any stage of the proceedings, allow either party to alter his statement of claim or defence or reply, or may order to be struck out or amended any matter in such statements respectively which may be scandalous, or which may tend to prejudice, embarrass, or delay the fair trial of the action, and all such amendments shall be made as may be necessary for the purpose of determining the real questions or question in controversy between the parties.[130]

It remained in these terms until 1962, when it was broadened out through the deletion of the reference to pleadings.[131] The latter was not originally intended to form part of the RSC. It was an innovation of the RSC's 1875 redraft, the original 1873 version never having come into force.[132] There was no comparable common law provision to RSC Ord. 59. It did, however, codify the approach taken in equity to relief from procedural default, and as the *Annual Practice*, through explaining its application by reference to *Ferrand v. The Mayor, Alderman and Burgesses of Bradford*[133] made clear, it was intended to operate in the same way as equity's power to set aside where justice required it.[134] It provided that:

---

[129] The 1868 Report at 11: 'the Judge should, at any stage of the proceedings, permit such amendment in or addition to the pleadings as he may think necessary for determining the real question or controversy between the parties, upon such terms, as to costs and otherwise, as he may think'.

[130] RSC (1873) Ord. 18; RSC (1883) Ord. 28 r. 1; RSC (1962) Ord. 20 r. 8.1; RSC (1965) Ord. 20 r. 8.

[131] The rule was redrafted so that until the close of pleadings parties could amend without reference to the court. Once pleadings had closed, parties would have to apply to the court to amend, at which time the RSC (1962) Ord. 20 r. 8 would apply.

[132] Judicature Act 1874 s. 2 amended the 1873 Act, to which the original RSC were annexed, so that it would not come into force until 1 November 1875, the same day as the Judicature Act 1875, s. 16 of which specified that the rules of court annexed to that Act would come into force at the time the Act came into force and would replace any previous rules. The RSC originally drafted were thus never operative.

[133] 8 De G M & G 93, 44 ER 324.

[134] For instance, T. Snow (ed.), *Annual Practice* (Sweet & Maxwell, 1894) Vol. I, at 1164; RSC Ord. 70, r. 1.2: 'Whenever the Court is satisfied that substantial justice requires any of its own regulations to be waived, or any slip to be remedied, it will interfere for the

> Non-compliance with any of these Rules shall not render the proceedings in any action void unless the Court or a Judge shall so direct, but such proceedings may be set aside either wholly or in part as irregular, or amended, or otherwise dealt with in such manner and upon such terms as the Court or Judge shall think fit.

It remained substantively unaltered until the CPR replaced the RSC in 1999, when it became CPR 3.10.[135] These two provisions formed the basis on which the courts enforced the commitment to doing complete justice.

The first significant decision to interpret and apply RSC Ord. 27 r.1 was that of *Tildesley* v. *Harper* in 1876.[136] Bramwell LJ gave the leading judgment, and as the High Court of Australia noted in 2009 in a decision that finally repudiated the approach he took in so far as its jurisdiction was concerned, he took a liberal approach to amendment.[137] Bramwell LJ, as a past member of the Second Common Law Commission, co-drafter of the Common Law Procedure Act 1852, and Judicature Commissioner, might well have been expected to approach the provision so as to ensure that it facilitated complete justice's achievement. He was well-versed in its provenance and what both the 1850 and 1870 reforms sought to achieve. He did as might have been expected, and held the correct approach to amendment to be one that required the court to:

> give leave to amend unless ... satisfied that the party applying has been acting mala fide, or, by his blunder, has done some injury to the other side which cannot be compensated by costs or otherwise.[138]

In a concurring judgment, Thesiger LJ added that:

> it is important that the rules of the court as to pleading should be enforced, but this may be done at too great a price. The object of these rules is to obtain a correct issue between the parties, and when an error has been made it is not intended that the party making the mistake should be mulcted in the loss of the trial.[139]

---

purpose ... (*Smith v Baker*, 2 H & M 498; *Ferrand v Mayor of Bradford*, 8 De G. M & G 93.'

[135] It became RSC (1883) Ord. 70 r. 1 in 1883 and then RSC (1965) Ord. 2 r. 1.

[136] 10 ChD 393; *Baker* v. *Medway Building & Supplies Ltd* [1958] 1 WLR 1216 at 1235; see also, J. Sorabji, 'Late Amendment and Jackson's Commitment to Woolf: another attempt to implement a new approach to civil justice' 31(4) (2012) *CJQ* 393.

[137] *Aon Risk Services Australia Ltd* v. *Australian National University* [2009] HCA 27 at [18].

[138] 10 ChD 393 at 396.   [139] Ibid. at 397.

This approach was not confined to amendment. Bramwell LJ returned to the theme in *Collins* v. *The Vestry of Paddington*, on an application made under RSC Ord. 59.[140] He held there that relief from the consequences of procedural default should be granted where the

> mistake, error, or carelessness of the applicant, had been real and unintentional, and no damage had been done to the other side that could not be repaired by payment of costs or otherwise.[141]

The same approach was thus to be taken to both rules. Bramwell LJ went on to explain the rationale underpinning the court's approach. It was an explanation redolent of equity's commitment to complete justice and particularly the way in which it was implemented through decisions.[142] It was as applicable to RSC Ord. 27 as it was RSC Ord. 59. The rules existed, and were to operate, so as to enable the court 'to do justice between the parties; . . . to bring out the result that the litigant succeeds according to the goodness of his cause and not according to the blunders of his adversary'.[143] Claims were not to be determined on the basis of procedural default. They were to be determined on their substantive merits. The new rules were not to be interpreted, as the Hilary Term Rules had been, consistently with the old common law formalist approach. Equity's approach was to guide the litigation culture.

Bramwell LJ may have introduced the proper approach to amendment and relief from sanction and offered the first explanation of the rationale underpinning it; however, it was two other Court of Appeal decisions that embedded it, and the commitment to complete justice, into the RSC's DNA. The first of those decisions was *Clarapede & Co* v. *Commercial Union Association*.[144] It concerned both RSC Ord. 27 r. 1 and Ord. 59. Brett MR, with whom Bowen LJ agreed, applied the approach endorsed in *Tildesley*, and explained that it required the court to grant relief under the provisions:

> However negligent or careless may have been the first omission, and however late the proposed amendment, the amendment should be allowed if it can be made without injustice to the other side. There is no injustice if the other side can be compensated in costs.[145]

---

[140] (1879–80) LR 5 QBD 368.   [141] Ibid. at 379.

[142] T. Snow (ed.), *Annual Practice* (Sweet & Maxwell, 1894) Vol. I, at 1164; RSC Ord. 70. r. 1.2.

[143] (1879–80) LR 5 QBD 368 at 380.   [144] (1883) 32 WR 262.

[145] Ibid. at 263; cf. *Atwood* v. *Chichester* (1877) LR 3 QBD 722 at 744.

This approach was then applied in *Cropper* v. *Smith*.[146] Bowen LJ explained its purpose and application once more. While his was the minority, dissenting judgment, there was no dissent from the nature of the test he articulated. He put it in this way:

> the object of the Courts is to decide the rights of parties, and not to punish them for mistakes they make in the conduct of their cases by deciding otherwise than in accordance with their rights ... I know of no kind of error or mistake which, if not fraudulent or intended to overreach, the Court ought not to correct, if it can be done without injustice to the other party. Courts do not exist for the sake of discipline, but for the sake of deciding matters in controversy, ... It seems to me that as soon as it appears that the way in which a party had framed his case will not lead to a decision of the real matter in controversy, it is as much a matter of right on his part to have it corrected, if it can be done without injustice.[147]

He went on to say it would only be very rarely that a party could not be compensated in costs for any injustice caused by granting the remedy sought by their appointment. In his words, 'in my experience ... there is one panacea which heals every sore in litigation, and that is costs.'[148]

The principle articulated in *Tildesley* and endorsed and elaborated in *Collins*, *Clarapede* and *Cropper* was subsequently followed and applied in a series of Court of Appeal decisions, such as *Steward* v. *North Metropolitan Tramways Company*, where Brett MR, by then Lord Esher, explained that the principle Bowen LJ and he had set out in *Clarapede* was the one laid down by Bramwell LJ in *Tildesley*.[149] The clearest subsequent explanation of the court's role under the RSC, through the application of the two rules and the manner in which they were to be applied was, however, given in *Indigo Company* v. *Ogilvy*.[150] In that case, the plaintiffs had improperly added a new cause of action to their claim. The defendant applied to have the amendment set aside. Its application was granted on the grounds that it '[opened] up a new field of litigation ... not covered

---

[146] (1884) 26 ChD 700.

[147] Ibid. at 710–711. On appeal to the House of Lords, Bowen LJ's statement of principle was approved by Lord Selbourne in an *obiter dictum*: *Smith & Hancock* v. *Cropper* (1884–85) LR 10 App Cas 249 at 259.

[148] Ibid.

[149] 16 QBD 556, and see Lopes LJ at 560. See further, *Weldon* v. *Neal* 19 QBD 395 at 396; *Shoe Machinery Company* v. *Cutlan* [1896] 1 Ch 108; *Australian Steam Navigation Company, Owners of S.S. 'Victoria'* v. *William Howard Smith & Sons, Owners of S.S. 'Keilawarra'* (1889) LR 14 App Cas 318 at 320.

[150] [1891] 2 Ch 31.

by the original writ at all'.[151] The plaintiff appealed and was subsequently granted permission to amend their original writ in order to put it, in the words of the Court of Appeal, 'in the right form'.[152] In allowing the appeal, the Court did two things. First, it applied the test laid down in *Tildesley*. In doing so, it explained how the rationale underpinning it was the same as that which had underpinned the introduction of section 222 of the Common Law Procedure Act 1852. There was thus continuity rather than a break with the past. The rationale behind this was that such an approach would enable the court to determine all issues between the parties in a single set of proceedings. In other words, it was to enable the court to do complete justice in a single claim. This was, of course, equity's approach, as Lord Redesdale had previously explained.[153] It was again an approach alien to common law formalism. But equally, it was one that illustrates the continuity between the RSC, equity and the post-1850 common law, which Jolowicz highlighted. Secondly, it presented a forthright condemnation of common law formalism. Lindley LJ, who gave the leading judgment in the Court of Appeal, first explained that North J at first instance had correctly concluded that the plaintiffs had erred in adding the new claim. There had been an error of form. He went on to say, however, that in reaching his decision, North J had failed to approach the litigation process properly. He had adopted a common law formalist approach. He had treated the plaintiffs as if they were playing a game, and were to be punished for their failure to abide by its rules. Lindley LJ put it this way:

> then comes the question what is to be done? It is not right for this Court, or any Court to play at battedore and shuttlecock with suitors, and Mr Justice North ought, it appears to me, to have given the Plaintiffs liberty to amend their writ in such a way as they could without doing any injustice to the Defendants, and I propose now to state the order which we think he ought to have made, and to make that order.[154]

A formalist approach to procedure might have justified North J's approach. Rules, however, did not exist, as Bowen LJ had made clear, for the sake of discipline. They existed in order to ensure that the court could determine disputes between parties on their substantive merits.

---

[151] Ibid. at 38.   [152] Ibid. at 46 *per* Kay LJ.

[153] The 1868 Report at 12; *Kurtz* v. *Spence* [1887] LR 36 ChD 770 at 773–774.

[154] [1891] 2 Ch 31 at 39. A point echoed in the USA in *Connor* v. *R. Co.* 133 NW 1003, cited in 46 (1912) *American Law Review* 761: 'litigation is not merely a game to be played, but a serious effort to do justice on the merits'.

While rules were to be observed, they were not to be applied so as to undermine the court's ability to do so. They were to be applied, and Ords. 27 and 54 were specifically to be applied, to ensure that the real issue or issues between the parties were identified and determined by the court on their merits. Rule-compliance was, as in equity previously, a means to an end. To secure that end, they were to be applied consistently with the liberal approach to applications for relief from any failure to comply with those rules outlined in *Tildesley* and the cases that followed it.

Despite the general approach established by RSC Ord. 27 and Ord. 59 when the RSC was introduced, one formal limitation on the power to cure procedural default remained despite this line of authority. The power contained in RSC (1875) Ord. 59 could not be relied on to cure procedural defaults that rendered proceedings void or a nullity.[155] It could only be relied on to cure procedural irregularities. On a superficial level, this limitation might look to be a final hangover from the common law's formalist approach.[156] It was, however, a limitation that arose as a consequence of the RSC's adoption of equity's approach to default. Equity had no power to cure nullities.[157] Where default rendered proceedings void or a nullity, the Court of Chancery had no jurisdiction. It therefore had no lawful basis on which to apply its liberal approach to non-compliance. The RSC, in adopting equity's commitment to complete justice, had carried over this approach to such default; a point emphasised by the Court of Appeal in 1963 in *Re Pritchard (deceased)*, where Danckwerts LJ described an incorrectly issued originating summons as being of no more use than a dog licence in the context of providing the court with jurisdiction. As such, RSC (1875) Ord. 59, or as it was in 1963 RSC (1883) Ord. 70 r. 1, could not be relied on.[158] This formal limit was, however, removed as a consequence of that decision, when Ord. 70 was revised and became RSC (1965) Ord. 2 r. 1. Consequently, as Lord Denning MR explained in *Harkness* v. *Bell's Asbestos & Engineering Ltd*, the RSC provided that:

> Every omission or mistake in practice or procedure is henceforward to be regarded as an irregularity which the court can and should rectify so long as it can do so without injustice. It can at last be asserted that 'it is not possible for an honest litigant in Her Majesty's Supreme Court to be

---

[155] *Craig* v. *Kanssen* [1943] KB 256.
[156] Zuckerman, *Zuckerman on Civil Procedure: Principles of Practice*, at 28.
[157] Daniell, *The Practice of the High Court of Chancery*, Vol. I at 298ff.
[158] [1963] Ch 502, 527.

defeated by any mere technicality, any slip, any mistaken step in his litigation.'(*Pontin v. Wood* [1962] 1 Q.B. 594: per Holroyd Pearce L.J. at p. 609 citing Bowen LJ). That could not be said in 1963: see *In re Pritchard, decd.* But it can be in 1966. The new rule does it.[159]

Apart from a small number of limited circumstances where procedural default was held to be so fundamental it could not be cured, the RSC by 1965 had overcome the formal limitation on the *Tildesley* test.[160] Its approach to amendment and default was thereafter entirely focused on enabling the real issues to be considered by the court and claims determined on their substantive merits. It was finally, as Edmund-Davies LJ would later describe it in a way reminiscent of Holdsworth's description of equity's approach, an 'all-embracing principle ... [to which] ... all other considerations must be subordinate'.[161]

2.5 Conclusion: complete justice and its consequences

The English civil justice system has been characterised as having adopted three different approaches to vindicating rights. It is said initially to have adopted a formalist approach, which required absolute compliance with procedural rules. This, however, led to a denial of justice, as it resulted in claims failing on technical grounds rather than being determined on their substantive merits. It is then said to have rejected that approach in the 1870s in favour of an approach that adopted as strict an approach to ensuring claims were determined on their merits as it had previously taken to securing formal rule-compliance. Formalism was replaced by the aim of securing substantive justice. Finally, it is said to have rejected that second approach in 1999 in favour of one that balanced substantive justice against two procedural aims: securing procedural economy and efficiency.[162] Such accounts are flawed. They are flawed because, throughout its history, the

---

[159] [1967] 2 QB 729 at 735–736.

[160] See *Bernstein v. Jackson* [1982] 1 WLR 1082, which stated that as the RSC provided a complete code for the renewal of writs, it had to be relied on rather than the power to cure procedural default. Also, defaults which undermined the court's ability to arrive at a decision on the merits through, for instance, amounting to a denial of the right to a proper hearing, could not be cured, see *Charlesworth v. Focusmulti Ltd, The Independent*, 15 March 1993, CA; transcript 1993 0228 CA, 17 February.

[161] *Associated Leisure v. Associated Newspapers* [1970] 2 QB 450 at 457.

[162] A. Zuckerman, 'Quality and Economy in Civil Procedure: The Case for Commuting Correct Judgments for Timely Judgments' 14 (1994) *Oxford Journal of Legal Studies* 353.

justice system has aimed to secure substantive justice. It did not suddenly discover, and start acting consistently with, that aim in the 1870s.

Prior to the 1870 reforms, it took two different approaches to securing substantive justice: formalism at common law and what was known as complete justice in equity. The former treated strict rule-compliance as an essential if it was to decide claims on their substantive merits because of its failure to separate substantive and procedural law. Procedure was part of the substantive merits. The latter took a strict approach to rule-compliance, but married it with a liberal approach to procedural amendment or the grant of relief from the adverse consequences of procedural error. It did so because equity treated securing substantive justice above all other considerations. These very different approaches to securing justice were the subject of scrutiny over the course of the nineteenth century. From the 1830s, that scrutiny saw common law formalism start to weaken, as it began to be appreciated that it was an inadequate mechanism to secure substantive justice. From the 1850s, it produced an initial attempt to replace formalism with equity's approach. In the 1870s, with the formal merger of procedural common law and equity, common law formalism was finally rejected in favour of equity's complete justice approach.[163] That equity-based approach remained in place until 1999. The reality is not as discontinuous as the generally accepted picture suggests.

The adoption of equity's approach to securing substantive justice as the RSC's implicit overriding objective was not straightforward. The initial attempt to do so from the 1850s did not succeed. It took the RSC's introduction in 1875, followed by a twenty-year line of Court of Appeal authority, to ensure that the justice system operated consistently with it. It took time and concerted effort, but that effort successfully produced a paradigm shift in justice. Common law formalism, which had formed part of the justice system's framework, was rejected as a means to securing substantive justice in favour of the adoption of equity's complete justice approach to securing it. This paradigm shift succeeded so well that by 1996 the approach taken from equity was understood to represent a universal and timeless theory of justice.[164] Given its origin, it was, in fact, neither. It was simply one of two historical approaches taken to securing substantive justice.

---

[163] Judicature Act 1873, s. 24.
[164] *Gale v. Superdrug* [1996] 1 WLR 1089 at 1098–1099. See Chapters 6 and 7.

The RSC's adoption of equity's approach to securing substantive justice had a fatal consequence for its efficacy. It undermined its ability to secure its very aim. It resulted in a justice system where satellite procedural litigation was endemic, with the costs and delays that generated equally endemic. The structural and procedural reforms of the nineteenth and twentieth century might have gone a long way to ensuring that litigation could progress efficiently and economically on the way to a judgment on the substantive merits of the claim. What they did not and could not deal with, however, was the level and degree of delay and cost generated as a consequence of the RSC adopting equity's approach to securing substantive justice. The theory of justice taken from equity robbed the RSC's rules (which, applied properly, could have delivered substantive justice economically and efficiently),[165] of any normative value.[166] This in turn led to an overly adversarial approach to litigation; one that ultimately and ironically undermined the system's very aim through fostering procedural litigation, producing delay and expense that was 'often excessive, disproportionate and unpredictable'.[167] It did so because, as the Woolf Review concluded, the RSC operated so that its rules were 'flouted on a vast scale', while litigation timetables were generally ignored and procedural obligations and requirements 'complied with when convenient to the interests of one of the parties and not otherwise'.[168] That this was the case was, as rightly argued by Zuckerman, an inevitable consequence of the RSC's overarching aim of securing substantive justice in each individual claim.[169] It was because the *Tildesley* test, as it applied to amendment and relief from the consequences of non-compliance, as well as its adoption in *Birkett* v. *James* regarding dismissal of proceedings for excessive delay,[170] bred a

---

[165] H. Woolf (1995), at 7.

[166] A point made on a number of occasions by Zuckerman, e.g., A. Zuckerman, *Civil Procedure* (1st edn) (Butterworths, 2003) at 31.

[167] H. Woolf (1995), at 7–8.   [168] Ibid. at 8.

[169] A. Zuckerman, 'Compliance with Process Obligations and Fair Trial' in M. Andenas, N. Andrews and R. Nazzini, *The Future of Transnational Civil Litigation* (British Institute of International and Comparative Law, 2004); Sorabji, 'The Road to New Street Station' at 78; *Ketteman & Others* v. *Hansel Properties & Others* [1987] AC 189 at 203; *Atkinson* v. *Fitzwalter & Another* [1987] 1 WLR 201 at 204; *Bobolas & Another* v. *Economist Newspaper Ltd* [1987] 1 WLR 1101 at 1107; *Costellow* v. *Somerset County Council* [1993] 1 WLR 256 at 264–265; *Begum* v. *Yousaf* [2002] EWCA Civ 187 at [38]–[40].

[170] [1978] AC 297. The test for relief from the consequences for failing to properly prosecute claims laid down in *Birkett* v. *James* [1978] AC 297 was a direct application of the

complacent attitude to compliance with procedural rules, especially process time limits.[171] It effectively rendered them optional. Absent one of the justifications set out by Bramwell LJ in *Tildesley*, which was both affirmed by Fry LJ in *Kurtz v. Spence*,[172] who explained that the policy underpinning the RSC was to ensure that claims were decided on their substantive merits, and applied in *Birkett*, relief had to be granted. To do otherwise would undermine the RSC's substantive aim.

Procedural complacency on the part of litigants gave rise to the *Tildesley* test's second effect. It resulted in the generation of an inordinate amount of protracted satellite litigation concerning amendment, relief from non-compliance or procedural delay. The necessary corollary of such satellite litigation was the accretion of an equally large amount of case law interpreting procedural rules. This accretion, of necessity, required courts to draw very technical distinctions between present cases and prior precedent in order to ensure that the court fulfilled its duty to achieve substantive justice. A prime example of this accretion, which itself further fuelled ever-more satellite litigation and its attendant cost and time disbenefits, was that which arose surrounding the court's power to strike out cases for want of prosecution following *Birkett*. The problem this approach posed for cost- and time-effective claim disposal was highlighted by the Woolf Reports as one of the central elements of the RSC that contributed to unnecessary litigant cost and delay.[173] It gave rise to such cost and delay because it necessarily required courts and litigators to examine each rule often on a line-by-line and word-by-word basis in order to arrive at the sought-for distinguishing feature to allow precedent to be circumvented in order to enable a decision consistent

---

Tildesley test. Delay would result in a strike-out if it was such as to demonstrate *mala fides* on the part of the defaulter, i.e. because it was so intentional and contumelious that it amounted to an abuse of process, or if it rendered the pursuit of accuracy impossible, i.e. because there was a serious risk that a fair trial could not take place or that it was likely to result in serious prejudice to the non-defaulting party. Questions of prejudice raised the question of whether costs were an adequate cure. Where a fair trial could take place, rarely would a strike out be justified, as in such an instance it would simply transform rules of court into the means to discipline parties, which was implicitly contrary to the *Tildesley* test, as explained in *Cropper: Department of Transport v. Chris Smaller (Transport) Ltd* [1989] AC 1197 at 1207.

[171] RSC (1965) Ord. 6 r. 8; CPR 7.5: RSC (1965) Ord. 18 r. 2; CPR 15.4; P. Middleton, *Civil Justice and Legal Aid* (HMSO, 1997) at 2.35; M. Zander, 'The Government's Plans on Civil Justice' 61 (1998) *Modern Law Review* at 388.

[172] *Kurtz v. Spence* [1887] LR 36 ChD 770 at 776; RSC (1965) Ord. 19 r. 1; Ord. 24 r. 16.1

[173] H. Woolf (1995), at 15, 208 and 215.

with the aim of securing substantive justice to be made. So great was this problem that *Birkett* generated such a degree of nuanced parsing that it resembled less a legal rule than an example of medieval scholasticism.[174]

Complacency instituted a vicious circle of complexity, satellite litigation, delay and increased costs in the individual claim. In turn, this resulted in individual claims utilising more than necessary and more than reasonable court resources. Excessive court resource allocation to a number of extant claims precluded fair resource allocation to other claims. It did so because it monopolised scarce judicial resources. Complacency and its attendant consequences gave rise to substantive justice's denial to the many, while securing it for the few. The equity-based approach to securing justice through the *Tildesley* test and *Birkett* v. *James* gave rise to such complacency and its consequences in the following way.

First, it should be remembered that neither litigants nor their legal representatives are perfect. It is inevitable that process obligations will, inadvertently, be breached. Mistakes will always happen. Incorrect forms will always be completed. Procedural rules will always be breached, time limits missed.[175] Pleadings are, to a certain extent, always going to call for amendment. Equally, absent an effective disincentive, deliberate tactical non-compliance will take place. Where one litigant fails to comply with process obligations, it is practically inevitable that, again absent a disincentive, the opposing party will seek to take advantage of that fact. It is so; as such, applications potentially have a number of consequences. They could, under the RSC, result in their opponent's case being struck out or, due to the increase in cost and delay they engendered, they could

---

[174] The reawakening of this aspect of *Tildesley* was, in fact, *Allen* v. *Sir Alfred McAlpine & Sons Ltd* [1968] 1 All ER 543, which led on to *Birkett*. *Birkett* itself generated, for instance, the following leading authorities, in which it was either applied, distinguished or discussed: *Firman* v. *Ellis* [1978] QB 886; *Acrow (Engineers)* v. *Hathaway* [1981] 2 All ER 161; *Hytrac Converoys Ltd* v. *Conveyors International Ltd* [1982] 3 All ER 415; *United Bank Ltd* v. *Maniar* [1988] Ch 109; *Logicrose Ltd* v. *Southend United Football Club* [1988] 1 WLR 1256; *Department of Transport* v. *Chris Smaller (Transport) Ltd* [1989] AC 1197; *Barclays Bank Plc* v. *Miller* [1990] 1 WLR 343; *Costellow* v. *Somerset CC* [1993] 1 WLR 256; *Trill* v. *Sacher* [1993] 1 All ER 961; *Roebuck* v. *Mungovin* [1994] 1 All ER 568; *Rastin* v. *British Steel* [1994] 1 WLR 732; *Shtun* v. *Zalejska* [1996] 3 All ER 411; *Jackson* v. *Slater Harrison and Co Ltd* [1996] 1 WLR 597; *Marchday Group Plc, Re* [1998] BCC 800; *Choraria* v. *Sethia* [1998] CLC 625; *Arbuthnot Latham Bank Ltd* v. *Trafalgar Holdings Ltd* [1998] 1 WLR 1426.

[175] E.g., *Re Pritchard (deceased)* [1963] Ch 502; *Parsons* v. *George* [2004] 1 WLR 3264; *Steele* v. *Mooney* [2005] 1 WLR 2819.

pressurise the opposing party into settling the litigation disadvanta-geously, or even withdrawing it without settlement.

Secondly, under the RSC, the court on such applications was con-cerned to assess whether it was in the interests of justice to exercise its discretionary power to forgive non-compliance, grant permission to amend, or strike out for delay. The central question for the court in such cases was always fundamentally the same: was it fair to grant relief? A judge asking that question will, and did, tend to answer it by reference to the RSC's aim. In other words, was it in the interests of justice, for instance, to frustrate the court's ability to determine a claim on its substantive merits because of technical default? The problem with such an approach is that it institutionalises a strong presumption that party failure to comply with process obligations would be forgiven, the amend-ment granted:[176] a problem just as prevalent in other jurisdictions that adopted the RSC's approach as it was in England.[177] The creation of such a culture, however, denudes process rules and obligations of any real normative value. This was particularly the case where questions of non-compliance or delay in the prosecution of claims was concerned because, in general, striking out the claim was the only genuinely available sanc-tion for non-compliance and, as that conflicted with the aim of securing substantive justice, it would not be exercised.[178] This in turn led to a great deal of satellite litigation centred on the question of whether the pre-sumption in favour of forgiveness or permission to amend should be acted on or not. It did so because while the presumption existed, parties could not take it for granted that in their individual case the court would exercise it in their favour. The court might always decide that the *Tildesley* and *Birkett* tests were not satisfied. The tension between the presumption and the existence of the discretion therefore bred uncer-tainty. That uncertainty bred procedural litigation. As Zuckerman put it:

> the desire not to allow matters of procedure to stand in the way of doing justice on the merits created extensive scope for litigation that had nothing to do with the merits but which could well obstruct a merits based resolution to the dispute.[179]

---

[176] *Holmes* v. *SGB* [2001] EWCA Civ 354 at [33].

[177] A. Lyons, 'Recasting the Landscape of Interlocutory Applications: *AON Risk Services Australia Ltd v Australian National University*' [2010] *Sydney Law Review* 549 at 550–51.

[178] H. Woolf (1995), at 7–8 and 207.   [179] Zuckerman, *Civil Procedure* at 31.

The RSC, as a consequence, resulted in too great a number of such applications and appeals of decisions arising out of such applications, which did not deal with progressing a claim towards a merits-based hearing, but on the contrary, either sought to avoid such a hearing, or sought to ensure that such a hearing took place in order to deal with the procedural issue.[180]

The inevitable consequence of this was that the justice system following the 1870 reforms was as riven with excess cost and delay as its predecessors. By embedding equity's approach to securing substantive justice into the RSC, with painful irony it undermined the RSC's ability to achieve it in individual cases. That it did so was a consequence of its very aim; a consequence which, due to its effect on rule-compliance and amendment, ignored financial and temporal considerations both for the immediate parties to any claim and for litigants as a whole. Excess cost and delay thereby arose as a consequence not of structural and procedural flaws, which the nineteenth and twentieth century spent their entire focus on, but rather, as a consequence of the system's aim. Substantive justice was antipathetic to economy and efficiency either in the individual case or in respect of access to justice for other litigants who suffered the adverse effects of litigation conducted inefficiently and uneconomically. The effect granting relief from the consequences of procedural error had on other litigants was, however, of no concern. The only relevant consideration, as it had been under equity, was to avoid injustice, arising out of the application of procedure, between the immediate parties to any one claim.[181] The inevitable consequence of this was that no matter what procedural improvements were made through the many reforms, described in Chapter 1, carried out during the twentieth century to render it better able to achieve substantive reforms at necessary litigation cost they were doomed to failure: none of them tackled the source of the problem. Only if normal science was rejected, and an extraordinary investigation embarked on might the problems of cost and delay be remedied, as only such a step would examine justice's aim. The Woolf Reports took that step and rejected the RSC's equity-based approach in favour of a novel theory of justice. It took the first step. To successfully replace one paradigm with another would require more. It would require an understanding of the nature of what was to be done and a concerted effort to secure the desired result. It would require not just the adoption of the approach taken by the Judicature Commission.

---

[180] N. Andrews, *English Civil Procedure* (Oxford University Press, 2003) at 35.
[181] *Saunders* v. *Pawley* (1885) 14 QBD 234.

It would need the same approach as that taken to implement its recommendations in the years following the Judicature Acts. There would have to be both proper understanding and concerted effort to give effect to that understanding. In order to prepare the ground for the discussion in Chapters 4 to 6 of the nature of Woolf's new theory, and how it differs from the RSC's equity-based theory of justice, it is necessary to consider Bentham's theory of justice.

3

Bentham: substantive justice is no end in itself

In England ... at no time has the system of procedure acted upon been in fact
directed to the ends of justice.[1]

the whole body of the Law has for its object the greatest happiness of the
greatest number.[2]

3.1 Introduction

The nineteenth century did not only see the gradual adoption of structural
and procedural reforms to the justice system intended to improve its
ability to determine individual cases on their substantive merits. It also
saw Jeremy Bentham develop a sustained critique of all aspects of the
English legal system, not least the operation of its civil courts and
the aim that they pursued.[3] As part of that critique, as Postema rightly
noted, he set out the first serious 'attempt in the English language ... at a
philosophical account of the law of procedure'.[4] This chapter examines that
account and the ways in which it differed from the equity-based theory of
justice that was being embedded into English civil justice through the
Victorian reforms and the RSC's introduction. It does so in order to
demonstrate: that a theory of justice can take as its predominant policy
aim the achievement of something other than substantive justice; and that
in doing so it can legitimately deny substantive justice's achievement in

---

[1] J. Bentham, 'Principles of Judicial Procedure, with the outlines of a Procedure Code' (PJP),
   in *The Works of Jeremy Bentham* (ed. Bowring) (William Tait, 1843) Vol. II (hereinafter
   J. Bentham (1843) PJP) at 8.
[2] Ibid.
[3] For an overview of the breadth of Bentham's criticism of all aspects of English law, see:
   W. Holdsworth, *A History of English Law* (7th edn)) (Sweet & Maxwell, 1966) Vol. XIII;
   G. Postema, *Bentham and the Common Law World* (Clarendon Press, 1986).
[4] G. Postema, 'The Principle of Utility and the Law of Procedure: Bentham's Theory of
   Adjudication' 11 (1976–77) *Georgia Law Review* 1393, 1393.

order to further that new policy aim. In doing so a framework for properly conceiving Woolf's new theory of justice can be constructed.

In contrast to that equity-based theory, Bentham's theory of justice had as its substantive policy aim the maximising of general welfare or happiness: the principle of utility. It was a theory of distributive justice rather than individual justice. Rather than being focused on securing substantive justice in the individual case, it was concerned to secure a fair distribution of utility across society by, in so far as the justice system was concerned, maximising its production.[5] Bentham's substantive policy aim for the justice system was, primarily, implemented by its procedural law being designed and operated consistently with three subsidiary, instrumental, policy aims. These were:

- a commitment to achieving substantive justice, which for Bentham included a commitment to securing the effective enforcement of the substantive law;
- a commitment to securing substantive justice achievement at no more than necessary litigation cost and delay, where necessary meant the minimum required to achieve that direct end; and finally,
- a commitment to ensuring, either partially or absolutely, the frustration of substantive justice in order to maximise utility.

3.2   Bentham's utilitarian critique

Bentham's primary philosophical concern throughout his career was the development of a particular form of utilitarian, consequentialist theory of ethics, known as welfare-hedonism.[6] Such theories posit that the moral value of any action depends not on its intrinsic qualities, but rather, on the sum of its effects. For a welfare-hedonist, a morally good action is one that produces more happiness, or pleasure, than suffering. Conversely, a morally bad action is one that produces more suffering than happiness.[7] Assessing the moral value of any act requires an assessment of the global sum of its effects. An assessment is therefore required to ascertain whether any particular act maximises happiness or utility generally, rather than for any particular individual: it focuses on the whole of society rather

---

[5] S. Fleischacker, *A Short History of Distributive Justice* (Harvard University Press, 2005) at 103ff.

[6] T. Mulgan, *Understanding Utilitarianism* (Acumen, 2007); R. Dworkin, *A Matter of Principle* (Harvard University Press, 1985) at 274ff; R. Dworkin, *Law's Empire* (Hart, 2007).

[7] J. S. Mill, *Utilitarianism* (Fontana Press, 1962) (M. Warnock, ed.) at 257.

than any particular individual.[8] As J. S. Mill described it: 'The happiness which forms the utilitarian standard of what is right in conduct is not the agent's own happiness but that of all concerned. As between his own happiness and that of others, utilitarianism requires him to be as strictly impartial as a disinterested and benevolent spectator.'[9]

There are, however, different versions of utilitarianism. The most basic form which Bentham did not develop, although there are passages where he appears to commit himself to it, is that which is now known as act, or direct utilitarianism.[10] This focuses the assessment of value entirely on each act carried out by each individual. The morally right action is the one that produces the most happiness or pleasure by way of contrast with other acts that the individual in question could have carried out at that time.[11] Bentham developed a more sophisticated form of utilitarianism: rule or indirect utilitarianism, which focused on institutional design, not specific, individual action. Rather than focus on the question of which acts maximise happiness, indirect utilitarianism focuses on which social institutions are best able to maximise pleasure. As Rawls summed it up, in his critique of utilitarian ethics, its 'main idea [was] that society is rightly ordered so as to achieve the greatest net balance of satisfaction summed over all the individuals belonging to it'.[12] In Bentham's terms, how should society, its institutions, their rules and procedures be ordered to produce the greatest happiness for the greatest number?[13] Which institutions and rules would maximise the generation of behavioural norms that would maximise aggregate utility? As Bentham explained it:

> By the principle of utility is meant that principle which approves or disapproves of every action whatsoever, according to the tendency which it appears to have to augment or diminish the happiness of the party whose interest is in question: or, what is the same thing in other words, to

---

[8] J. Bentham in ibid. at 33ff; Goodin in P. Singer, *Practical Ethics* (Cambridge University Press, 1993) at 241.

[9] J. S. Mill in Mill, *Utilitarianism* at 268 and 262; Bentham in ibid. at 37 (addition added to text in July 1822) and 64ff; J. Bentham (1843) PJP at 8.

[10] Ibid. at 34. Postema, *Bentham and the Common Law World*; J. Dinwiddy, 'Adjudication under Bentham's Pannomion', in W. Twining, *Bentham: Selected Writings of J. Dinwiddy* (Stanford University Press, 2004).

[11] G. Moore, *Ethics and the Nature of Moral Philosophy* (Oxford University Press, 2005) at 1–39; B. Williams, *Ethics and the Limits of Philosophy* (Fontana, 1985) at 75–7; Mulgan, *Understanding Utilitarianism* at 115ff.

[12] J. Rawls, *A Theory of Justice* (Oxford University Press, 1972) at 22.

[13] J. Bentham (1843) Vol. IX, *The Constitutional Code* (hereinafter CC) at 5; L. Solum, 'Procedural Justice' 78 (2004) *Southern California Law Review* 181, 251.

promote or to oppose that happiness. I say of every action whatsoever: and therefore not only of every action of a private individual, but of every measure of government.[14]

Bentham's assessment of the early nineteenth-century justice system, as a consequence of his utilitarianism, was concerned with the question of whether it was consistent with the principle of utility, i.e. was it best able to maximise aggregate happiness or utility?[15] His answer, in a coruscating, even if disorganised, attack on the common law, equity, the court structure and its operation and the conduct of the legal profession, was a resounding 'no'.[16] In his view, the justice system was in no way consistent with the principle of utility. He understood it to be fundamentally corrupt, paying no more than lip service to the vindication of rights. While it might claim to secure substantive justice, in reality, as he saw it, the system existed and operated solely to satisfy the financial self-interest of lawyers and judges.[17] To that end, its processes were overly complex and spread across an unnecessarily complicated web of courts of competing jurisdiction.[18] Courts, judges and lawyers contrived to ensure that decisions would be arrived at on 'grounds avowedly foreign to the merits',[19] and at too great a cost, delay and vexation.[20] Where

---

[14] J. Bentham in Mill, *Utilitarianism* at 34.

[15] J. Bentham in ibid. at 59ff and 64ff.

[16] The destructive aspect of his critique would ultimately play a positive part in the nineteenth-century reform process even if, for a significant period, he was, as Sunderland put it, no more than a critical 'voice crying in the wilderness'; see E. Miller, 'The English Struggle for Procedural Reform' 29 (1925–26) *Harvard Law Review* 725, 728; Miller, 'The Formative Principles of Civil Procedure I' 18 (1923–24) *Illinois Law Review* 1, 3; Mill, *Utilitarianism* at 113–14.

[17] J. Bentham (1843) PJP, at 7, 13, 48–9 and at 63: 'In all cases, the object being to put money into the pockets of the judges, the object, and that alone, except the like benefit to the other members of the firm Judge & Co (i.e., lawyers), the mode of procedure is made subservient'; Vol. V, *Letters on Scotch Reform* (hereinafter SR) at 2 and 7; CC at 40; Vol. VI, *An Introductory View of the Rationale of Judicial Evidence; for the use of non-lawyers as well as lawyers* (hereinafter IRE) at 10–11 and 37.

[18] J. Bentham (1843) PJP, at 48–9, 173ff, and see 7 and 13, where he makes the same point where he characterises English procedure as presenting 'no other object than a system of absurdity directed to no good end'; SR at 10; although see SR at 17 for his positive view of the existence of competing courts of co-extensive jurisdiction.

[19] J. Bentham (1843) SR at 11; PJP at 32: 'Of the judicatories self-styled Equity courts, dilatoriness is, to the knowledge of everybody, the characteristic and most cardinal vice.'

[20] For Bentham, vexation referred to an unintended negative outcome, or evil produced by a justice system, see J. Bentham (1843) Vol. VI, *Rationale of Judicial Evidence* (hereinafter RJE) at 345; this could include unnecessary time, expense, worry, commercial difficulties caused by unjustifiable litigation or unnecessarily incurred time and expense during

proceedings ended in a merits-based decision, they did so more by accident than by design.[21] It was, in his view, a justice system as divorced from the pursuit of substantive justice as it was from the pursuit of utility.

3.3   Substantive law reform: applying the principle of utility

Bentham did not, however, simply develop a negative critique of the justice system. Having identified its ills, he went on to set out, across a range of writings, a constructive account. That account had a number of elements. First, substantive civil law, e.g. the law of contract, tort, property etc., had to be fully codified and drafted consistently with the principle of utility.[22] As he put it:

> Of the substantive branch of the law, the only defensible object or end in view, is the maximization of the happiness of the greatest number of the members of the community in question.[23]

If substantive law was designed consistently with this aim, individuals acting consistently with it would generate a utility value (x), where (x) is the maximum possible amount of utility. Assume, for instance, that two individuals enter a contract for the supply of goods and that contract law is designed consistently with the principle of utility. By fulfilling their contractual obligations, those individuals will maximise aggregate utility. Their acts will have a utility value of (x): substantive law's full utility value will have been realised.

Substantive law was not only to be drafted in order to maximise utility. It was also to be drafted in a simple, straightforward manner so that all members of society could readily understand its provisions without

litigation prior to final judgment. And see J. Bentham (1843) SR at 47; IRE at 11 and 40; PJP at 48–9, 76, 87, and 111–14.

[21] Ibid. at 8: 'In England ... at no time has the system of procedure acted upon been in fact directed to the ends of justice ...'; SR at 11; IRE at 5–6. With this in mind, it is unsurprising that Bentham would highlight as one of technical procedure's negative consequences the ease with which meretricious claims and defences could be pursued, see SR at 22 and PJP at 13, 48–9 and 63, where he states that if judges were paid by salary, their interest would become one focused on minimising the number of actions commenced and that the court's aim was to cast its net wide to let in 'the whole tribe of insincere litigants on both sides of the case', and the litigant whose 'object is to do wrong'.

[22] J. Bentham (1843) PJP at 6–8 and 13; RJE at 205; Vol. I, *Principles of the Civil Code* (hereinafter PCC) at 301; Postema, 'The Principle of Utility and the Law of Procedure' at 1395; Dinwiddy, 'Adjudication under Bentham's Pannomion'.

[23] J. Bentham (1843) PJP at 6.

needing recourse to a lawyer. Each member of society was to be their own lawyer,[24] thus maximising the prospects that they would act according to the law, while minimising the prospect of their having to seek costly legal advice regarding the proper implementation of the law which, if it were necessary, would tend to undermine utility maximisation. A necessary corollary of this was that the common law would have to be abolished: the only valid law was to be simple, easy to understand code law.[25] While this would mean that courts were to be prohibited from developing the law through judgments, they were still to play a positive role in ensuring that the law was capable of maximising utility. They were to be given a power to suspend legal proceedings where they concluded that the substantive law they would otherwise have to apply, did not permit utility-maximisation, i.e. they were given a power to stay proceedings indefinitely.[26] In addition to this, they were also to be given a power to issue advisory recommendations to the legislature. These could be issued where the court considered there was a gap in the law or that it required amendment to bring it in line with utility.[27] The courts could not develop the law, but they could invite the legislature to do so.

3.4   Adjective law reform: utility the predominant policy aim

Bentham recognised, however, that properly designed substantive law was a necessary but not sufficient condition for maximising utility. This was so because substantive law, no matter how well designed, is not self-executing.[28] Through inadvertence, ignorance (notwithstanding the law being drafted so each could be their own lawyer), genuine dispute or deliberate conduct, individuals can act inconsistently with substantive law. Such conduct frustrates its aim. It is not necessarily the case, for instance, that the parties to the contract for the supply of goods would fulfil their obligations under it. In order to maximise utility in such circumstances, it would be necessary to issue legal proceedings. If the

---

[24] Postema, *Bentham and the Common Law World*, at 425.

[25] J. Bentham (1843) RJE at 205 (per Bowring's note); PJP at 6–8 and 13; PCC at 301; Postema, 'The Principle of Utility and the Law of Procedure' at 1395; Dinwiddy, 'Adjudication under Bentham's Pannomion'; F. Ferraro, 'Direct and Indirect Utilitarianism in Bentham's Theory of Adjudication' 12 (2010) *Journal of Bentham Studies* 1.

[26] Dinwiddy, 'Adjudication under Bentham's Pannomion' at 158–61.   [27] Ibid.

[28] Postema, 'The Principle of Utility and the Law of Procedure' at 1402; J. Lever, 'Why Procedure is More Important than Substantive Law' [1999] *International & Comparative Law Quarterly* 285.

justice system remained in its unreformed, nineteenth-century state, however, there was, for Bentham, no real prospect that it would be able to determine disputes concerning the proper application of substantive law in a way that would maximise utility. Through the law's delays, its expense, complication and lack of genuine desire to secure substantive justice, it would produce more harm than good through attempting, or rather, purporting, to give proper effect to substantive law. The justice system, then, just like the substantive law, had to be redesigned consistently with the principle of utility.[29] It would have to be redesigned to permit the proper enforcement of substantive law at least cost and with minimal time expended. In that way, it would maximise utility through the positive enforcement of the law, whilst generating the least cost in terms of disutility that would inevitably arise through the resort to litigation. This would require a number of things to be done.

First, the court structure would have to be simplified.[30] Bentham thus anticipated the structural reforms that in 1870 saw the creation of the High Court and Court of Appeal. Simplification would reduce the time taken to provide, and the cost of giving proper effect to substantive law. Equally, the link between the judiciary and the legal profession had to be broken. This was to be achieved through the introduction of a salaried career judiciary: a career that would not be open to the legal profession. No longer should there be any mutual interest between judge and lawyer to artificially prolong proceedings and inflate legal fees.[31] Structural reform of the courts and legal profession was not, however, sufficient. If the justice system were to fulfil its purpose,[32] its processes as well as its structure would have to change.[33] As the substantive law was to be revised and codified, so was procedural, or as he described it, adjective law. A new 'code of judicial procedure' would have to be designed.[34] This new code was, unlike the common law, equity or the RSC, not to

---

[29] J. Bentham (1843) PJP at 5–6, 13–15 and 20; IRE at 7; RJE at 7; CC at 25–6; Postema, 'The Principle of Utility and the Law of Procedure' at 1396.

[30] J. Bentham (1843) SR at 7; PJP at 7, 11–13 and 169ff; RJE at 213ff; Postema, *Bentham and the Common Law World* at 345ff.

[31] J. Bentham (1843) PJP at 22, 63, 111–12 and 173; SR at 6–7, 10–11, 29 and 32–3; RJE at 203–4; IRE at 12–13 and 88–9; 41. H. Hart, *Essays on Bentham* (Oxford University Press, 2001).

[32] J. Bentham (1843) PJP at 6 and 20; Postema, 'The Principle of Utility and the Law of Procedure' at 1396.

[33] Ferraro, 'Direct and Indirect Utilitarianism in Bentham's Theory of Adjudication' at 6.

[34] J. Bentham (1843) IRE at 7; RJE at 7; CC at 25–6; PJP at 5–6, 13 and 15 and 19–20; M. Mack, *Jeremy Bentham: An Odyssey of Ideas 1748-1792* (Heinemann, 1962) at 287.

have as its ostensible aim the production of substantive justice. It was not to be consistent with a traditional theory of justice. In fact, Bentham would have preferred to see references to 'justice' removed entirely from his reformed justice system and replaced by references to 'utility'. Courts were not to achieve justice. They were to achieve utility and to be judged by whether they did so, not by whether they achieved, as he viewed it, some vague and shifting notion of justice.[35] As he explained the position in *Principles of Judicial Procedure*:

> Of the adjective branch of law, the only defensible object, or say end in view, is the maximisation of the execution and effect given to the substantive branch of the law.[36]

Adjective law was to secure its aim, not through giving effect to the principle of utility directly, as the substantive law was to do if acted on properly. It was to do so indirectly, through securing compliance with substantive law.[37] Rather than a theory of justice in the traditional sense, Bentham wanted to recast adjective law – the procedural code – as a specific application of his theory of utility: justice was utility. The question then was how the new procedural code was to maximise utility. In terms of institutional design, how was it to conform to Bentham's theory of justice as utility? It was to do so through being designed and operated consistently with two subordinate policy aims, 'the ends of justice upon the occasion of judicature'.[38] Those subordinate aims were, as Bentham described them, justice's positive or direct end and its negative or collateral ends:[39]

> When the whole body of the Law has for its object the greatest happiness of the greatest number, the whole of the adjective branch taken together may be said to have two specific ends: the one positive, maximizing the execution and effect given to the substantive branch; the other negative, minimizing the evil, hardship, in various shapes necessary to the accomplishment of the main specified end.[40]

These two ends were the instrumental means by which justice – utility – was to be done. A system that could realise these aims was one that maximised utility.

Adjective law because procedure stands in relation to substantive law as an adjective does to a noun, see Postema, 'The Principle of Utility and the Law of Procedure' at 1399.

[35] J. Bentham (1843) RJE at 8; Postema, 'The Principle of Utility and the Law of Procedure' at 1409ff.

[36] J. Bentham (1843) PJP at 6.   [37] Ibid.   [38] J. Bentham (1843) RJE at 8.

[39] J. Bentham (1843) PJP at 6; SR at 5; RJE at 213.   [40] J. Bentham (1843) PJP at 8.

3.5 Justice's direct end: maximising utility through enforcing substantively just decisions

The primary means by which the justice system was to maximise utility was through the procedural code being designed and operated so that it could achieve justice's positive, direct end.[41] It was to do so in the first instance by ensuring that individual legal proceedings ended in a substantively just decision. Bentham's theory of justice thus incorporated, as a subordinate and instrumental aim, what for the traditional theory of justice was its predominant aim. As he put it:

> On the occasion of each individual course of judicial procedure, there are two necessarily distinguishable questions, – the question of law, and the question of fact: whether the state of the law is as alleged, and whether the state of fact is as alleged.[42]

Having identified true fact and right law, the court seized of a claim was to apply one to the other. Judgments were to be reached only 'upon appropriate grounds; viz on the joint consideration of the law ... and of the evidence'. There were to be no decisions except 'upon the merits'.[43] In this way, the court would reach the 'right decision'.[44] Substantive justice would be achieved. It would not, however, be sufficient to maximise aggregate utility. Like substantive law, court judgments are not self-executing. Effective enforcement is sometimes necessary. In order to meet this practical point, Bentham understood justice's direct end to have a second aspect: a commitment to ensuring that substantively just decisions were enforced effectively. Justice's direct end required both 'right decision and conformable execution. . . Decision is right, in so far as, by giving execution and effect to it, the will expressed by the law is conformed to – the eventual predictions delivered by the law, carried into effect.'[45] Only through effective enforcement of individual judgments could the justice system give effect to substantive law, and thereby maximise utility. If it were able to do so, it would also help maximise utility in another, again indirect, way. It would do so by ensuring that the substantive law maintained its normative force generally. A justice system readily able to secure justice's direct end in individual proceedings is one that can provide an effective mechanism for deterring individuals

---

[41] Ibid. at 20 and 29.   [42] J. Bentham (1843) CC at 26; RJE at 203–4 and 210; IRE at 7.
[43] J. Bentham (1843) SR at 10–11; PJP at 15.
[44] J. Bentham (1843) CC at 25; PJP at 29ff and 174 and 178; SR at 5; IRE at 88–9.
[45] J. Bentham (1843) CC at 25–6; RJE at 203–4.

from breaching contracts, committing torts or otherwise acting contrary to the demands of utility as given life in the substantive law. Through promoting voluntary compliance – or deterring non-compliance – with substantive law, as a consequence of its ability to maximise utility in individual proceedings, justice's direct end's achievement thus has a wider effect than that which it had in any individual proceeding. The strength of the system's ability to secure this wider effect was, however, a function of its ability to secure substantive justice and effective enforcement. Its ability to maximise utility was not, however, simply a function of its ability to do so: justice's direct end was supported by a further policy aim: justice's collateral ends, which were equally important a means to secure the wider aim.

3.6   Justice's collateral ends: maximising utility through minimising litigation's disutility cost

The achievement of justice's direct end was the primary means by which utility was to be maximised. Bentham recognised, however, that this aim, and its achievement, was not without price. Enforcing substantive law through legal proceedings was expensive, time-consuming and caused, in Bentham's terms, vexation. A certain amount of each was both a necessary and an inevitable consequence of litigation. Litigants require sufficient time to marshal evidence or otherwise prepare their claims properly. This in turn, naturally enough, generates expense. Both time and expense give rise to vexation. Taken together, these three inevitable consequences of litigation produced a certain amount of disutility. If utility were to be maximised, such disutility had to be minimised. The reason for this is obvious. The more disutility generated during the course of litigation, the greater the reduction in utility produced in enforcing a substantively just decision. In order to maximise utility through the legal process, then, justice's direct end had to be produced at the least disutility cost. The least cost, the closest the amount of utility produced by effective enforcement of the law would be to that which would have been produced if the substantive law had been given effect without recourse to litigation.[46]

Justice's direct end was not, however, concerned with minimising disutility. Its sole focus was on securing the proper enforcement of

---

[46] J. Bentham (1843) PJP at 8 and 19; CC at 29; SR at 5 and 17.

substantive law. In order to ensure that utility could be maximised through the legal process, Bentham's theory had to go beyond justice's direct end. On its own, and just like equity and its pursuit of complete justice, the pursuit of justice's direct end provided no express break or limit on the amount of disutility cost that could properly be generated by legal proceedings. In order to maximise utility it also therefore had to contain a commitment to minimising such costs. The theory had to have a secondary aim. This was contained in what Bentham termed the collateral ends of justice. As he described their role by way of contrast with justice's direct end:

> These principles are – the ends, the direct and collateral ends, of justice, the proper and legitimate ends of procedure: on the one hand, rectitude of decision; which may be said to have place when rights are conferred, and obligations imposed, by the judge, on those persons, and those only, on whom the legislator intended that they should be conferred and imposed: on the other hand, the avoidance of unnecessary delay, vexation, and expense. The first may be called the direct end; the three latter, the collateral ends of justice.[47]

This collateral aim had a number of roles to play within Bentham's theory of justice. Its primary role was to support the achievement of justice's direct end. It was to ensure that delay, vexation and expense, and the disutility they generated, did not frustrate its achievement. Bentham described this aspect of it in this way:

> every moment beyond what is necessary to the direct ends is detrimental to the direct ends ... To the direct ends, by the intermediate eventual decease of the pursuer, by chance of deperition [destruction] of sources of evidence on both sides; and in case of personal evidence, not already in writing, danger of diminution of clearness or correctness, and completeness, by faultiness of recollection.[48]

This aspect of its role recognised the point inherent in Magna Carta's imprecation against denying justice: too great a delay in the litigation process can denude evidence of probative value, thus frustrating the court's ability to find true fact. Equally, such delay can render substantive justice's achievement valueless if judgment comes too late to be enforced effectively.[49] Similarly, unnecessary expense can undermine the court's

---

[47] J. Bentham (1843) RJE at 212–13; SR at 5; CC at 25; IRE at 10; PJP at 6–8.
[48] Ibid. at 29–30; IRE at 90.
[49] J. Bentham (1843) PJP at 17ff, 30, 111, 178; SR at 5; IRE at 86ff and 101.

ability to secure justice's direct end by causing potential litigants to refrain from issuing proceedings, causing them to abandon their claim prior to judgment, or through producing an incorrect decision by reducing the amount of probative evidence obtained and put before the court.[50] In each case, the substantive law goes unexecuted. Utility is not maximised. In the first instance, then, the collateral ends were a secondary means of securing justice's direct end. They set the boundary line beyond which delay, expense and vexation would undermine the system by frustrating the direct end's achievement. They required litigation to be conducted within the scope of that outer limit.

This, the primary and positive, role they played, was intended to ensure delay, cost and vexation did not frustrate the court's ability to reach, and enforce, a substantively just decision. In this it acted to stop utility-maximisation being frustrated. Justice's collateral ends also played a secondary positive role in Bentham's theory. This secondary role sought to promote the minimisation of the disutility cost of delay, vexation and expense: to ensure that, as far as possible, litigation was conducted at no greater cost than was absolutely necessary to secure the direct end's achievement. This was not an absolute commitment. Minimisation to no greater cost than strictly necessary was, consistently with utility-maximisation, the aim, but a degree of flexibility over and above the bare minimum was permissible. This was the case because, in some circumstances, greater cost than strictly necessary to achieve and enforce a substantively just decision could still be justifiable. Utility-maximisation need not be frustrated by the generation of unnecessary disutility costs. This can be illustrated by considering the following circumstances.

First, unnecessary delay does not always, for instance, reduce or destroy the probative value of evidence. A fair trial, in today's terms, may still be possible after many years, even though litigants have failed to prosecute a claim efficiently. Expense may be greater than strictly necessary, but justice's direct end may still be achievable. The same points can be made in respect of complexity-generated vexation.[51] Secondly, a certain degree of such unnecessary disutility cost may, in some circumstances, also be required in the pursuit of justice's direct end. Assume, for instance, that one of the parties to the breach of contract claim outlined earlier fails or is simply, for reasons outside their control, unable to obtain or submit

[50] Ibid. at 9–10.   [51] J. Bentham (1843) PJP at 30 and 178; SR at 5.

evidence in time. They are therefore unable to ensure that judgment can be reached with no more than minimal, necessary delay. An otherwise unnecessary adjournment is thus requested, which, if granted, would generate an additional, strictly unnecessary cost. The evidence is, however, of fundamental importance. If the court is to determine the dispute on its substantive merits it needs to have the evidence before it. Refusing to grant the adjournment, keeping the evidence from the court, would frustrate justice's direct end's achievement. In such circumstances, even though the adjournment generates costs that are, strictly speaking, unnecessary, it should still be allowed. Equally, the same conclusion can be reached regarding further such applications in the course of proceedings. If such applications were refused, the court would either consequently fail to maximise utility through reaching the right decision, or, by reaching the wrong decision, maximise disutility. Even if it reached no decision, that, too, would increase overall disutility as, not only would the proceedings have failed to give effect to the substantive law, but they would also have generated a degree of overall disutility as a consequence of all the work done in the litigation up to the point at which the proceedings were abandoned. These two types of unnecessary disutility cost are not rendered impermissible by a commitment to act in conformity with justice's collateral ends, as long as they do not produce disutility equal to or beyond the boundary line set by the primary aspect of justice's collateral ends. The secondary role they played was one that policed the amount of disutility generated within that boundary line. Ideally, it would require the justice system to be designed and operated so that no more than the minimum amount of delay, vexation and expense necessary to achieve justice's direct end was generated in each set of proceedings. However, the system was to be flexible enough to enable more than minimal costs to be incurred, where to do so would still tend to maximise utility. Its secondary role was one focused on minimising costs as far as possible in the pursuit of justice's direct end.[52]

3.7   Justice's collateral ends: maximising utility through frustrating justice's direct end

If Bentham's theory simply had as its aim the enforcement of substantively just decisions at minimal cost, it would have differed in no real

---

[52] J. Bentham (1843) PJP at 30.

respect from the express aims that lay behind nineteenth- and twentieth-century civil justice reform. It would have been a theory whose predominant aim was securing substantive justice, and would have promoted the minimisation of cost and delay so as not to frustrate that aim. Bentham's utilitarianism, however, required justice's collateral ends to play a further role, one that did not seek to maximise utility through ensuring the enforcement of substantive law. On the contrary, it was a reductive aim. It was concerned with ensuring that, in appropriate circumstances, justice's direct end was not achieved. It was, as Bentham described it, an aspect of the collateral ends of justice that was in 'all pervading and perpetual' conflict with the direct end, which was always to 'a greater or lesser degree obstructive to the attainment of the [direct] end'.[53] It might be thought that anything that was obstructive or antagonistic to the achievement of justice's direct end would be incompatible with Bentham's theory. A system that was explicitly intended to be the means to an end that was said to be 'the execution of the commands issued, the fulfilment of the predictions delivered, of the engagement taken, by the system of substantive law' might reasonably be thought to be entirely at odds with any aim antagonistic to it.[54] This would certainly appear to be the case given the fact, as Dinwiddy has rightly pointed out, that the courts had no power to refuse to implement the strictures of the substantive law if they arrived at the conclusion that doing so would be inconsistent with the aim of maximising utility.[55] They had no such power because, as a matter of proper institutional design, it was for the legislature to consider how substantive law should be drafted so that it maximised utility. Once the legislature had determined that certain substantive laws were the optimum means of maximising utility, the only role for the courts was to give effect to the law.[56]

The restriction Bentham wanted to see imposed on the justice system's ability to develop the substantive law was as consistent with his utilitarianism as was the third role he ascribed to justice's collateral ends. The power to frustrate justice's direct end was a fundamentally important aim of institutional design consistent with Bentham's utilitarianism. It was an aim that was equally committed to and justified by reference to maximising utility. It was because, as Bentham rightly recognised, there would be circumstances where achieving justice's direct end at minimal, even at no

---

[53] Ibid. at 8; IRE at 88–9.   [54] J. Bentham (1843) RJE Vol. VII at 335
[55] Dinwiddy, 'Adjudication under Bentham's Pannomion' at 159ff.   [56] Ibid. at 160–1.

more than strictly necessary disutility cost, would still produce greater disutility than it would utility. He described the issue in these terms:

> The quantity of vexation, expense, and delay, without which the course necessary to the execution of the article of substantive law in question cannot be pursued with effect, – the price thus necessary to be paid for the chance of obtaining the benefit in question, – does it exceed the value of that benefit, or rather of that chance? In such case the price ought not to be paid the law ought rather to remain unexecuted . . . A competition has place between two of the ends of justice: one or other of the contending branches of the public interest must yield: one or other of them must for the moment fall a sacrifice.[57]

Bentham recognised that in certain circumstances a cost–benefit analysis would require a court to decide that a further adjournment, for instance, to obtain evidence, must be refused, even though it would increase the prospect that the judgment reached at trial would not be the right one. Equally, he recognised that in other circumstances the cost–benefit analysis would require the court to bring the proceedings to an end before trial and judgment. There were circumstances where, on his utilitarian theory, the price of justice should not be paid. The justification for this was that utility maximisation, the substantive policy aim of Bentham's theory of justice, required it. There would be cases where the utility gained by enforcing the law would not and could not outweigh the cost to society in general of enforcing the law. In today's terms, there would be cases where the cost of litigation would be entirely disproportionate to the amount at stake. The third aspect of justice's collateral ends ensured, then, that the courts took the hard decision to maximise utility through denying justice's direct end's achievement. The difficult question for the courts, and for Bentham, was how this was to be achieved. How was the procedural code to be designed and operated so that the court knew when the public interest required the pursuit of substantive justice to yield to its denial in order to maximise utility? The answer to that question lay, as with the rest of Bentham's theory of justice, with the principle of utility.

3.8   Mediating the competition between the two ends of justice

Bentham could have adopted a number of different possible approaches to resolve the tension between justice's direct end and the third aspect of

---

[57] J. Bentham (1843) RJE Vol. 7 at 335.

its collateral ends. He could, for instance, have specified that justice's direct end should always take precedence. Such an approach might even have been expected. It is entirely consistent with the limitation he imposed on the court's ability to set aside substantive law where it was, in the court's view, inconsistent with the demands of utility. A stance that gave privileged status to justice's direct end, requiring it always to take precedence over the collateral ends, could have been straightforwardly justified on the ground that the court's role was simply to implement the substantive law. Such an approach would have required the code of procedure to incorporate an absolute rule to that effect. Alternatively, Bentham could have adopted a discretionary approach. Reflecting the importance his theory gave to justice's direct end, this could have ceded it *de facto* priority. The discretion would thus make it first amongst equals.

Bentham's theory could, however, neither adopt an absolutist, non-discretionary approach, nor could it adopt a discretionary approach that in some way gave more weight to the need to resolve the tension between it and the third, reductive, aspect of the collateral ends in the direct end's favour. He could not adopt either of these approaches, because both were inconsistent with his utilitarianism. A non-discretionary approach would fail to maximise utility in those cases where the price to be paid for enforcing substantive justice outweighed the benefit to be derived from enforcing the substantive law. Equally, a weighted discretion might also result in the enforcement of substantively just decisions in circumstances where doing so produced greater disutility than utility. These practical considerations reflect a deeper truth. Any form of weighting, absolute or otherwise, in favour of justice's direct end could only arise if it played the same role for Bentham as substantive justice played in equity's and the RSC's theory of justice. It would render it the predominant policy aim or end of justice. For Bentham it was not. For Bentham it was a means to a wider end, and one that its achievement could only partially secure. In order to ensure that the competition between the direct and collateral ends of justice was resolved so as to maximise utility a discretionary approach was necessary; one that relied on no presumption in favour of either of the two ends and relied on the utility principle to determine the outcome of the competition between them.[58]

The reliance on the utility principle as the mechanism to mediate the conflict between the two ends of justice is apparent from Bentham's

---

[58] J. Bentham (1843) PJP at 15 and 31–2; IRE at 90; RJE, Preface – Prospective View and 204 (footnote).

approach to the presentation of evidence in proceedings. In order to ensure that the court was able to properly determine true fact in reaching substantively just decisions, Bentham believed that there should be no exclusionary rules of evidence or privileges against disclosure.[59] So long as it could properly be called evidence, Bentham believed it should be admissible. As he explained it, 'The theorem is this: that, merely with a view to rectitude of decision, to the avoidance of the mischiefs attached to undue decision, no species of evidence whatsoever, willing or unwilling, ought to be excluded.'[60] This might seem to suggest that Bentham believed no limits should be imposed on the admission of evidence. If his theory were only concerned with furthering the achievement of justice's direct end, such a conclusion would be justified. However, in the *Introductory View of the Rationale of Judicial Evidence*, he explained that his theory did, in some circumstances, require the exclusion of evidence. He explained it in this way:

> the following rules will, it is hoped be found neither altogether devoid of practical use, nor in any respect open to dispute: –
>
> 1. Produce not a greater evil in pursuit of the means of excluding a lesser evil.
> 2. Exclude not a greater good in pursuit of the means of obtaining a lesser good.
> 3. Produce not any preponderant evil in pursuit of the means of obtaining any good.
> 4. Exclude not a preponderant good in pursuit of the means of excluding any evil.
>
> These rules being taken for a standard and a guide – for a standard of reference, and for a guide to practice – are any cases to be found (it may be asked,) in which exclusion put upon this or that article of evidence would be conducive upon the whole to the ends of justice? Answer: yes; beyond doubt there are. Question: What are these cases? Answer: All such cases in which, in a quantity preponderant over that which would be produced by such exclusion, a mass of evil, composed of any evils in the avoidance of which the ends of justice respectively consist, would be produced by admission given to that same article of evidence.[61]

If the admission of a piece of evidence would produce greater disutility through delay, expense or vexation than the utility it could give rise to

---

[59] Ferraro, 'Direct and Indirect Utilitarianism in Bentham's Theory of Adjudication'; Dinwiddy, 'Adjudication under Bentham's Pannomion'.
[60] J. Bentham (1843) RJE at 203–4; IRE at 12 and 88–9.   [61] Ibid.; PJP at 10.

through helping to facilitate a substantively just decision, then it can properly be excluded.[62] To do otherwise would be unreasonable. It would be unreasonable because it would undermine the aim of maximising utility, as it would produce more disutility than it would utility. Utility determined the issue. It mediated the conflict between the two ends. The 'standard or guide' provided no more than a bare test for the exercise of discretion. A court acting consistently with Bentham's standard, assessing whether a decision maximised the good whilst it minimised harm is still left with the substantive question of how it is to determine the degree to which a particular decision will maximise utility and minimise harm. How the standard operates needed to be fleshed out.

Bentham fleshed out how the standard was to be applied by expressly incorporating the felicific calculus into his theory of justice.[63] This was central to his utilitarian philosophy. It was the means by which decision-makers were supposed to calculate the sum total of the utility, or disutility, generated by actions or institutions.[64] They were to do so through an assessment of the positive and negative utility value of seven factors, each of which were to be weighed against each other to produce an overall total. Bentham described the calculus in these terms:

> the value of a pleasure or pain ... will be greater or less, according to seven circumstances ...
>
> 1. Its intensity.
> 2. Its duration.
> 3. Its certainty or uncertainty.
> 4. Its propinquity or remoteness.
> 5. Its fecundity.
> 6. Its purity.
>   ...
> 7. Its extent; that is, the number of persons to whom it extends; or (in other words) who are affected by it.[65]

In the *Principles of Judicial Procedure*, Bentham expressly incorporated the felicific calculus into his theory of justice. Judicial decision-making, as he explained, was to be exercised in conformity with the utility principle.[66] Where a judge had to resolve a conflict between the direct and collateral ends of justice he should, as Bentham put it, carry out the following exercise:

---

[62] J. Bentham (1843) IRE at 12.   [63] M. Warnock in Mill, *Utilitarianism* at 19.
[64] Ibid. at 64ff.   [65] Ibid. at 65–6.
[66] J. Bentham (1843) PJP at 8 and 29–32.

as a security for the maximization of the aggregate of good, and the minimization of the aggregate of evil, he [the judge] will settle in his own mind, and make public declaration of, the reasons by the consideration of which his conduct has been determined; which reasons will consist in the allegation of so many items in the account of evil, on both sides: magnitude, propinquity, certainty, or say probability, and extent, – being in relation to each head of good and evil taken into account.[67]

The judge should thus ensure the felicific calculus was applied when, for instance, it was necessary to determine whether a specific piece of evidence should be obtained and put before the court. Equally, it should be applied where the court needed to consider whether to grant adjournments; whether to grant relief from sanctions imposed for non-compliance with utility-consistent procedural time limits or allow pleadings to be amended; and, most importantly, whether to allow a claim to proceed to judgment or to be brought to a halt prior to judgment. In determining these and similar questions, the court will not afford the direct or collateral ends *a priori* precedence over the other. Which end is given precedence is determined by the amount of utility and disutility generated, as determined by an application of the felicific calculus. The competition between the two ends is mediated, determined by reference to the wider, substantive policy aim that they both are intended to serve and promote. Utility, independent of both ends of justice, was for Bentham the criterion by which the justice system would ensure that justice was done. It would because, as stated earlier, for Bentham, doing justice meant doing utility.

3.9   Substantive justice tempered

Bentham developed a theory of justice that placed significantly less weight on the pursuit of substantive justice than either equity or the RSC. He did so because whatever the question regarding institutional design, there was only one criterion for decision-making: the principle of utility. Whether the question was how to structure the health care system, how to structure national taxation, or how to codify the law and revise the structure and operation of the justice system, there was only one means by which that question could be properly determined. The decision was dictated by the need to secure the greatest happiness for the greatest number, to maximise overall aggregate utility. As a consequence

---

[67] M. Warnock in Mill, *Utilitarianism* at 29.

of his wider philosophical commitment Bentham developed a theory of justice that, of necessity, had as its sole substantive policy aim utility-maximisation. This had a number of consequences.

The first was that Bentham's theory of justice would stand or fall with his utilitarianism. This is particularly problematic as his wider philosophical theory is not without a number of fundamental and arguably intractable problems that render it unusable as a guide or standard for decision-making or institutional design.[68] Bentham's equation of utility with pleasure or happiness, for instance, is strongly, arguably unjustified and unjustifiable.[69] Equally, it is questionable whether there is a simple, straightforward or even workable definition of pleasure or happiness. If utility is not pleasure what, then, is it? Is it a unitary concept? If not, how are different pleasures or kinds of happiness compared with each other? How are different people's valuations of pleasures compared to each other? Is pleasure or happiness coterminous with that which is right or good?[70] Seeking pleasure might promote utility, but does that promote actions that can properly be said to be the right actions? Drug-taking promotes pleasure, but if it were to promote overall happiness would that mean it would be morally right? Is it enough simply to define that which is good by reference to the consequences of action?[71] More fundamentally, how can utility in promoting overall happiness be reconciled with a distribution of benefits that leaves some members of society with very little and others with a great deal? Examples can, of course, be multiplied. The exact nature of those problems is outside the scope of this book. It is properly the subject of detailed philosophical debate, as it has been since Bentham and then J. S. Mill developed their version of hedonistic utilitarianism in the nineteenth century. What can be said, though, is that it remains to be seen whether

---

[68] For an outline of those problems and an introduction to the wider debate concerning utilitarianism and its critics, see: W. Kymlicka, *Contemporary Political Philosophy* (Clarendon Press, 1990) at 9–50; R. Goodin, 'Utility and the Good' in P. Singer, *A Companion to Ethics* (Blackwell, 1993); J. Smart and B. Williams (eds), *Utilitarianism: For and Against* (Cambridge University Press, 1973) B. Williams, 'Ethics', in A. Grayling (ed.), *Philosophy: a guide through the subject* (Oxford University Press, 1995) at 550ff; P. Hurley, *Beyond Consequentialism* (Oxford University Press, 2011); S. Scheffler (ed.), *Consequentialism and its Critics* (Oxford University Press, 1988).

[69] R. Nozick, *Anarchy, State and Utopia* (Basic Books, 1974); at 42ff.

[70] A. Baujard, 'A Return to Bentham's Felicific Calculus: From moral welfarism to technical non-welfarism' 16(3) (September 2009) *European Journal of the History of Economic Thought* 431–3; see Chapter 7.

[71] Hurley, *Beyond Consequentialism*.

a workable version of utilitarianism can be developed that answers these and various other problems. At a theoretic level, then, Bentham's theory of justice is, absent such a development, as theoretically flawed and unworkable as his overall utilitarian philosophy.

There is a second problem with Bentham's theory, both in general terms and as it applies to his theory of justice. That problem arises from his reliance on the felicific calculus as a means to assess the utility of actions. Simply put, as a means of determining how to maximise aggregate utility the calculus is unworkable; a point Bentham recognised.[72] It raises a number of its own fundamentally intractable problems. First, if the only valid decision is one that maximises utility, where is the line drawn in so far as consequences are concerned? What are the ultimate consequences of any action? How does a moral actor, or a utilitarian legislator, determine those consequences in order to determine the right action to do or the right institutions and laws to develop? If the total range of consequences of any specific action is unknown and unknowable, how is it possible to assess the amount of utility each would produce? How is it possible to construct laws that maximise utility? Moreover, how is it possible to determine the utility value ascribable to each of the seven factors in the felicific calculus? How are they to be measured? What values and weighting should be ascribed to them in assessing each possible action or decision? Are some more important than others? If so, are they more important in all circumstances or just some? If only in some circumstances, how do we know which ones? Might it be the case, as J. S. Mill argued, that there ought to be qualitative values ascribed to the seven factors in addition to quantitative ones?[73] If so, how are quality and quantity to be assessed? Assuming they can be ascribed values that all can validly be agreed, how are they then to be weighed against each other?[74] Assuming that that is possible, what is the ambit of assessment? Applied to the justice system, should a court applying the felicific calculus to the question whether to grant an adjournment to enable a party to obtain further evidence assess the utility value of granting or denying the application to adjourn by reference to the parties, to all litigants presently using the justice system, or all potential future litigants? If the second of

---

[72] Baujard, 'A Return to Bentham's Felicific Calculus'.

[73] J. S. Mill in Mill, *Utilitarianism* at 258ff.

[74] For an outline of criticisms raised against Bentham's reliance on the felicific calculus, see J. Harris, *Legal Philosophies* (2nd edn) (Oxford University Press, 2004) at 44–5; Baujard, 'A Return to Bentham's Felicific Calculus'.

the three choices is made, which might well have been Bentham's choice, how is the court to assess the utility value of the decision? Assuming that this is possible, what guarantees are there that individual judges will apply the calculus consistently when faced with similar decisions at different times and involving different litigants? It is one thing to ascribe common values to the various factors and common mechanisms by which they are to be assessed. It is another thing to guarantee that judicial decision-making will then be carried consistently with those factors and mechanisms.[75]

Taken together, the problems both with Bentham's utilitarianism *per se* and various elements of it, have led to a general rejection of it by many as a fundamentally flawed and unworkable philosophical theory.[76] Even if they could be overcome, problems over its practical applicability would remain. As a specific application of it, his theory of justice must fall for those very same philosophical and practical reasons. This would be a serious problem if any attempt were made to implement Bentham's theory of justice. There has been no such attempt. It is unlikely that there ever will be. It is not, for instance, suggested that the Woolf Reforms implemented or attempted to implement Bentham's theory of justice. Woolf did not adopt utilitarianism. Nor did he attempt to incorporate the felicific calculus into the CPR. Whatever criticisms there are of Bentham's theory of justice and its utilitarian basis, they are not ones that can straightforwardly be applied to the Woolf and Jackson Reforms. The relevance of Bentham's theory today rests not in the utility of its philosophical roots. It rests in two further consequences that flow from Bentham's adoption of a theory of justice that had utility as its substantive policy aim: first, its hierarchical structure; and secondly, its incorporation of a nascent commitment to proportionality.

Bentham's theory of justice broke from the traditional theory. Rather than adopt a structure that had as its predominant substantive policy aim the achievement of substantive justice, it relegated it to a subsidiary role. In this it was revolutionary. Its relegation was important for another reason. By creating a hierarchical structure, which placed utility as the

---

[75] See the following for an assessment of the problem of consistent application of discretionary factors: M. Zander, *The State of Justice* (Sweet & Maxwell, 2000) at 43ff; I. Scott, 'Caseflow Management in the Trial Court' in A. Zuckerman and R. Cranston (eds), *Reform of Civil Procedure: Essays on 'Access to Justice'* (Clarendon Press, 1995) at 23ff; R. Dworkin, *A Matter of Principle* (Clarendon Press, 1985) at 89ff.

[76] Nozick, *Anarchy, State and Utopia*; Rawls, *A Theory of Justice*; Dworkin, *Law's Empire*.

predominant aim and substantive justice and its achievement and considerations of cost and delay as subordinate aims the pursuit of which was justified and justifiable only by reference to utility, it provided the means by which substantive justice's achievement could legitimately be denied by the justice system on the grounds of cost, delay or the adverse effect the continued pursuit of justice in the individual case would have on other litigants or society more generally. It did so both because it treated substantive justice as an aim equivalent to other policy aims against which it was to be balanced, but equally because those aims were subordinate to a wider public policy aim, it provided an independent criterion – utility – by which they could be weighed against each other. Again, this provided a stark contrast with the traditional theory, where neither substantive justice nor the aims of reducing cost and delay could be in competition with each other (the latter only playing the role played by the positive aspect of justice's collateral ends), nor was there an independent criterion by which any notional competition between them could be determined. Assuming they could come into conflict, absent an independent criterion, there would be no proper way in which to determine which was to prevail. In such circumstances, the likelihood would be that substantive justice would prevail over considerations of cost and time, given that that was the system's aim.

That it did so enabled substantive justice to be denied through a process that remained fair despite that, where to achieve it in the individual case was in today's terms disproportionate. It would be disproportionate where the disutility cost of achieving it outweighed its achievement's utility value. This was something that the traditional theory could not properly do. Bentham's theory could do so, however, because its incorporation of utility as its predominant aim required the justice system to focus on something more than the immediate interests of parties to litigation. Unlike the traditional theory it was not, nor could it be, a theory predicated on securing individual justice. It had to look beyond the interests of the immediate parties to litigation, and consider how best individual litigation could be managed by the court – and given Bentham's view that the courts should operate quasi-inquisitorially rather than on an adversarial basis, it was for the court to manage litigation – to secure the optimum distribution of society's resources across all litigation so as to maximise utility.[77]

---

[77] W. Twinning, 'Alternative to What? Theories of Litigation, Procedure and Dispute Settlement in Anglo-American Jurisprudence: Some Neglected Classics' 56 (1993) *Modern Law Review* 380 at 384.

The traditional theory, with its singular devotion to substantive justice, could only ever properly consider the interests of individual parties. It could not consider the effect of its decisions in individual cases on the justice system as a whole, or on other litigants in unrelated proceedings. Bentham's theory, because it focused on overall utility rather than individual utility, had a wider focus. Unlike the traditional theory, it did not permit the court to focus solely on the litigants in front of it on the particular application.[78] While the effect its decision would have on the litigants immediately before it would necessarily form part of its assessment of the overall utility of exercising discretion one way or the other, it was only part of the equation. The felicific calculus required the court to assess the overall utility value of its decision, as it affected not just the individual litigants before it, but society as a whole. It required an assessment of the price to be paid for securing substantive justice in each case, and whether that was justifiable by reference to the overall benefit to be obtained by it. While the substantive and adjective law were both to be designed so as to maximise utility if properly applied, there would be cases on an application of the felicific calculus where it would be disproportionate to permit litigation to continue to judgment and enforcement; disproportionate because the disutility cost would outweigh its utility value.

3.10   Conclusion

Bentham's theory of justice differed profoundly from the traditional theory accepted by the common law, equity and then the RSC. Rather than being a theory of substantive justice, it was a theory of applied utilitarianism, hence Bentham's (unimplemented) desire to replace references to justice with references to utility. It may have used some of the same language and concepts inherent in the traditional theory, but for Bentham they had different meanings and different roles to play. Substantive justice was a subordinate aim within the theory, rather than its predominant aim. Minimising delay, expense and vexation was equally a subordinate aim, albeit again not in the same way as it was for the traditional theory. It played a wider role than simply ensuring that substantive justice was not frustrated by, for instance, too great a delay in reaching trial and judgment. It also justified the court refusing to proceed to a merit-based decision. It did so because the substantive

---

[78] J. Bentham in Mill, *Utilitarianism* at 35.

policy aim of his theory, its overriding objective, was utility: substantive justice was no more than a means to an end, and one which in turn was limited by that wider end.

Given the fundamental differences between Bentham's theory and the traditional theory of justice, it is not possible to compare them directly. As Kuhn put it, in describing the tension between advocates of two competing scientific theories, the two theories of justice cannot engage with each other because they are 'always slightly at cross-purposes'.[79] Just like competing scientific theories, the two theories of justice see the world through different eyes. They interpret it through concepts that, while they use the same language, are markedly different and serve different aims. Both refer to justice. But for each theory the term means something profoundly different. A conversation between Bentham and an adherent of the traditional theory of justice would seem to be one concerning the same thing, but in truth, they would fail to understand each other. Mutual misunderstanding would be the order of the day. There are two consequences of this. First, it is easy to mistake Bentham's theory as simply a more sophisticated version of the traditional theory. A commentator who, for instance, focused on Bentham's emphasis on the importance of justice's direct ends and the role the collateral ends had in supporting its achievement could mistake his theory as one that simply put the traditional theory into more exacting language.[80] This problem leads inexorably to the second consequence. Such an impoverished view of Bentham would inexorably undermine its promotion as a replacement for the traditional theory. For one scientific paradigm to replace another failed or failing paradigm rests on an appreciation of the fact that the new paradigm is just that: a new paradigm. If it is wrongly understood – as Woolf's theory of justice has been understood by some to be no more than a restatement of the traditional one – simply to be a new version, variation or restatement of the original paradigm, its proponents will not be able to argue for, or secure, its adoption. As a scientific, or in this case jurisprudential revolution, it will fail.[81]

Bentham may have had a degree of influence over nineteenth-century law reform. His theory of justice was not, however, influential. This was

---

[79] T. S. Kuhn, *The Structure of Scientific Revolutions* (3rd edn) (University of Chicago Press, 1996) at 112.

[80] A. Zuckerman, *Zuckerman on Civil Procedure: Principles of Practice* (2nd edn) (Thomson, 2006) at 5.

[81] See Chapter 4.

hardly surprising given the lack of clarity in its exposition. More fundamentally, though, it is unsurprising due to the fact that it was rooted in
his commitment to utilitarian philosophy. The manifest failings of that
philosophical idea could not but have ensured that Bentham's theory of
justice gained no real support, even if it had been properly appreciated
and garnered the support of reform's advocates at the time. As a legal
revolution it is an example of one that failed before it began. However, as
an alternative theory of justice it provides a basis for both interpreting
and elucidating the nature of the reforms applied to the English civil
justice system as a consequence of the Woolf Reforms. It also provides a
warning. If the Woolf Reforms are to successfully introduce a new,
alternative theory of justice, they – and the Jackson Reforms that seek
to build on them must ensure that such an alternative theory of justice is
properly understood and then implemented.

PART II

Introduction: Woolf's new theory of justice

> there must be reform of a fundamental nature ... if you are going to achieve
> what is necessary to have a civil legal system which is appropriate for the next
> century, then you have to start off with the fundamentals and ask yourself
> what the civil justice system should seek to achieve and then produce a
> system which will fit in with those needs, and that involves looking at what
> you mean by civil justice.[1]

Justice reform from the 1850s to the 1990s was predicated on ensuring that the justice system was better able to deliver substantive justice through reducing litigation cost and delay. The Woolf Reports, like their predecessors, could easily have worked within this framework. They could, as Jolowicz had it, have done no more than engage in yet more petty tinkering with the system.[2] Rather than take that tried and failed approach, the reports engaged in a form of extraordinary investigation, one that examined the justice system's aims and revised them. The failure of past reforms had given rise to a consensus that favoured fundamental reform.[3] A new theory of justice, underpinned by new principles, would replace the one that had been in place since the Judicature Act reforms.[4] Securing substantive justice was no longer to be the justice system's aim.[5] Proportionate justice

---

[1] H. Woolf, 'A New Approach to Civil Justice', in *Law Lectures for Practitioners* (*Hong Kong Law Journal* special edn) (Sweet & Maxwell Asia, 1996) (H. Woolf (Hong Kong, 1996)) at 2.

[2] J. Jolowicz, '"General ideas" and Procedural Reform', in *On Civil Procedure* (Cambridge University Press, 2000) at 364, 370.

[3] H. Woolf (1995) at 5; H. Woolf (1996) at 12; H. Woolf (Hong Kong, 1996) at 2.

[4] H. Woolf (1996) at 24; H. Woolf (Hong Kong, 1996) at 9: 'The principles which have controlled litigation in the past have to give way to the five principles which I have identified.'

[5] Jolowicz, '"General ideas" and Procedural Reform' at 355–9, 370.

was to become its aim.[6] The basis on which this reform was to be achieved was through Woolf's adoption of the approach to reform taken by the Judicature Commissioners in the 1870s. They explicitly adopted equity's aim of doing complete justice as the guiding principle of their reforms and of the new system of justice they recommended and then saw introduced via the Judicature Act reforms. Woolf also identified and adopted a guiding principle for reform and a newly reformed system of justice, one that rejected the legacy of the 1870 reforms. That principle was encapsulated in what would become rule 1 of the CPR. Its overriding objective: rather than seeking to secure substantive justice, the justice system was to operate so as to deal with cases justly. The imperative of dealing with cases justly required the system to operate so as to balance a number of individual principles: substantive justice; equality (it should be fair and be seen to be so, all litigants should have adequate and equal opportunity to state their case and answer their opponents); expense; expedition; efficiency; and most importantly, proportionality.[7] Each of Woolf's specific structural and procedural reform recommendations, i.e. the introduction of case management, the creation of procedural case tracks that matched procedure to the value and complexity of individual proceedings, court control of evidence, was to be consistent with those principles, as were the new rules of court, which would ultimately come into force on 26 April 1999 and replace the RSC.[8] In full, the rule specified that:

(1) The CPR is a . . .new procedural code with the overriding objective of enabling the court to deal with cases justly.

(2) Dealing with a case justly includes, so far as practicable –
    (a) ensuring that the parties are on an equal footing;
    (b) saving expense;
    (c) dealing with the case in ways which are proportionate –
        (i)   to the amount of money involved;
        (ii) to the importance of the case;
        (iii) to the financial position of each party;
    (d) ensuring that it is dealt with expeditiously and fairly; and

---

[6] H. Woolf (1995) at 25–6; H. Woolf (1996) at 11.

[7] H. Woolf (1995) at 2–3; H. Woolf (Hong Kong, 1996) at 3–5.

[8] Civil Procedure Act 1998; CPR 1.1 (SI 3132/1998); *Biguzzi v. Rank Leisure plc* [1999] 1 WLR 1926.

(e) allotting to it an appropriate share of the court's resources, while taking into account the need to allot resources to other cases.[9]

However, there were unfortunately a number of crucial differences between the approach taken by the Judicature Commissioners and that adopted by Woolf. The former's recommendations came as the culmination of a twenty-year period of prior reform that was committed to the same idea: ensuring that every court was capable of achieving complete justice. That idea was well understood. It was explicitly identified as underpinning their recommendations. Perhaps most importantly, individual judges, such as Bramwell LJ, who had served on both the 1850 and 1873 Commissions and been involved in drafting the Acts of Parliament that implemented their recommendations, were able to ensure that the then new RSC operated in accord with the Commissioners' intentions through authoritative decision.[10] The same points cannot be made regarding the Woolf Reforms. It is true that in the mid-1990s England had undergone a similar period of reform to that which preceded the appointment of the Judicature Commissioners. There was, however, prior to Woolf, no comparison to the 1850 common law reforms. Unlike the Judicature Commissioners, the decision to start from first principles, set out what those principles were, and most significantly, depart from the previous orthodoxy, was not the culmination of a long-term shift to a new theory of justice. It was the start of that process. If anything, the Jackson Review marks the point for Woolf's new theory of justice that the 1870 reforms marked for the adoption of the equity-based theory in the nineteenth century. Linked to this is the nature and understanding of what the Woolf Reforms meant to achieve. As the first attempt at introducing a new theory, it could not be as well understood as complete justice was in the 1870s. Such a problem is inevitable. It was further compounded by the fact that the principles Woolf identified as underpinning his new theory of justice were and are vague and open-textured. They can be variously interpreted, as can their relationship to each other. This is in stark contrast to the RSC's theory and its commitment to substantive justice. Securing a substantively accurate decision is easy to understand. Its predominance over factors such as efficiency and economy, which are simply understood as facilitative mechanisms akin

---

[9] H. Woolf (1996) at 274–5; *Orange Personal Communications Services Ltd* v. *Hoare Lea (A Firm)* [2008] EWHC 233 (Admin) at [31].

[10] See Chapter 2.

to the positive role Bentham accorded to justice's collateral ends, is equally easy to understand and apply. The same cannot be said for Woolf's new theory, its aim of dealing with cases justly and the relationship between the principles to which that aim gives expression.

These problems are further compounded by the fact that none of the principles Woolf identified were novel. They all bring with them prior understanding; one that can too easily lead to the false conclusion that they are intended to operate as they did under the RSC. This is obviously true of substantive justice, equality, expense, expedition and efficiency. It is perhaps less obviously true of proportionality. It has, for instance, been said by two of Woolf's successors as Master of the Rolls, Lords Clarke and Neuberger, that proportionality was the one novel principle Woolf identified and then introduced into the CPR.[11] In this, they were mistaken. Proportionality is not a new concept, either broadly speaking or in respect of the operation of civil justice systems; what novelty there was in Woolf's use of it was to place it at the heart of civil justice.[12] It has underpinned European Union law since 1956.[13] It has been a feature of private law for far longer than that.[14] It also underpinned, for instance, the existence of England's hierarchical court structure: lower value, relatively simpler claims being dealt with in the County Courts via the simpler procedure contained in the County Court Rules, while higher value, more complex claims were dealt with in the High Court under its more detailed procedure set out in the RSC.[15] From a wider perspective, since 1983 rule 26 of the US Federal Rules of Civil Procedure has included the express requirement that discovery should be no more than

[11] A. Clarke, *Proportionate Costs from Woolf to Jackson* (The Law Society, London) (10 July 2009) at [8]; D. Neuberger, 'A New Approach to Justice – From Woolf to Jackson', in G. Meggitt (ed.), *Civil Justice Reform: What has it Achieved?* (Sweet & Maxwell, 2010) at 15; CPR rr. 1.1, 1.3 and 1.4. Given that these rules were implemented in 1999, it is clear that C. Piche's claim that Quebec, which adopted the same approach in 2002, is perhaps the only country in the world take this approach is clearly wrong, see C. Piché, 'Figures, Spaces and Procedural Proportionality' 1 (2012) *IAPLH RIDP* 145, at 155.

[12] *Callery v. Gray (Nos 1 and 2)* [2002] 1 WLR 2000 at [3]; H. Brooke, 'The "Overriding Objective", Procedural Sanctions and Appeals', in M. Andenas, N. Andrews and R. Nazzini, *The Future of Transnational Civil Litigation* (British Institute of International and Comparative Law, 2004) at 55.

[13] Article 5(4) Treaty on the European Union; see Piche, ibid. at 150.

[14] D. Kennedy, 'A Transnational Genealogy of Proportionality in Private Law', in R. Brownsword et al., *The Foundations of European Private Law* (Hart, 2011) at 187.

[15] I. R. Scott, *Proportionality – Cost Effective Justice* (Keynote Address, 22nd AIJA Annual Conference, 2004) at 8 <http://www.aija.org.au/ac04/papers/IanScott.pdf>.

proportionate.[16] In a manner akin to the CPR's overriding objective, it requires the US federal courts to take account of 'the needs of the case, the amount in controversy, the parties' resources, the importance of the issues at stake' when deciding the extent to which discovery should be ordered in any particular case.[17] Just like the other principles identified as underpinning Woolf's new theory, proportionality brings with it an historical legacy; one in respect of civil justice that, due to its limited application within a system whose overarching theory was committed to securing substantive justice was, like efficiency and economy, a subordinate one. The fossil record of the principles is one that sees that substantive justice was conceived as first amongst equals. That was not Woolf's intention. It does, however, pose a problem of interpretation.

From these issues the third difference between the Judicature and Woolf Reforms arises. Individual judges secured the effective implementation of their recommendations in the 1870s and 1880s. They understood the nature of the reform, what it was intended to achieve, how it differed from common law formalism and how it was meant to embed equity-based complete justice as the guiding principle of the RSC. As such, it was possible for a consistent line of Court of Appeal authorities to ensure the new approach became the established approach. The same cannot be said of the Woolf Reforms and their new theory of justice. These differences, combined with the open-textured nature of the principles underpinning Woolf's new theory of justice, create a significant problem. It can be and has been interpreted in two different ways, as either a new theory of proportionate justice, or as no more than an explicit statement of the traditional commitment to substantive justice. The chapters in Part II focus on these competing interpretations and argue that the former is the one that properly captures Woolf's intentions. It does so because, as Kuhn pointed out, not all revolutions succeed.[18] They need to be recognised as such, accepted, and then implemented.[19]

---

[16] J. Carroll, 'Proportionality in Discovery: A Cautionary Tale' 32 (2010) *Campbell Law Review* 455.

[17] Ibid. 458.   [18] Kuhn (1996) at 84.   [19] See Chapter 7.

Woolf's new theory: a traditionalist view

to do justice but to achieve it by means which minimise cost and delay.[1]

the overriding principle is that justice must be done.[2]

4.1 Introduction

When the RSC was introduced after 1873, it was an open question how it would operate. Liberalising reforms had failed in the past, and it was possible they would do so again. In Kuhn's terms, there is always the possibility that a scientific revolution will fail because it is interpreted consistently with the established paradigm. In the event, they succeeded, despite attempts to the contrary.[3] The Woolf Reforms adopted a different approach to that taken in 1873. They did something the RSC failed to do and, consequently, should have stood an even stronger chance of success.[4] They did not leave the successful implementation of their new theory of justice entirely to chance: they provided explicit guidance

---

[1] H. Woolf (1995) at 214–15.
[2] *Mortgage Corporation* v. *Sandoes* (CA 26 November 1996, unreported) at 30.
[3] E.g. *Ward* v. *The Mayor and Town Council of Sheffield* (1887) 19 QBD 22 at 29.
[4] H. Woolf (1995) at 207ff and 214–15; H. Woolf (1996) at 274–5; D. Greenslade, 'A Fresh Approach: Uniform Rules of Court' in A. Zuckerman and R. Cranston (eds), *Reform of Civil Procedure: Essays on 'Access to Justice'* (Clarendon Press, 1995) at 127; J. Jacob, *Civil Justice in the Age of Human Rights* (Ashgate, 2007) at 31–2; J. Sorabji, 'The Road to New Street Station: fact, fiction and the overriding objective' [2012] *EBLR* 1–77; *Orange Personal Communications Services Ltd* v. *Hoare Lea (A Firm)* [2008] EWHC 233 (Admin) at [31]; *Holmes* v. *SGB* [2001] EWCA Civ 354 at [27]; *Clarkson* v. *Gilbert (Rights of Audience)* [2000] 2 FLR 839; *Totty* v. *Snowdon* [2002] 1 WLR 1384 at (34); *Stewart* v. *Engel* [2000] 1 WLR 2268 at 2291; *Flynn* v. *Scougall* [2004] 1 WLR 3069 at [10]; *Cala Homes (South) Ltd* v. *Chichester District Council* (20 August 1999) TLR 15 October 1999; *Jones* v. *University of Warwick* [2003] 3 All ER 760 at 764; *Garratt* v. *Saxby* [2004] 1 WLR 2152 at [18]; *Flynn* v. *Scougall* [2004] 1 WLR 3069 at [10]; *Konkola Copper Mines Plc* v. *Coromin* [2005] ILPr 39 at [106] and [114].

within the reformed rules of court – the Civil Procedure Rules (CPR), which would replace the RSC. As the Final Report explained it:

> Although the rules can offer detailed directions for the technical steps to be taken, the effectiveness of those steps depends upon the spirit in which they are carried out. That in turn depends on an understanding of the fundamental purpose of the rules and of the underlying system of procedure.
>
> In order to identify that purpose at the outset, I have placed at the very beginning of the rules a statement of their overriding objective. This is intended to govern the operation of all the rules and in particular the choices which the court makes in managing each case and in interpreting the rules.[5]

While this was innovative in England, there is nothing inherently novel about explicit overriding objectives.[6] Prior to the Woolf Reforms' endorsement of the idea, such objectives had been introduced in a number of common law jurisdictions, e.g. the United States of America, Australia and Canada. In each case, these common law overriding objectives guided the operation of rules of court through articulating the theory of justice according to which they were to be applied. In each case, that theory was the same as the RSC had adopted from equity. Before turning to Woolf's overriding objective, it is instructive to examine its predecessors.

The first common law overriding objective was introduced as rule 1 of US Federal Rules of Civil Procedure in 1938.[7] It provides that the Federal Rules 'should be construed and administered to secure the just, speedy, and inexpensive determination of every action and proceeding'.[8] From 1987, a similar rule governed the South Australian Supreme Court Rules, and now governs the operation of its Supreme Court Civil Rules. In its original form, it specified that the rules were

> made for the purpose of establishing orderly procedures for the conduct of litigation in the Court and of promoting the just and efficient determination of such litigation. They are not intended to defeat a proper claim or defence of a litigant who is genuinely endeavouring to comply with

---

[5] H. Woolf (1996) at 274; *Swain v. Hillman* [2000] 1 All ER 91 at 92–94.

[6] Sorabji, 'The Road to New Street Station', at 79.

[7] Federal Rules of Civil Procedure, r. 1; R. Bone, 'Improving Rule 1: A Master Rule for the Federal Rules' 87 (2010) *Denver University Law Review* 287.

[8] Federal Rules of Civil Procedure, r. 1; *In re Paris Air Crash*, March 3, 1974, 69 F.R.D 310, 318 (C.D. Cal. 1975), cited in Bone 'Improving Rule 1' at 288, rule 1 is the 'command that gives all the other rules life and meaning and timbre in the realist world of the trial court'.

the procedures of the Court, and are to be interpreted and applied with the above purpose in view.[9]

In its revised, post-2006, form it directs that:

The objects of these rules are—

(a) to establish orderly procedures for the just resolution of civil disputes; and
(b) to facilitate and encourage the resolution of civil disputes by agreement between the parties; and
(c) to avoid all unnecessary delay in the resolution of civil disputes; and
(d) to promote efficiency in dispute resolution so far as that object is consistent with the paramount claims of justice; and
(e) to minimise the cost of civil litigation to the litigants and to the State.[10]

Finally, from 1990, the Rules of Civil Procedure for the Ontario Superior Court of Justice and Court of Appeal have also been subject to a similar provision. In a much more generalised fashion than either the US or South Australian rules, it specifies that the Ontario Rules 'shall be liberally construed to secure the just, most expeditious and least expensive determination of every civil proceeding on its merits'.[11] These three common law overriding objectives, despite their different language, have a number of features in common, not only with each other, but also with the RSC's implicit overriding objective.

First of all, they each require civil process to be conducted in order to bring about merit-based determinations of individual claims. Rules were not to hinder the pursuit and achievement of substantive justice through being applied in a formalist way. Ontario's overriding objective states this explicitly. It requires the liberal, rather than technical or formal, application of the rules in order to secure such decisions. South Australia's overriding objective, in both its versions, does the same, albeit in a slightly more oblique fashion. Claims are not to be determined on formal grounds, but rather, justly, at minimal cost, i.e. on their merits rather than on technicalities. The US Federal Rules'

---

[9] (South Australia) Supreme Court Rules 1987, r. 2.01.
[10] (South Australia) Supreme Court Civil Rules 2006, r. 3.
[11] (Ontario) Rules of Civil Procedure (R.R.O. 1990, Reg. 194, r. 1.04 (1)). Amended in 2008 to add a requirement to take account of proportionality as r. 1.04(1.1): 'In applying these rules, the court shall make orders and give directions that are proportionate to the importance and complexity of the issues, and to the amount involved, in the proceeding.' (O. Reg. 438/08, s. 2.).

overriding objective makes the same point again, albeit more obliquely still. It simply refers to the just determination of claims. As Bone has described it, as drafting goes the language used is 'hopelessly vague'.[12] That might be so, but as he goes on to clarify, its purpose was clear, given its drafting history. Just as with the other two overriding objectives, and most significantly, the RSC's implicit overriding objective, it was intended:

> to make clear that the Federal Rules should be construed liberally, that procedural decisions based on technicalities should be avoided, and that trial judges should exercise the broad discretion given them by the Federal Rules 'to the end that controversies may be speedily and finally determined according to the substantive rights of the parties'.[13]

It was intended to do for the US Federal Rules what the 1850 and 1873 reforms were intended to achieve in England: replace an approach to achieving substantive justice predicated on strict compliance with procedural rules with a more liberal approach that had as its 'sole aim ... deciding cases on the substantive merits according to the facts and the evidence'.[14] It was expressly intended to ensure the Federal Rules operated so as to secure 'just decisions on the merits'.[15] More than that, though, at the time of its introduction in 1938, it was understood to be functionally equivalent with what was at that time the Federal Rules' version of RSC (1875) Ord. 59. It was thus equivalent to the RSC's rule that specified that procedural error or default did not render the proceedings void, and which specifically incorporated equity's approach to procedural error into the RSC.[16] The basis through which the RSC's implicit overriding objective was given life in England was understood, in the United States, as being of the same effect as rule 1 of its Federal

---

[12] Bone, 'Improving Rule 1' at 288.   [13] Ibid. at 289.

[14] Ibid. at 290; M. Rosenberg, 'Sanctions to Effectuate Pretrial Discovery' 58 (1958) *Columbia Law Review* 480 at 480: 'Literally the first rule of federal civil procedure is that the rules be interpreted to promote just, speedy, and inexpensive decisions. Rightly, the framers saturated the federal rules with their premise that procedural rules exist to aid, not abort, determination of the merits of legal controversies.'

[15] Bone, 'Improving Rule 1' at 293; L. Solum, 'Procedural Justice' 78 (2004) *Southern California Law Review* 181 at 244; *Mahler v. Drake*, 43 F.R.D. 1, 3 and n. 8 (D.S.C. 1967).

[16] Bone, 'Improving Rule 1' at 293, n. 25; see Federal Rules of Civil Procedure, rule 61: 'The court at every stage of the proceeding must disregard any error or defect in the proceeding which does not affect the substantial rights of the parties.' A provision explicitly derived from equity's provisions regarding amendment: Notes of Advisory Committee on Rules 1937 at http://www.law.cornell.edu/rules/frcp/rule_61; cf. Chapter 2, n. 134.

Procedure Rules. More clearly than the South Australian and Ontarian overriding objectives, and despite the language used, the Federal Rules' overriding objective articulated the same theory of justice that implicitly governed the RSC.

The second point concerns the role the three rules understood economy and efficiency had in the conduct of litigation. All three treat the relationship between these two principles and substantive justice in the same way. Just as Bentham understood the primary role of justice's collateral ends to be subordinate to its direct ends, they understand the former to be subordinate to, and facilitative of, the latter. The more economical and efficient the litigation process the better able to produce justice, and conversely the less chance that its achievement would be frustrated as a consequence of excess cost and delay. In all three cases, they are part of what it means to secure a merits-based decision.

In their different ways the three explicit overriding objectives set out exactly the same approach to litigation which England adopted following the RSC's introduction. They simply make explicit what implicitly governed it as a consequence of the *Tildesley* line of authorities. This was particularly the case in so far as the US Federal Rules' overriding objective was concerned, given its history and the intention behind its introduction. If the RSC's drafters had considered introducing their own rule 1, they could easily have adopted the same approach as the Federal Rules' draftsman, or indeed, that taken in South Australia or Ontario. If the Woolf Reforms had been an exercise in normal science and simply adopted the same approach to reform as its many predecessors it, too, could have adopted such an approach. It could have borrowed the language used in the common law overriding objectives and imported them into a revised RSC. If it had done so, it would have done no more than formalised the status quo. That it recommended that the RSC should be replaced by a new procedural code might seem to suggest that it could not have taken such an approach. There is nothing in principle, however, to preclude the introduction of a new code with a traditional, substantive justice-based, overriding objective.[17]

It has been claimed that the common law overriding objectives, and specifically the US one, played no part in the CPR overriding objective's creation.[18] That may be correct, although it would be remarkable if true.

---

[17] See Chapter 7.

[18] R. Turner, "'Actively': The Word that Changed the Civil Courts' in Dwyer (ed.), *The Civil Procedure Rules Ten Years On* (Oxford University Press 2009) at 77–88.

Notwithstanding that claim, there is a significant degree of support for the view that the Woolf Reforms intended to do no more than introduce such an overriding objective into the new code of procedure. Notwithstanding the Woolf Reforms' explicit aim of conducting fundamental reform, a strand of interpretation has arisen that sees it as having done no more than introduce an explicit version of the RSC's implicit overriding objective. This – traditionalist – interpretation of the overriding objective poses a significant difficulty for the success of both the Woolf and Jackson Reforms. If it becomes the accepted interpretation, then the CPR will operate so as to ensure that individual claims result in substantive justice. The problems that undermined the RSC will, as a consequence, continue unabated, as the Jackson Review noted in its criticism of the court's failure post-1999 to develop a more robust approach to rule-compliance.[19] As a consequence, any attempt to properly implement a commitment to proportionality will inevitably fail. It will fail, and the attendant benefits, in so far as reduction in litigation cost and the efficient conduct of litigation will not be realised, because any tension between proportionality and the need to secure substantive justice at the very least will be weighted in the latter's favour; an issue discussed further in Chapter 7.[20] That a traditionalist interpretation of the overriding objective has arisen is unsurprising. Experience from the nineteenth-century reforms points to the persistence of pre-existing approaches to litigation, as reform is simply seen as an attempt to make the established system operate more effectively without changing what it seeks to do. Equally, and as noted earlier, Kuhn's understanding of scientific revolutions equally points to the difficulty that new theories have in being understood as distinct from those they seek to replace, not least due to the use of similar concepts to those used by the established theory. There is, however, one fundamental reason why a traditionalist interpretation of the overriding objective was inevitable. The Woolf Reforms, to a large degree, originally conceptualised it in such terms.

4.2 A traditional overriding objective

The overriding objective was first introduced in the Interim Report. At that time it was described as a general objective, which was to guide the interpretation of the, then, proposed new rules of court. It was to do so in

---

[19] R. Jackson (2009) at 386ff.
[20] *State of Queensland* v. *JL Holdings Pty Ltd* (1997) 189 CLR 146.

order, as its initial clause specified, to 'enable the court to deal with cases justly'. This was explained as requiring proceedings to be dealt with so as to reduce party inequality, save expense and time, secure proportionality and ensure claims were provided an appropriate share of the court's resources.[21] Saving expense and time obviously referred to the principles of economy and efficiency. At best, it was understood to mean that litigants should expend no more resources than necessary to secure a merits-based decision. What was necessary was determined by reference to the nature and value of the claim.[22] The idea that any significant tension might arise between proportionality and substantive justice was, at the least, latent at this stage. What might be deemed necessary by reference to a claim's value is not synonymous with what might be necessary to secure a merits-based decision. The former is potentially more limited than the latter. Referring to what is necessary by reference to the need to secure a merits-based decision suggests that that aim predominates, as it did under the RSC. Merits trumps proportionality.

The exact role proportionality was to play in the overriding objective was, however, thinly developed at this stage, and the two most important aspects of what was meant by dealing with cases justly were the need to ensure that the new rules were applied in ways that would render litigation more economical and efficient. In this, there was no real difference between the Woolf and previous reforms. This new economical and efficient approach was one that simply required litigation to be conducted in a less technical and more purposive approach to it. Rather than litigants taking procedural points in order to argue that the liberal

---

[21] H. Woolf (1995) at 216–17:
  - The general objective of these rules is to enable the court to deal with cases justly.
  - The court shall apply these rules so as to further the general objective.
  - Dealing with a case justly includes:
    - (a) making allowances for any inequality between the parties;
    - (b) saving the parties expense;
    - (c) handling the case in ways which are proportionate:
      - (i)   to the amount of any money involved;
      - (ii) to the importance of the issues; and
      - (iii) to the parties' financial position;
    - (d) ensuring that the case is handled and completed expeditiously; and
    - (e) allotting an appropriate share of the court's resources to the case while taking into account the need to devote resources to other cases.

[22] See for instance, A. May, 'The ALI/UNIDROIT Rules of Transnational Civil Procedure in the Perspective of the New English and Welsh Rules', in M. Andenas, N. Andrews and R. Nazzini, *The Future of Transnational Civil Litigation* (British Institute of International and Comparative Law, 2004) at 45; Greenslade, 'A Fresh Approach' at 128.

discretion should not be exercised, or simply to increase litigation cost
and delay as a consequence of taking such a point to thereby obtain a
tactical advantage that had nothing to do with furthering the pursuit of a
merits-based decision, litigation was to be conducted and managed by
the court, so that justice was achieved at minimal cost and with minimal
delay.[23] In all of this there was little, if anything, to obviously take the
Woolf Reforms beyond the realms of normal science. As the Interim
Report explained, the new general objective was intended to ensure that
the courts could 'do justice but . . . achieve it by means which minimise
cost and delay'.[24] It captured, in the words of Greenslade, a member of
the Woolf Review's enquiry team:

> the need to do justice in the instant case – this is the function of the courts
> and is the stated overriding objective of the new rules.[25]

The Interim Report's and Greenslade's explanations would not have been
out of place in the Evershed Report as a description of its new approach
to justice, or the Judicature Committee's reports as a description of what
doing complete justice meant. Nor would it have been out of place as a
description of what the common law overriding objectives, and the
RSC's, aimed to do. The new policy aim, in the light of this, looked very
much like the old one. All that had changed, and in this there was no real
change at all, was that there was a greater emphasis on efficiency and
economy.[26]

That the overriding objective, as originally conceived, had the look of a
traditional one was not confined to the Interim Report and the views of
a member of the Woolf Review's enquiry team. If it had been, it could
more easily have been dealt with. It was borne out by the Court of Appeal
shortly after the Final Report was published, in the case of *Mortgage*

---

[23] H. Woolf (1995) at 215: 'A paramount consideration of those applying the rules must be
saving cost and reducing delay. It is this new approach to procedural matters which will
be the cornerstone of the new rules because the rules will be applied to save expense and
avoid delay. The new rules are being deliberately framed so that the approach of those
construing them can be more purposive and less technical. It will thus be the responsibility of the judiciary to make the new system work.'

[24] H. Woolf (1995) at 214–15.   [25] Greenslade, 'A Fresh Approach' at 130.

[26] As Lord Bingham would describe it in *Callery* v. *Gray* [2002] 1 WLR 2000 at [3]: 'The
objects underlying these rules [the CPR] were not new, but the rules gave a sharply
increased emphasis to the need for expedition in the conduct of legal proceedings, to the
need for simplicity and to the need to avoid unnecessary and disproportionate costs. To
achieve these ends new and detailed procedures were devised to moderate the traditional
adversarial approach to the making and defending of claims.'

Corporation v. *Sandoes*.[27] The case centred on the question whether it was permissible for the court to grant an extension of time to exchange witness statements and expert reports, to vacate the trial date at very short notice and permit further expert evidence to be obtained. It thus focused on the question of compliance, or rather, non-compliance, with procedural obligations. Ought the application to be granted, or should the court take a stricter approach to rule-compliance, and thus, as the Woolf Reforms intended, reduce litigation cost and delay? A stricter approach would have been inconsistent with the *Tildesley*-inspired lax approach to rule compliance and the adverse and unnecessary cost and delay that that engendered. It would have been contrary to the RSC's overriding objective. Such an approach was rejected. It was rejected on the basis that the new stricter approach that the Woolf Reforms were about to introduce was subject to the overriding principle of securing substantive justice. The new overriding objective, when it was introduced, would give expression to this idea, it was suggested. It would simply make explicit what had always been implicit under the RSC.

When the proceedings had been dealt with at first instance, the judge had taken what he thought was the required stricter approach. The application was refused. In reaching this decision, the judge relied on guidance given by Lord Woolf in *Beachley Property Limited* v. *Edgar*. In that case, he had taken a tougher, less indulgent, attitude to such applications and did so in the light of the change of approach required by his Reports' recommendations.[28] The importance of *Beachley* is considered further in the following chapter. The point taken from it by the first instance judge in *Mortgage Corporation* was that, in the absence of a good reason explaining the default, the applications had to be refused; that was what the Woolf Reforms required. The Court of Appeal rejected that approach. In doing so Millett LJ set out ten principles which, before the judgment was delivered, had been endorsed by both Lord Woolf and Scott VC, the then Head of Civil Justice responsible for implementing the Woolf Reforms. Those principles were described as setting out 'the future approach which litigants can expect the court to adopt to the failure to adhere to time limits contained in the rules or directions of the court'.[29] They were thus to be understood as consistent with what would be required by the overriding objective when it came into force. Those principles were that:

---

[27] CA 26 November 1996, unreported.   [28] CA 6 June 1996, unreported.
[29] CA 26 November 1996, unreported, at 30.

1. Time requirements laid down by the Rules and directions given by the Court are not merely targets to be attempted; they are rules to be observed.
2. At the same time, the overriding principle is that justice must be done.
3. Litigants are entitled to have their cases resolved with reasonable expedition. Non-compliance with time limits can cause prejudice to one or more the parties to the litigation.
4. In addition, the vacation or adjournment of the date of trial prejudices other litigants and disrupts the administration of justice.
5. Extensions of time which involve the vacation or adjournment of trial dates should therefore be granted only as a last resort.
6. Where time limits have not been complied with the parties should cooperate in reaching an agreement as to new time limits which will not involve the date of trial being postponed.
7. If they reach such an agreement, they can ordinarily expect the court to give effect to that agreement at the trial and it is not necessary to make a separate application solely for this purpose.
8. The court will not look with favour on a party who seeks only to take tactical advantage from the failure of another party to comply with time limits.
9. In the absence of an agreement as to a new timetable, an application should be made promptly to the court for directions.
10. In considering whether to grant an extension of time to a party who is in default, the court will look at all the circumstances of the case including the considerations identified above.[30]

The principles give the clear impression that the new approach required by the Woolf Reforms was intended to be traditional in nature and that the RSC's theory of justice would remain in place. At each point, the centrality of securing substantive justice in individual cases is emphasised. The new focus on rule-compliance may have been stressed, but only in order to emphasise the need to resolve claims in reasonable time. This was necessary so as to ensure that the court's ability to ascertain true fact, through, for instance, permitting delay to cause prejudice to the parties to the litigation, was not undermined. Tactical applications and objections were deprecated. Attempts to obstruct the determination of claims on their substantive merits were not to be countenanced. In the same vein, parties were to seek to agree between themselves how to resolve a failure to comply with procedural time limits. Rather than taking procedural points, they were to get on

---

[30] CA 26 November 1996, unreported, at 30–31.

with the case and ensure it was resolved at trial. Where they could not agree, the court was to give directions on how to proceed i.e. to set a new timetable that would enable the dispute to proceed to trial. The principles thus read look like an exhortation to avoid common law formalism in favour of securing substantive justice; a point that was emphatically emphasised by the relationship between the first two principles Millett LJ outlined.

The first principle Millett LJ articulated emphasised the normative role that procedural rules play. They were to be complied with, rather than to be treated as if they were simply aspirational targets. The second principle, however, immediately undermined the claim to normativity; just as the *Tildesley* test undermined the normative nature of the RSC's rules. Rule-following – and the same was true of the other principles – was to be subject to the same overriding principle (or objective) that governed the RSC and, according to the Interim Report, the general (or overriding) objective of the reformed system: that substantive justice must be done. Reform was apparently to go no further than make clearer than had previously been the case how substantive justice was to be achieved through rendering litigation more efficient and economical. As it was originally understood, and as Millett LJ articulated principles that were consistent with it, it looked no different from the common law overriding objectives. It simply made explicit the traditional theory of justice that had governed the RSC. Apparently, nothing was to change.

4.3   Implementing a traditional overriding objective post-1999

The idea that the overriding objective's introduction was to bring about no significant change was not confined to a reading of its early development in the Interim Report and Millett LJ's Lord Woolf-approved guidance. If it was, it might not have become problematic. Unfortunately, it gained credence after the CPR was introduced in April 1999. It influenced both influential textbook and academic writers and the Court of Appeal. It has thus influenced lawyers who rely on the textbook writers to gain an understanding of how the CPR is intended to operate, and a less than virtuous circle has then both influenced and been influenced by authoritative guidance from the courts, which in turn is based on a flawed understanding of the nature of the rule.

It was pointed out in Chapter 2 that the *Annual Practice* after the RSC was introduced properly articulated the equity-based origin and intention behind the, then, new rule on the effects of procedural non-compliance. It articulated the new theory of justice, which the *Tildesley* test would then articulate authoritatively. Its twenty-first century successor, *Civil Procedure*, i.e. *The White Book*, has failed to play the same role. It has consistently articulated a traditionalist interpretation of the overriding objective. Its editors have, for instance, consistently described it in terms that have emphasised the primacy of substantive justice over all other considerations, e.g.:

> the overriding consideration must be the doing of justice in the individual case and the application of the several aspects of the overriding objective as particularised in r.1.1 (2) is subject to that consideration.[31]

Any conflict between economy, efficiency and even proportionality on this view, as it was in Millett LJ's guidance, are subordinate to the aim of securing substantive justice; a point emphasised at the time the Jackson Reforms were implemented. Relying on both Collins MR's classic statement that procedure is the handmaiden of justice and its restatement in *NML Capital Ltd* v. *Republic of Argentina*,[32] it has re-emphasised the flawed view that substantive justice, which it understands to be articulated by the imprecation in CPR r. 1.1(1) that the procedural code should enable the court to 'deal with cases justly', is superior to the principles articulated in CPR r. 1.1(2), i.e. to economy, efficiency and proportionality.[33] Its predecessor helped embed the RSC's theory of justice. It has continued to do so.

An equivalent approach has been taken by Sime, who has described the overriding objective in terms redolent of Bowen LJ's statement of principle from *Cropper*:

> The main concept in CPR, r1.1, means the primary concern of the court is doing justice. Shutting a litigant out through a technical breach of the rules will not often be consistent with this, because the primary purpose of the civil courts is to decide cases on their merits, not to reject them through procedural default.[34]

---

[31] See for instance, *Civil Procedure 2007* (Sweet & Maxwell) (M. Waller, ed.) Vol. I at 1.3.3; *Civil Procedure 2009* (Sweet & Maxwell) Vol. II at 11.8; *Civil Procedure 2013* (Sweet & Maxwell) (R. Jackson, ed.) Vol II at 11.8; see Chapter 7.

[32] [2011] 1 WLR 273.

[33] *Civil Procedure 2013* Vol. II at 11–18; see criticism of this view in Chapter 7.

[34] S. Sime, *A Practical Guide to Civil Procedure* (13th edn) (Oxford University Press, 2010) at 35. Emphasis added.

The same points regarding the subordinate nature of the commitments to economy, efficiency and proportionality and their status in respect of the court's primary concern are clearly articulated. The overriding objective is once again presented as nothing more than an express statement of the RSC's theory of justice. It is, again, another common law overriding objective. For Sime, as for the *White Book*'s editors, Millett LJ, Greenslade and the Interim Report, the overriding objective may encourage the pursuit of economy, efficiency and proportionality, but it does so in order to promote the achievement of substantive justice. Should they come into conflict with it, then doing justice must win out, just as it did under the RSC. An entirely traditional picture is given. The overriding objective is an expression of continuity, not change. On this view, there could be no realistic expectation that the problems of complexity, cost and delay would be resolved by the CPR's introduction. Rendering explicit the source of the RSC's problems cannot properly be considered to be a viable basis on which reform could succeed.

The Court of Appeal has further compounded the problem posed by the textbook writers' flawed understanding of the overriding objective. It has endorsed it on a number of occasions. On each of those occasions, the question in issue concerned rule-compliance, relief from the consequences of procedural default or error and late amendment. If the overriding objective had introduced a new theory of justice, a new approach to such applications should have been taken. If, however, the overriding objective was an explicit statement of the RSC's theory of justice, no appreciable difference in approach should have become apparent following the CPR's introduction. In *Hannigan* v. *Hannigan & Others*,[35] *Thurrock Borough Council* v. *Secretary of State for the Environment, Transport & the Regions*,[36] *Sayers* v. *Clarke-Walker*[37] and *B* v. *B*,[38] the Court of Appeal took the latter approach. It interpreted the overriding objective in entirely traditional terms.

Hannigan presented an early opportunity for the Court to explain the proper application of Woolf's new approach to doing justice. It concerned an application, issued in June 1999, under the Inheritance (Provision for Family and Dependants) Act 1975. The applicant's solicitor inadvertently issued the application using a pre-CPR court form. The respondent subsequently applied to have the proceedings struck out on nine technical grounds arising out of the wrong form's use. A district

---

[35] [2000] 2 FCR 650.   [36] [2001] CP Rep 55.   [37] [2002] 1 WLR 3095.
[38] [2005] EWCA Civ 237.

judge granted the application. An appeal followed. Dismissing the appeal, the circuit judge emphasised how the CPR was intended to 'ensure that civil litigation was brought up to a higher degree of efficiency than possibly pertained before'.[39] The failure to use the newly introduced form undermined that aim: the claim had to be struck out for procedural non-compliance. Looked at in the light of Millett LJ's principles, the decision gave precedence to the first one: the rules were to be followed, they were not simply targets or aspirations. A further appeal followed. Brooke LJ, who was one of the appellate judges entrusted with dealing with appeals arising out of the new rules, gave the Court of Appeal's principal judgment. In doing so, he noted that the approach taken by the district judge and upheld by the circuit judge was reminiscent of the technical approach to litigation that was finally laid to rest in 1965 through the reforms that created RSC Ord. 2.[40] Those reforms, he noted, had ensured that Bowen LJ's *dictum* from *Cropper*, albeit the extra-curial version cited in both *Pontin v. Wood*[41] and *Harkness v. Bell's Asbestos & Engineering Ltd*[42] was finally true of all English civil procedure. In other words, it was reminiscent of common law formalism rather than the equity-based commitment to securing substantive justice that governed the RSC. The CPR, he stressed, was not intended to take civil justice back to the days of common law formalism, where form took precedence over substance.[43] Lord Woolf did not, as he described it, intend procedure to form an obstacle to effective access to justice.[44] In this, he was obviously correct. The Woolf Reforms were not intended to reintroduce common law formalism or a modern version of it. Having made these points, Brooke LJ went on to consider the overriding objective. He said this:

> the Civil Procedure Rules were drawn to ensure that civil litigation was brought up to a higher degree of efficiency. But one must not lose sight of the fact that the overriding objective . . . is to enable the court to deal with cases justly, and this means the achievement of justice as between litigants whose dispute it is the court's duty to resolve. . . CPR 1.3 provides that the parties are required to help the court to further the overriding objective, and the overriding objective is not furthered by arid squabbles about technicalities such as have disfigured this litigation and eaten into the quite slender resources available to the parties.

---

[39] Cited at [2000] 2 FCR 650 at [18].   [40] Ibid. at [30]; see Chapter 2, n. 159.
[41] [1962] 1 QB 594 at 609.   [42] [1967] 2 QB 729 at 735–736.
[43] [2000] 2 FCR 650 at [30].   [44] Ibid. at [21]–[31].

. . .

> If we do not make an order directing the correction of all these errors and we leave the judge's order to stand, . . . the result would be the antithesis of justice, [the] claim would be struck out in its infancy without any investigation into its merits and the defendants would receive a completely unjustified windfall simply because of a number of technical mistakes made by a solicitor in the very early days of a new procedural regime.[45]

Brooke LJ's stance here is clearly correct as to its result. The district and circuit judges' decision was patently over-zealous. On any reading of the overriding objective it was unjustified. The respondent's conduct evidenced all the characteristics of the tactical approach to procedure the Woolf Reforms had criticised and which the overriding objective and the duty imposed on parties to assist the court to further it were intended to bring to an end. Equally, although Brooke LJ did not refer to it, neither the district judge's nor the circuit judge's approaches were consistent with the approach to relief from the consequences of default set out in *Biguzzi* v. *Rank Leisure*,[46] which had been handed down in July 1999, shortly before the respondent's application was considered at first instance. In *Biguzzi*, Lord Woolf had emphasised how, under the new rules, there was greater emphasis on keeping to procedural time limits. That did not mean, he explained, that the overriding objective required cases to be struck out for procedural error or default. The CPR provided the court with a variety of means to deal with the consequences of default, and it should tailor the measures used to the nature of the default. The punishment should, in other words, fit the crime.[47] In *Hannigan*, the punishment clearly did not fit the crime. It was disproportionate.[48] It rewarded the respondent who, if the order stood, would succeed in its defence of the claim on purely formal grounds. More importantly, it would do so even though in bringing the application the respondent had failed to further the overriding objective in breach of its duty to assist the court required by CPR r. 1.3. Equally, there was no question of the applicant's error having caused any significant

---

[45] Ibid. at [36]–[38]; *Kesslar* v. *Moore & Tibbits (A Firm)* [2005] PNLR 17 at [27]; May, 'The ALI/UNIDROIT Rules of Transnational Civil Procedure in the Perspective of the New English and Welsh Rules', at 44.

[46] [1999] 1 WLR 1926.

[47] A point Brooke LJ would reiterate in *Jones* v. *T Mobile (UK) Ltd* [2003] EWCA Civ 1162; [2004] CP Rep 10 at [28].

[48] [2000] 2 FCR 650 at [38].

increase in cost or delay, nor had it resulted in any adverse effect on the proper administration of justice. The claim had just been issued.

There is nothing in the manner in which the appeal was dealt with that can properly be criticised. On its facts, it was the right decision. The underlying tenor of Brooke LJ's judgment is, however, consistent with the traditionalist view of the overriding objective. In the first instance, he explained the requirement that the court deal with cases justly in entirely traditional terms. It meant no more than that the court must do justice between parties whose dispute the court has to resolve. It focused on the immediate parties. Furthermore, it required parties to assist the court to secure such a resolution. They were to do so by avoiding technical disputes. In other words, they were required to assist the court to resolve disputes by ensuring that litigation is carried out with one aim: to secure a decision on the merits rather than on formal grounds. If they did so, they would ensure that litigation costs were kept to a minimum and rendered more efficient than had been the case under the RSC. This was nothing more than the traditional approach. Substantive justice remained the aim. Economy and efficiency were to be promoted in pursuing it. Procedural applications and technical points were not to be taken. They frustrated justice's achievement. They were, as Brooke LJ put it, in terms entirely consistent with the sentiment that lay behind Bowen LJ's *dictum* from *Cropper* and the rationale behind its citation in *Pontin* and *Harkness*, the very antithesis of justice. Determining the claim on formal grounds arising from procedural error with no consideration of the substantive merits was no part of securing justice. As dealing with cases justly meant doing justice between the parties, such a consequence, by necessary implication, would be contrary to the overriding objective. The court's duty remained under the CPR to resolve disputes through doing justice, through securing merits-based decisions. The one difference between the RSC and the CPR was that the efficiency and the economy the former had strived to secure was within reach. Securing substantive justice remained the aim. Brooke LJ returned to this in *Thurrock*.

Thurrock concerned a challenge to a planning decision under the Town and Country Planning Act 1990. The defendant appealed a decision to grant the claimants permission to amend their claim to enable them to bring a statutory appeal. If the question had arisen prior to the CPR's introduction, it would have been one that would have been dealt with straightforwardly under the *Tildesley* test. The Court of Appeal dismissed the appeal; the amendment was to stand. Brooke LJ once more gave the principal decision. In doing so, he adverted to *Hannigan*.

He first noted that the amendment power had to be exercised consistently with the overriding objective.[49] He then asked whether the claimants should be denied an opportunity to proceed to judgment because they initially failed to formalise their claim properly. The answer to that question was to be decided by reference to *Hannigan*, consistently with the gloss it gave to the overriding objective: formalism was not to be reintroduced, the court's predominant aim was still to secure substantive justice. The same principle that applied to relief from the consequences of default applied to the power to amend: the position was the same under the CPR as it was under the RSC.[50]

The only point of apparent departure from the RSC these two decisions suggested the overriding objective introduced was the role parties were to play in the conduct of litigation. Litigants were to cooperate and they were to help the court further the overriding objective. They were no longer to engage in conduct that undermined it and its aim of securing justice. A laissez-faire attitude to rule-compliance, tactical skirmishing and procedural litigation had undermined the RSC's ability to secure justice. This was to stop as a consequence of this new duty placed on litigants to assist the court in securing substantive justice. The overriding objective thus effected an instrumental change designed to do what the RSC in practice could not: achieve its aim of securing substantive justice.[51] It did so by doing no more than placing its faith in the fact that litigants would act consistently with this duty to assist the court further the overriding objective.

The overriding objective's traditionalist interpretation was next supported in *Sayers*. In that case, the court faced the question how it was to operate where substantive justice, economy and efficiency came into conflict. If it simply enunciated the RSC's theory of justice, the answer would be straightforward. It would be the same answer that Millett LJ in *Mortgage Corporation*, the *White Book* and *Hannigan* and *Thurrock* had all given: the former would take precedence, as it remained the predominant policy aim. Economy and efficiency, as subordinate aims, could not legitimately be relied on to call into question its achievement. Alternatively, if the overriding objective set out something other than the traditional theory of justice, the three policy aims might have been

---

[49] [2001] CP Rep 55 at [25]; see CPR r. 17.
[50] Ibid. at [27]–[30]; see the discussion of the application of the *Tildesley* test to both amendment and relief from sanction for non-compliance in Chapter 2.
[51] [2000] 2 FCR 650 at [36]; H. Woolf (1995) at 27.

treated as equals. They might then have been weighed against each other as such, and the application for an extension of time within which to seek permission to appeal might have been decided on the grounds that one or two of the principles outweighed the other or others. Substantive justice could have outweighed the other two principles. Equally, economy or efficiency could have outweighed it. The question, though, would not have been weighted in substantive justice's favour, as the traditional interpretation required. On the alternate view, it would not have been first amongst equals. It would have been one amongst equals.

Brooke LJ once more gave the principal judgment. The approach taken was once again consistent with a traditionalist interpretation. Substantive justice was not one aim amongst equals. It remained the predominant aim. When it came into conflict with economy and efficiency, it was to be given precedence. In the words of the *White Book*, CPR 1.1(2) was subject to CPR 1.1(1). In other words, the end trumped the means by which it was to be achieved, as was the case under the RSC and equity before it. The extension of time was granted, notwithstanding the additional, unnecessary litigation cost it engendered. Brooke LJ reached this conclusion by first noting something Lightman J had set out in *Commissioners of Customs and Excise* v. *Eastwood Care Homes*.[52] In that decision, delivered shortly after the CPR was introduced, the point had been accepted that pursuing efficiency and economy in the course of litigation were not independent aims. They were simply facilitative ones, pursued in so far as they promoted substantive justice's achievement. This was the RSC's approach. As Lightman J described it, it:

> was ... correct ... to say that one of the important features in deciding what justice requires is to bear in mind that time limits are there to be observed, and that justice may be seriously defeated if there is any laxity in that regard.[53]

Economy and efficiency were not ends in themselves. They were, through an increased emphasis on rule-compliance, the means by which justice could be done. Nothing had changed with the replacement of the RSC by the CPR. Having noted this, Brooke LJ moved on to consider whether to grant relief from the consequences of the appellants' failure to issue their substantive application within the prescribed time limit. He said this:

---

[52] CA 18 January 2000; TLR 07 March 2000.   [53] [2002] 1 WLR 3095 at [23].

the overriding objective is to deal with cases justly, so that resource considerations should not carry very much weight if fairness demands that an extension of time should be granted.[54]

Fairness was the fulcrum on which substantive justice, economy and efficiency turned. It was a seemingly independent criterion against which they were weighed, and through which conflict between them could be resolved.[55] Why would fairness require an extension of time to be granted? Why would it be a more important consideration than the pursuit of economy and efficiency? It would, because what was fair was determined by reference to securing substantive justice. As had been made clear in *Air Canada*: 'In a contest purely between one litigant and another, . . ., the task of the court is to do, and be seen to be doing, justice between the parties – a duty reflected by the word "fairly"'.[56] If the court in *Sayers* was to do justice between the parties, to treat them fairly, it had no choice: substantive justice had to be done. Even if resource considerations pointed towards frustrating its achievement, fairness to the parties required it. Resource considerations, just like considerations of technical default, should not stand in the way of justice: as equity had taught the RSC, so the CPR would codify what the RSC had learnt. If resource considerations did stand in the way of justice, then litigants would have been treated unfairly: they would not have received justice. In *Sayers*, in order to deal with the case justly, an extension of time had to be granted, notwithstanding the fact that by doing so the pursuit of economy and efficiency would be frustrated. Fairness required this, just as it did under the RSC. Reliance on fairness emphasised that nothing had changed.

The strongest endorsement of the overriding objective's traditionalist interpretation is found in *B* v. *B*.[57] The substantive claim arose out of proceedings relating to alleged sexual abuse during the early 1990s. It was issued in 1997 and was dealt with by way of cross-undertakings before a district judge later that year. No further action was taken, and the claim became subject to an automatic stay under CPR 51 in early 2000. In May 2003, shortly before limitation expired, the claimant issued new proceedings seeking damages. An issue arose as to whether the second set of proceedings had been issued in abuse of process given the continued,

---

[54] Ibid. at [25].

[55] D. Galligan, *Discretionary Powers* (Clarendon Press, Oxford) (1990) at 57–61.

[56] *Air Canada & Others* v. *Secretary of State for Trade & Others* [1983] 2 AC 394, 438.

[57] [2005] EWCA Civ 237; J. Sorabji, '*B v B*: Forwards or Backwards for the Overriding Objective' 24 (2005) *CJQ* 414, 414ff, for an earlier version of this critique.

albeit stayed, existence of the initial proceedings. The claimant argued that if the second set of proceedings were an abuse of process, the stay on the first claim ought to be lifted. Guidance regarding the correct approach to applications under CPR 51 had been given on a number of prior occasions. Each had adopted an approach sympathetic to the traditionalist interpretation, not least because claims dealt with under CPR 51 had all begun prior to the CPR's introduction and had therefore been prosecuted, at least initially, under the previous regime and its litigation culture.[58]

The Court of Appeal lifted the stay and approved the traditionalist interpretation of the overriding objective. It abandoned any pretence that it was anything other than an explicit statement of the RSC's implicit overriding objective, which rendered explicit the principle that underpinned the approach endorsed by *Tildesley*. Giving the principal judgment, Longmore LJ, with whom Brooke and Arden LJJ agreed, said this:

> ... [the DJ's] exercise of discretion was flawed because the district judge proceeded at once to the factors in CPR Part 3.9 without giving any weight to the overriding objective of CPR (see 1.1(1)) that cases between litigants should be determined justly... I would regard the overriding objective of determining cases justly as being dominant. If there were irreparable prejudice to the defendant, it might be more just to prevent these matters from being determined...[59]

The first, and substantive, point made equated the overriding objective with the commitment to arriving at a merits-based decision. Claims were to be 'determined justly' rather than dealt with justly or fairly. Determining rather than dealing with cases justly saw the overriding objective express the court's commitment to 'decide cases on their merits'. Claims were determined at trial. It was only permissible to refuse to determine a claim at trial where to do so would irreparably prejudice the non-defaulter. It is the reference to irreparable prejudice that clarifies that determining cases is a reference to substantive justice's achievement. Under the RSC, and equity before it, irreparable prejudice was prejudice that could not be compensated in costs, as had been made clear by *Tildesley, Clarapede* and *Cropper*. The sole consideration for the court

---

[58] *Taylor* v. *Anderson* [2002] EWCA Civ 1680; TLR, 22 November 2002; *Hanson* v. *E Rex Makin* [2003] EWCA 1801; *Flaxman-Binns* v. *Lincolnshire County Council* [2004] 1 WLR 2232. For criticism, see *Khatib* v. *Ramco International* [2011] EWCA Civ 605; *Ryder Plc* v. *Dominic James Beever* [2012] EWCA Civ 1737.

[59] [2005] EWCA Civ 237 at [18]–[19].

when asked to exercise its discretion to permit forgiveness for non-compliance with a procedural requirement or to permit a party to amend its pleadings was the effect that granting or refusing the application would have on the parties and their right to receive a merits-based determination. No consideration was given to any wider effects that the decision might have. Justice in the individual case was the sole consideration that only irreparable prejudice could trump. Determining cases justly, for Longmore LJ and the Court of Appeal, through the reference to irreparable prejudice, meant no more than the *Tildesley* test. The overriding objective was no more than a restatement of that and the RSC's theory of justice.

Longmore LJ's judgment goes on to reinforce this interpretation in his explanation of how CPR r. 3.9 which, as noted earlier, is the CPR's provision dealing with relief from the consequences of procedural default, ought to be applied.[60] CPR r. 3.9 in its original form, which was in force at the time of the decision, set out nine factors that were supposed to be consistent with the overriding objective. In theory it provided detailed criteria, which if properly applied, could enable the court to reach decisions that properly balanced substantive justice with the other principles set out within the overriding objective.[61] That was the theory. Longmore LJ's judgment understood CPR r. 3.9's application

---

[60] CPR r. 3.9 in its original version permitted the court, amongst other things, to take account of the following criteria:

'(a) the interests of the administration of justice;
(b) whether the application for relief has been made promptly;
(c) whether there failure to comply was intentional;
(d) whether there is a good explanation for the failure;
(e) the extent to which the party in default has complied with other rules, practice directions, court orders, and any relevant pre-action protocol;
(f) whether the failure to comply was caused by the party or his legal representative;
(g) whether the trial date of the likely trial date can still be met if relief is granted;
(h) the effect which the failure to comply had on each party; and
(i) the effect which the granting of relief would have on each party.'

[61] A revised version of the rule came into force in April 2013, to implement recommendations made in the Jackson Review. It simply provides that:
'r. 3.9(1) On an application for relief from any sanction imposed for a failure to comply with any rule, practice direction or court order, the court will consider all the circumstances of the case, so as to enable it to deal justly with the application, including the need–

(a) for litigation to be conducted efficiently and at proportionate cost; and
(b) to enforce compliance with rules, practice directions and orders.'

as having three parts to it. First, that the overriding objective should be applied. An assessment must be made whether the claim can be determined justly, i.e. the *Tildesley* test must be applied. If relief ought to be granted according to that test, then and only then could an assessment of CPR r. 3.9's specific requirements be made. Having gone through this exercise, the court had then to look once more to the overriding objective and note that this was the '*dominant*' of the two processes. It was not just dominant over the resource considerations set out in CPR r. 1.1(2), which Longmore LJ failed to deal with, but it was dominant over CPR r. 3.9. Describing it as the dominant of the two processes made plain that the overriding objective could be deployed to trump any, but in reality only any adverse conclusion reached at the end of the second, CPR r. 3.9, limb of the process.

This approach rendered the exact provisions in CPR r. 3.9 superfluous. The twin-track assessment envisaged by Longmore LJ had three possible outcomes: both the overriding objective and r. 3.9 suggested that relief should be granted; the overriding objective suggested that relief should be granted, but r. 3.9 did not; or, the overriding objective suggested relief should not be granted while r. 3.9 suggests it should. In the first situation, CPR r. 3.9 had no role to play. It merely confirmed the decision made by the dominant element. In the second situation, it was trumped by the overriding objective's commitment to securing a merits-based determination of the claim. Again, it had no role to play as the decision whether to grant relief was actually taken by the conclusion reached by applying the overriding objective. The same point again arises, *mutatis mutandis*, under the third scenario. In all three situations it is the overriding objective that does the real work by weighing up the relative prejudice to the parties of either a grant or refusal of relief; the abovementioned assessment's third limb. Two consequences flow from this. Longmore LJ's statement, by leaving no work for CPR r. 3.9 to do, effectively undermined the mechanism that was explicitly supposed to govern the process by which courts assessed whether to grant relief from sanctions. It rendered redundant the mechanism that took account of the need to arrive at a merits-based decision (CPR r. 3.9(a), (h) and (i)) as well the need to secure efficiency and economy in the course of litigation (CPR r. 3.9(b) to (i)). The only real considerations that were to be taken account of were those of the *Tildesley* test, i.e. whether the case could be determined justly as between the immediate parties; and whether the non-defaulting party could be compensated in costs. Nothing had changed. In reality, the *Tildesley* test remained in place. As such, the theory it gave life to also remained in place. Consequently, the judgment reinforced the idea that the overriding objective was no more than an express statement of the RSC's implicit overriding objective or an English version of the established overriding objectives. Building on *Hannigan, Thurrock* and *Sayers*, the decision in *B* v. *B* entrenched the overriding objective's traditionalist interpretation. It downgraded economy and efficiency's importance to no more than facilitative supports for substantive justice's achievement that could be set aside when they conflicted with it. Moreover, just like in *Mortgage Corporation, Hannigan, Thurrock* and *Sayers*, it gave no real role for proportionality to play either as between the parties or as CPR r. 1.1(2)(e) required. The focus was simply on economy and efficiency, and their subordinate role within the overriding objective.

Longmore LJ did not stop there. In his consideration of the specific elements of CPR r. 3.9, he offered an RSC-consistent account of what it meant to refer to the administration of justice. CPR r. 3.9(a) required the court to take account of the interests of the administration of justice in considering applications for relief from sanctions. Longmore LJ's gloss on it was that:

> (a) the interests of the administration of justice; these interests are that cases, brought within the time limits settled by Parliament, should be resolved...[62]

The administration of justice was based solely on a consideration that the individual claim is the court's immediate concern. Cases brought legitimately, i.e. within limitation, should be resolved; they should be determined on their merits. Other issues, such as the cost and length of time it might take to resolve such claims, had no real role to play. Again proportionality had no role to play, just as it had no role to play in the Court of Appeal's earlier decisions and the Interim Report's early development of the overriding objective, proportionality did not appear to enter the equation. CPR r. 1.1(2)(e), which required both the court and the parties to take account of the needs of other court users, had no role to play. Longmore LJ simply interpreted CPR r. 3.9(a) consistently with the approach to delay articulated by Lord Griffiths in *Department of Transport* v. *Chris Smaller (Transport) Ltd*, viz., that:

---

[62] [2005] EWCA Civ 237 at [19].

> The courts must respect the limitation periods set by Parliament; if they
> are too long then it is for Parliament to reduce them. I therefore com-
> mence my assessment of the present regime by concluding that the
> plaintiff cannot be penalised for any delay that occurs between the accrual
> of the cause of action and the issue of the writ provided it is issued within
> the limitation period.[63]

The consideration of what the administration of justice meant echoed
this. Wider considerations of the effect on other litigants in other claims
did not enter the frame. The consequences that individual case management decisions, to grant relief from sanction or to grant a late amendment, for instance, had on the wider public interest in the administration
of justice, had no role to play. The effect that furthering the pursuit of
individual justice had on the fair distribution of the court's resources
amongst all litigants had no real role to play. If a fair trial could still
be held, and hence a merits-based judgment given, and it is to be
assumed in all cases that lie within the ambit of a limitation that a fair
trial could still be held, then the courts were to ensure that such a trial
was held, cost, delay and the consequences for other litigants notwithstanding. Such considerations were of little consequence: the court was to
secure substantive justice. Just as fairness for Brooke LJ in *Sayers*
demanded considerations of economy and efficiency to be set aside whilst
issues of proportionality were ignored, so it was for Longmore LJ's
approach. It could be said fairness required it, but only because fairness
focused solely on securing substantive justice between the immediate
litigants. Once more, the Court of Appeal had endorsed an interpretation
of the overriding objective that understood it as nothing more than an
explicit statement of the RSC's implicit overriding objective: substantive
justice was to be done.[64]

4.4   Conclusion: the overriding objective – more of the same

In a lecture given at University College, London in 2005, Lord Woolf
explained how the overriding objective embodied three philosophies:
a commitment to reaching the right decision on the merits of the claim,
i.e. substantive justice; the commitment to economy; and the commitment to efficiency. In this, he echoed the way in which he described it in

---

[63] [1989] AC 1197 at 1207.

[64] *Less* v. *Benedict* [2005] EWHC 1643; *Di Placito* v. *Slater & Others* [2004] 1 WLR 1605;
Overseas & Commercial Developments Ltd v. *Cox* [2002] EWCA Civ 635 at [33].

Biguzzi v. *Rank Leisure* and *Swain* v. *Hillman* as the embodiment of three overriding objectives rather than the enunciation of an overriding objective.[65] The question was how those philosophies or objectives related to each other. Did they embody two different categories of commitment: a substantive and predominant policy aim and two subordinate policy aims that were simply the means by which the former was to be achieved? Did they embody equal substantive policy aims each of which was an end in itself? If the former, then the *White Book*'s claim that the overriding objective is nothing more than an expanded and particularised version of the statement of principles that govern arbitration procedure under the Arbitration Act 1996 might be right.[66] The traditionalist interpretation understands it in those terms; as nothing more than a generalised statement of the commitment to use the court's powers to dispose of claims 'fairly and expeditiously' as was previously required by RSC (1965) Ord. 38 r. 2A.[67] It was no more than an explicit version of the RSC's overriding objective.

The early development of the overriding objective supports this interpretation, as do the Court of Appeal's decisions from *Hannigan* to *B* v. *B*. What is emphasised is that the overriding objective articulated two ideas. First, that dealing with, or as it was misdescribed in *B* v. *B*, 'determining' cases justly was no more than an express endorsement of the RSC's theory of justice. That commitment remained the justice system's substantive and predominant policy aim. Secondly, that economy and efficiency, as set out within CPR r. 1.1(2), were intended to guide the court and litigants so that the predominant aim was achieved at the least possible cost and in the least time. The individual commitments set out in r. 1.1(2) are to deal with cases justly; what, for Bentham, the primary role of justice's collateral ends was to its direct end. It is servant to justice's master. This has consequences.

---

[65] [1999] 1 WLR 1926 at 1932.

[66] *Civil Procedure 2013* Vol. II at 11.5; Arbitration Act 1996 s. 1: 'the object of arbitration is to obtain the fair resolution of disputes by an impartial tribunal without unnecessary delay or expense...'; J. Sorabji, 'Prospects for Proportionality: Jackson Implementation', 32 (2013) *CJQ* 213, 221.

[67] I. Scott (ed.), *Supreme Court Practice* (Sweet & Maxwell, 1999) Vol. I; RSC (1965) Ord. 38 r. 2A (exchange of witness statements): '2A(1) The powers of the Court under this rule shall be exercised for the purpose of disposing fairly and expeditiously of the cause or matter before it, and saving costs, having regard to all the circumstances of the case'. CCR (1981) Ord. 20. r. 12A was drafted in identical terms.

The most important consequence if the traditionalists are correct, is that it remains the case under the CPR just as it was under the RSC that,

> A just result (or judgment or decision) is one which follows from the correct application of the law to the true facts and therefore gives the parties what is theirs. An unjust or incorrect result is one which does not achieve this end, which does not correctly apply the law or accurately determine the facts. An unjust decision is one where the plaintiff's rightful claim is denied or the defendant's rightful defence is denied.[68]

If correct, this view simply embeds an interpretation of the overriding objective, to borrow Jacob's phrase, into the fabric of English civil justice that is no different from its previous, implicit, overriding objective. The new theory of justice is no more than the old one. Just as under the RSC, the justice system will be committed to the theory that justice means the achievement of accuracy with the avoidance of cost and delay that could undermine its achievement in the individual case.[69]

This poses a substantial problem if correct. If the overriding objective really does no more than articulate the RSC's theory of justice, it is difficult to see exactly how the justice system might operate in a different manner than previously. It is difficult to see, for instance, how the courts could properly take a more rigorous approach to rule-compliance and procedural default. It is difficult to see how greater rigour might be imposed on party compliance where securing substantive justice remains the predominant aim and economy and efficiency are to be promoted as means to secure it.[70] It will inevitably be the case that, as in *Sayers*, where the three come into conflict, fairness will require justice to take precedence.[71] Any conflict, as it was in *Sayers* and *B* v.*B*, must be resolved in its favour. Just as Edmund-Davies LJ had it in *Associated Leisure*, securing substantive justice will remain the 'all-embracing principle' that governs the civil justice system and which economy and efficiency

---

[68] A. Zuckerman, 'Quality and Economy in Civil Procedure: The Case for Commuting Correct Judgments for Timely Judgments' 14 (1994) *Oxford Journal of Legal Studies* 353, 355.

[69] *B* v. *Reading Borough Council & Others* [2007] EWCA Civ 1313 at [48].

[70] May, 'The ALI/UNIDROIT Rules of Transnational Civil Procedure in the Perspective of the New English and Welsh Rules' at 44–5.

[71] A. Zuckerman, 'Compliance with Process Obligations and Fair Trial', in Andenas, Andrews and Nazzini, *The Future of Transnational Civil Litigation*, at 127; A. Zuckerman, 'A Colossal Wreck – the *BCCI*-*Three Rivers* Litigation' 25 (2006) *CJQ* 287; A. Zuckerman, *Weakness of Will – The Exercise of Case Management Discretion under the CPR* (unpublished paper presented at Atlantic Chambers, 24 May 2007).

and 'all other considerations must be [and will remain] subordinate'.[72] Nothing will have changed. Compliance will remain an optional extra and excess cost and delay will not be properly tackled as the Woolf Reforms intended. The same underlying theory could not but, ultimately, give rise to the same consequences; a point borne out in the Jackson Review, when it concluded that:

> There is a wide spread of views about this issue, amongst both practitioners and distinguished academic commentators. The conclusions to which I have come are as follows. First, the courts should set realistic timetables for cases and not impossibly tough timetables in order to give an impression of firmness. Secondly, courts at all levels have become too tolerant of delays and non-compliance with orders. In so doing they have lost sight of the damage which the culture of delay and non-compliance is inflicting upon the civil justice system. The balance therefore needs to be redressed.[73]

A mere six years after Brooke LJ, in *Southern & District Finance Plc v. Turner* had explained that the CPR required the court and litigants to take a more rigorous approach to rule compliance and to be more astute than previously to 'correct sloppy practice and to avoid at all costs slipping back to the bad old days when courts took a relaxed attitude to the need for compliance with rules and court orders, so that expensive and time-consuming satellite litigation was only too apt to flourish', the bad old days were back.[74] That this was the case should have been unsurprising. If the overriding objective is understood and applied as if it is no more than a restatement of the RSC's overriding objective, then the reformed system could not but give rise to the same litigation culture, its cost and delays, as was endemic under the RSC. Cultures grow from the fundamental characteristics of the system. The bad old ways were an inevitable symptom of giving priority to the need to secure substantive justice. If, as the traditionalist interpretation understands it, the Woolf Reforms effected an arch-conservative revision of the justice system, introducing into it an explicit commitment to the very theory of justice that Bramwell LJ had embedded into the RSC in the 1870s, then it

---

[72] [1970] 2 QB 450 at 457.
[73] R. Jackson (December 2009) at 397; R. Jackson, *Achieving a culture change in case management* (5th Lecture in the Implementation Programme) (22 November 2011) (http://www.judiciary.gov.uk/Resources/JCO/Documents/Speeches/lj-jackson-speech-achieving-culture-change-case-management.pdf).
[74] [2003] EWCA Civ 1574; (2003) 147 SJLB 136 at [34].

was inevitable that the new approach to justice would result in exactly the same consequences as the old; as Evershed's new approach and as the RSC's new approach had in 1870. The traditionalist interpretation, as one that sees the Woolf Reforms and, through its continuation of them, the Jackson Reforms as nothing more than an exercise in normal science, condemns those reforms to the fate visited on all previous reform. It transforms them into one more exercise in futility.

5

The overriding objective: a new theory of justice (I)

Since April 1999 there has been a completely new set of Rules of procedure, a new language and, if Lord Woolf's intentions are realised, the beginnings of a new legal culture . . .This is no 'petty tinkering', but does it have the 'general idea or legal philosophy', the absence of which from Anglo American law Roscoe Pound bemoaned almost a century ago?[1]

The principal objective of the English civil justice system up to now has always been justice, to get at the truth as to what happened, who said and did what and why. Until now all proposals to reform the system have been designed to further this objective, by for example reducing the importance of technicalities and avoiding surprise. [The Woolf Report] is I think the first to recommend proposals calculated to make the achievement of this objective less likely.[2]

5.1 Introduction

The traditionalist view is that the Woolf Reforms were simply a case of business as usual. They did no more than previous reforms. The overriding objective's introduction simply made explicit the historic commitment to securing substantive justice while seeking to minimise cost and delay. The crisis in civil justice was, as a consequence, to be cured through ensuring that the system operated more rigorously, cost-effectively and efficiently than it had in the past. If correct, the traditionalist view is one of hope triumphing over experience. This view is, however, difficult to reconcile with that expressed in 2002 by Sir Anthony May, at the time the deputy Head of Civil Justice, that the

[1] J. Jolowicz, 'The Woolf Reforms', in J. Jolowicz, *On Civil Procedure* (Cambridge University Press, 2000) at 386–7.
[2] C. Dehn, 'The Woolf Report: Against the Public Interest?', in A. Zuckerman and R. Cranston, *Reform of Civil Procedure: Essays on 'Access to Justice'* (Clarendon Press, 1995) at 162.

CPR was not just a new procedural code, but one that gave expression to a 'profound new philosophy'.[3] Nor is it easy to reconcile with similar views expressed by the House of Lords in *Three Rivers District Council and Others* v. *Governor and Company of the Bank of England (No 3)* the following year, or the Court of Appeal in *Hashtroodi* v. *Hancock* in 2004. In the former, Lords Hope and Hobhouse made the same point, more forcefully. In their judgments, they described how the CPR marked an 'important shift in judicial philosophy'. In particular, it was said to represent a shift away 'from the traditional philosophy that previously dominated the administration of justice' towards one where economy, efficiency and the need to ensure that each claim would only be allotted 'an appropriate share of the court's resources . . . taking into account the need to allot resources to other cases'[4] were given greater weight than previously. In the latter, Dyson LJ, by then deputy head of Civil Justice, described how the 'CPR ushered in a new era in which, in significant respects, the previous approach to civil litigation and former practices . . . were abandoned.'[5] These various statements, which follow on from the Woolf Reforms' claim that what they had engaged in was fundamental reform aimed at producing both a new approach to litigation and a new litigation landscape, do not suggest reform was a case of business as usual.[6] On the contrary, they more than suggest that the traditionalist view fails adequately to capture the true nature of reform.

   This and the next chapter explore the shift in judicial philosophy that the Woolf Reforms effected; a shift which replaced the RSC's theory of justice with one of proportionate justice. This new theory, unlike the RSC's, yet like Bentham's, is constituted of four elements. First, its primary, or predominant, policy aim is to secure effective access to the justice system by ensuring an equitable distribution of the court's resources amongst all litigants. As the Interim Report explained it by reference to the introduction of active case management, which was to be carried out by the court in order to further the overriding objective, that aim was to 'preserve access to justice for all the users of the system'.[7] Through this the justice system was to secure the court's constitutional

---

[3] A. May, 'The ALI/UNIDROIT Rules of Transnational Civil Procedure in the Perspective of the New English and Welsh Rules', in M. Andenas, N. Andrews and R Nazzini, *The Future of Transnational Civil Litigation* (British Institute of International and Comparative Law, 2004) at 44.

[4] [2003] 2 AC 1 at [106] and [153].   [5] [2004] 1 WLR 3206 at [16].

[6] H. Woolf (1995) at 6; H. Woolf (1996) at 4.   [7] Ibid. at 24.

aim of vindicating rights and upholding the rule of law.[8] The primary aim was then to be achieved through the implementation of two equal subordinate policy aims: the second and fourth elements of the new theory. The first of those aims was the achievement of substantive justice in individual cases. Its role was, in this way, diminished in contrast to that which it played under the RSC: it was no longer the predominant aim. This was then, as in Bentham's theory, supported by the new theory's third element: a secondary, or collateral, commitment to minimising litigation cost and delay.[9] Finally, and crucially, the theory's primary aim was to be achieved through the operation of the second of its two subordinate policy aims: proportionality. This element was to play the same role that the reductive role justice's collateral ends played in Bentham's theory. It was the means by which a reduction in the quality of substantive justice was justified. It was also the means by which substantive justice could legitimately be denied in its entirety. It was an aim that, as Conrad Dehn QC rightly noted, would mean that the justice system post-Woolf was less likely to get at the truth, to secure substantive justice in individual cases, than previously.[10] This chapter focuses on those elements that are common to it, Bentham's and the RSC's theories, and the traditionalist view of Woolf: the commitment to substantive justice and to its achievement in minimal time and at minimal cost. The following chapter moves on to a consideration of those elements of the new theory that are only shared with Bentham's: equitable access to justice and proportionality.

5.2   Substantive justice: justice's direct end

The Woolf Reforms, as noted in the previous chapter, intended the overriding objective to articulate the civil justice system's and its rules of procedure's purpose.[11] It should, therefore, incorporate all four elements of Woolf's new theory. It does not, however, contain any express reference to

---

[8] H. Woolf (1995) at 2.

[9] *Vinos* v. *Marks & Spencer plc* [2001] 3 All ER 784, 790: 'If you then look up from the wording of the rules and at a broader horizon, one of the main aims of the CPR and their overriding objective is that civil litigation should be undertaken and pursued with proper expedition.'

[10] Dehn, 'The Woolf Report' at 162, 166–7, where he argues that the Woolf Reforms would entail that 'achieving justice [would] no longer [be] the overriding objective of the system'.

[11] H. Woolf (1996) at 274.

securing substantive justice, the first of its two subordinate policy aims. Unlike its express references to equality, economy, efficiency and proportionality, in neither of the Woolf Reports was there any explicit reference to substantive justice in the overriding objective, nor is there in its 1999 or 2013 versions.[12] In this, it differs from its equivalent in England's Criminal Procedure Rules. They refer explicitly to the need to reach an accurate decision.[13] The suggested rationale for this regrettable error was that such a reference would have been otiose; albeit not apparently otiose in the case of criminal process. As explained by the draftsman of the overriding objective's third draft version, there was no need to make express reference to, as he put it, truth-finding, because 'seeking the truth is so obviously part of the court's role that it does not need to be stated expressly in the rules'.[14] Zuckerman has elaborated this point in his analysis of the overriding objective.[15] It would have been wrong, he has suggested, to specify in rules of procedure the court's constitutional role; a role that he then noted was to secure substantive justice. Rules simply set out how the constitutional role is to be carried out, not what that role is.[16] Again, it might be asked why it was then appropriate to refer to that constitutional role in the Criminal Procedure Rules. Both the draftsman's and Zuckerman's positions are, however, flawed.

The first problem with the draftsman's explanation is that it appears to rest on a misunderstanding. It suggests that the civil courts are under an obligation to seek the truth, e.g. to arrive at an accurate decision, when, as counter-intuitive as it might seem, they are under no such duty.[17] They are not, for instance, required to actively obtain evidence, nor do they have any power to obtain evidence independently of the parties, or to require parties to do so on their behalf.[18] They cannot

---

[12] H. Woolf (1995) at 214–16; H. Woolf (1996) at 274; H. Woolf, *Access to Justice – Draft Civil Proceedings Rules* (HMSO, July 1996) at 2; CPR r. 1.1 (SI 1998/3132 as amended in 2013 by SI 262/2013); A. Zuckerman, *Zuckerman on Civil Procedure: Principles of Practice* (Thomson, 2006) at 7; A. Clarke, 'The Role of the Expert after Woolf' 14(3) (May 2008) *Clinical Risk* 85, 89–90.

[13] Rule 1.1(2)(a) of the Criminal Procedure Rules (SI 2005/384), specifies that dealing with cases justly includes 'acquitting the innocent and convicting the guilty'.

[14] Cited at J. Jolowicz, '"General Ideas" and Procedural Reform', in Jolowicz, *On Civil Procedure* at 391. The third draft of the rule differed in no significant degree from its previous drafts in the Interim and Final Woolf Reports, or its final published version in the CPR.

[15] Zuckerman, *Zuckerman on Civil Procedure* at 7.   [16] Ibid. at 8.

[17] Jolowicz, '"General Ideas" and Procedural Reform' at 390–1.

[18] *Re Enoch and Zaretzky, Bock & Co.'s Arbitration* [1910] 1 KB 327.

descend into the arena and cross-examine witnesses.[19] Nor can they go behind the terms of the dispute set out by the parties, even if they come to the conclusion that the wrong issues, whether factual or legal, are being contested.[20] Nor are they able to go behind the evidence presented by the parties to litigation, even where they are aware of the existence of evidence that, for whatever reason, has not been placed before it, as emphasised by Lord Wilberforce in *Air Canada & Others* v. *Secretary of State for Trade & Others*.[21] Courts are simply required to resolve disputes through ascertaining true fact as best they can according to the evidence properly submitted.[22] They may be under a duty to arrive at a substantively just decision on the balance of probabilities in the light of such evidence put before the court and consequently arrive at as accurate a decision as that permits. That is not, however, the same as being required to seek the truth.[23]

Putting to one side this misunderstanding, the draftsman's explanation is flawed for another reason, one it shares with Zuckerman: that the aim of securing substantive justice is so obviously part of the court's role that it need not be set out within the court's rules. Unlike the draftsman, who provided no detailed elaboration of this claim, Zuckerman has been developing his view on this as part of a wider theory of justice, which he has argued for since the early 1990s. To fully understand his position, which in many ways mirrors the approach taken by the Woolf Reforms, requires a short discussion of that wider theory. The first aspect of it is based on the claim that the justice system's traditional commitment to achieving substantive justice should, to a certain extent, be diminished. It should no longer be the 'sole criterion by which we judge the justice and the effectiveness of civil procedure'.[24] His rationale for this is twofold. First, he has argued that the untrammelled pursuit

---

[19] *Jones* v. *National Coal Board* [1957] 2 QB 55.

[20] *Loveridge and Loveridge* v. *Healey* [2004] EWCA Civ 173 at [23]: *Al-Medenni* v. *Mars UK Ltd* [2005] EWCA Civ 1041 at [22]–[25]: 'By making findings for which the claimant was not contending, it seems to me that the judge crossed the line which separates adversarial and inquisitorial systems. What he did may have been legitimate in an inquisitorial system. It was, in my judgment, impermissible in our system.'

[21] *Air Canada & Others* v. *Secretary of State for Trade & Others* [1983] 2 AC 394 per Lord Wilberforce at 438–9.

[22] *Loveridge and Loveridge* v. *Healey* at [23], although see Buxton LJ at [30].

[23] *Harmony Shipping Co SA* v. *Davies* [1979] 3 All ER 177 at 181.

[24] A. Zuckerman, 'Quality and Economy in Civil Procedure: The Case for Commuting Correct Judgments for Timely Judgments' 14 (1994) *Oxford Journal of Legal Studies* 353, 386; H. Woolf (1995) at 19.

of substantive justice is simply too expensive a commitment for the State, which has other fiscal responsibilities. By reducing the amount of money spent on the justice system, its focus on achieving substantive justice and, as a consequence, reducing the quality of judgments, the State's sparse resources could be spent on other socially useful activities, i.e. funding the health system.[25] In this respect, it is a theory that, to a certain extent, views the provision of one branch of the State as being equivalent to the provision of socially beneficial welfare provision This is, at the least, a questionable position. Social welfare provision may be the hallmark of a civilised society; it is not, however, an essential element of a properly functioning democratic State. Secondly, he rightly identified the RSC's approach to securing justice as the primary cause of the excess cost and delay that afflicted it from its inception.[26] Through giving primacy to the need to secure substantive justice in each individual case, the system could not but develop into one that generated unnecessary litigation cost and delay.[27] The RSC's theory of justice was thus not merely too time-consuming and expensive for the State, but it was subject to a funda-mental flaw, and one which lay at the heart of the constant failure of twentieth-century reform.[28]

Having identified the privileged status given to substantive justice under the RSC, a point on which he agreed with the conclusion Woolf would draw his Interim Report,[29] as the cause of the problems of cost and delay endemic to the justice system, Zuckerman also drew the conclusion that it should be reoriented. The inherently flawed theory of justice the RSC was committed to should be abandoned.[30] Just as the Interim and Final Reports would do, he then argued for a genuinely new, in his terms, multi-dimensional approach to justice. Unlike Woolf's theory, Zucker-man's new approach was based on the belief that the justice system should operate consistently with not one, as was the case under the

---

[25] Zuckerman, 'Quality and Economy in Civil Procedure'; A. Zuckerman, 'A Reform of Civil Procedure – Rationing Procedure rather than Access to Justice' 22 (1995) *Journal of Law and Society* 155, 160.

[26] A. Zuckerman, 'Compliance with Process Obligations and Fair Trial', in Andenas, Andrews and Nazzini, *The Future of Transnational Civil Litigation*; see Chapter 2, n. 169.

[27] Zuckerman, 'Quality and Economy in Civil Procedure' at 131–3.

[28] Ibid. at 286; A. Zuckerman, 'Justice in Crisis: Comparative Dimensions of Civil Proced-ure', in Zuckerman (ed.), *Civil Justice in Crisis* at 17; Zuckerman, 'Compliance with Process Obligations and Fair Trial' at 131–4; Zuckerman, *Zuckerman on Civil Procedure* at 31–2.

[29] H. Woolf (1995) at 7 and 19.   [30] Zuckerman, 'Justice in Crisis' at 17.

RSC, but three equal, balanced aims: substantive justice, economy and efficiency.[31] While such a theory could not, he argued, hope to produce results as substantively accurate as those the RSC had been committed to achieve, it would, however, ensure claims were determined at greater speed and at less expense. A reduction in the quality of justice would, however, also produce a fairer and broader distribution of the justice system's limited resources across a broader spectrum of litigants. It would, in other words, rest on an acceptance that the justice system, like all public services, had to operate within limited financial constraints, while ensuring it was designed and operated so as to provide a fair and fairly managed distribution of its resources to the public. It would consequently increase access to justice, through securing a more effective distributive of the justice system's resources.[32]

Zuckerman's approach is clearly one that in no way can be described as an exercise in normal science. It rests on a rejection of the fundamental premise on which the RSC rested: that substantive justice was the justice system's predominant aim. He has not, however, simply developed this idea; he has explicitly ascribed it to Woolf, whom he has gone on to argue, introduced it via the overriding objective. As he has variously described it:

> The CPR break with [the RSC] tradition by establishing that doing justice on the merits is not the sole overarching principle. The overriding objective adds two other vital procedural imperatives to the imperative of doing substantive justice: deciding cases within a reasonable time, and using no more than proportionate resources.[33]

> Doing justice on the merits remains a major goal but it is supplemented by a concept of proportionality that consists of two goals: reasonable expedition and reasonable use of resources. The 'overriding objective' of dealing with cases justly represents, therefore, a three dimensional

---

[31] In this, it closely mirrored the traditionalist interpretation of the overriding objective.

[32] A. Zuckerman, 'Interlocutory Remedies in Quest of Procedural Fairness' 56 (1993) *Modern Law Review* 325; Zuckerman, 'Quality and Economy in Civil Procedure' at 163ff; Zuckerman, 'A Reform of Civil Procedure'; A. Zuckerman, 'Lord Woolf's Access to Justice: Plus ça change...' 59 (1996) *Modern Law Review* 773; A. Zuckerman, 'Dismissal for Delay – The Emergence of a New Philosophy of Procedure' 17 (1998) *CJQ* 223; A. Zuckerman, 'A Colossal Wreck – the *BCCI-Three Rivers* Litigation' 25 (2006) *CJQ* 287; Zuckerman, *Weakness of Will – The Exercise of Case Management Discretion under the CPR*; A. Zuckerman, 'Civil Litigation: A Public Service for the Enforcement of Civil Rights' 26 (2007) *CJQ* 1; A. Zuckerman, 'How Seriously Should Unless Orders be Taken?' 27 (2008) *CJQ* 1.

[33] Zuckerman, *Zuckerman on Civil Procedure* at 3.

strategy of justice: the court must aim to achieve not just a correct outcome, but must do so within a reasonable time and by a reasonable and proportionate use of procedural resources.[34]

The problem with Zuckerman's account can be put simply. It may appear to be a multi-dimensional theory of justice, but in reality it does no more than set out the traditional theory. It does so because of the way in which it explains the absence of any reference to substantive justice from the overriding objective. Just like the traditionalist interpretation of the overriding objective, it is a theory that treats achieving substantive justice as a commitment that is superior to economy and efficiency, albeit it does so implicitly. It does this because it treats the former commitment as being outside the rules. For Zuckerman, achieving substantive justice is the court's constitutional purpose. It stands above the rules of court, which simply set out how that purpose is to be realised.[35] It is to be achieved through the application of the CPR, which is to be guided by the overriding objective and its procedural imperatives of economy and efficiency. Substantive justice remains the aim, as it did for the RSC. The application of economy and efficiency are the means by which it is achieved.[36] This is exactly the position that underpins Millett LJ's *dicta* in *Mortgage Corporation*, Brooke LJ's *dicta* in *Sayers*[37] and Longmore LJ's in *B* v. *B*.[38] It is the position that understands doing justice to be superior to the procedural principles set out in the overriding objective.

By adopting this approach, Zuckerman's account cannot but collapse into the traditionalist account. It may expressly disavow the RSC's theory of justice, but it cannot escape it, given the way in which it was developed.

---

[34] Zuckerman, 'Compliance with Process Obligations and Fair Trial' at 134–5; J. Sorabji, '*B* v *B*: Forwards or Backwards for the Overriding Objective' 24 (2005) *CJQ* 414.

[35] Zuckerman, *Zuckerman on Civil Procedure* at 7–8: 'The right to court adjudication upon disputed rights is therefore derived from the constitutional arrangements not from subordinate legislation. The function of the CPR is quite different: to lay down the principles that will guide the court in carrying out its constitutional function. Doing substantive justice is the purpose of adjudication, but this must now be achieved by proportionate means, with reasonable expedition and consistent with principles of fairness.' This statement rests on the further conflation of the court's constitutional purpose with the means by which it gives effect to that purpose. The court's constitutional purpose is to vindicate rights and uphold the rule of law. It does this through arriving at correct decisions. Arriving at correct decisions, at substantive justice, is not its constitutional purpose, but rather, the means by which that is achieved. His account is further confused as he goes on to say that this constitutional purpose is implicit in the overriding objective. It becomes then both the end and the means to that end.

[36] Chapter 4, n. 24.   [37] [2002] 1 WLR 3095; see Chapter 4, n. 35.

[38] [2005] EWCA Civ 237; see Chapter 4, n. 36.

It cannot fail to do so because of the hierarchical relationship it posits between substantive justice, the court's constitutional purpose that sits outside and above the mere rules of court, and the overriding objective. Any attempt to reconcile a conflict between substantive justice and the procedural principles of the overriding objective cannot but follow the same route as that taken by the advocates of the traditionalist account: the former remains pre-eminent, and where it comes into conflict with economy and efficiency the latter must not, and in fact cannot, be given much weight. Put another way, Zuckerman's theory, just as the RSC's theory did and the traditionalist interpretation of the overriding objective also does, cannot but place greater weight on securing substantive justice. Any conflict between substantive justice and the procedural principles is a conflict between ends and means. No genuine balance can be struck between such categorically different concepts. To attempt to balance an aim with the means to achieve it is to commit a category mistake.[39] It is a fundamentally flawed exercise, akin to attempting to balance a journey's destination with the means of transport used to get there. The outcome of any such flawed exercise, setting aside the conceptual confusion, is inevitable: the aim, the end, will always trump the means.[40] Substantive justice on such an account cannot but be given precedence. Any account that treats the former as lying outside the overriding objective cannot but fall into this trap. As such, if it were the case that the overriding objective did not articulate a commitment to achieving substantive justice, it would collapse back into the RSC's theory of justice, with its attendant and intractable problems.

There is a further problem with Zuckerman's account, just as there is with that of the draftsman. They both rest on an inaccurate view concerning the court's role, its constitutional purpose. That purpose is not to achieve substantive justice, but to vindicate and enforce rights.[41] Substantive justice under the RSC was the means by which that wider constitutional purpose was achieved. Again, Zuckerman's and the draftsman's account conflates means and ends. Woolf's theory does not make this mistake. It did not challenge the view that the effective vindication and enforcement of rights is the court's constitutional purpose. It challenged the view that the only means by which that can be achieved was through the achievement of substantive justice in each individual case,

---

[39] J. Sorabji, 'The Road to New Street Station: fact, fiction and the overriding objective' [2012] *EBLR* 1–77, 85; G. Ryle, *The Concept of Mind* (Penguin, 1990) at 17–25.
[40] See Chapter 4.   [41] H. Woolf (1995) at 2.

as the RSC posited. It rested, therefore, on reforming the means by which the constitutional purpose, or end, was to be achieved. It reformed the rules' purpose and did so through the overriding objective's introduction, which articulated the 'fundamental purpose of the rules and of the underlying system of procedure'.[42] Given that the justice system's constitutional purpose remained rights-vindication, and the overriding objective set out how that purpose was to be achieved, it could not but articulate a commitment to substantive justice. Only through reaching an accurate decision on the merits of a claim could rights be properly vindicated. The nature of the relationship between the justice system's purpose and the instrumental nature of the rules of court's purpose entailed that to deal with a case justly could not but refer to securing substantive justice. That this was the case can, however, also be seen through an examination of a number of the individual reforms the Woolf Reports recommended. The fundamental purpose of the rules underpinned those reforms. As such, it is to them that we can look for further confirmation of the fact that the overriding objective, which expressed that purpose, maintained a continued commitment to substantive justice.

First, it is readily apparent that the Woolf Reforms were intended to increase the court's ability to secure substantive justice, given the recommendations made concerning information technology (IT). Like the subsequent Jackson Reforms, they recommended improved IT provision. Without such improvements, effective reform and the effective operation of the reformed justice system was said to be simply impossible.[43] While the specific recommendation was to help improve efficiency and reduce cost, it was to do so for a specific purpose. As the Interim Report put it:

> Many of the benefits to be offered by more widespread use of IT in the justice system are [e.g.] increased access to justice, speedier recourse to the courts, enhanced quality of judicial decision making and increases in substantive justice (including fewer cases being decided in ignorance of earlier appellate rulings).[44]

Improved IT promoted substantive justice's achievement through, for instance, increasing access to right law in the form of appellate decisions.

---

[42] H. Woolf (1996) at 274–5; *Orange Personal Communications Services Ltd* v. *Hoare Lea (A Firm)* [2008] EWHC 233 (Admin) at [31].

[43] R. Jackson (December 2009) at 434ff; R, Jackson, *Reforming the Civil Justice System – The Role of IT* (13th Lecture in the Implementation Programme) (Society for Computers and Law, 26 March 2012). The necessary IT upgrades remain unimplemented.

[44] H. Woolf (1996) at 89.

Increased access to right law would ensure that courts were better placed to apply it to true fact and reach a substantively just decision.[45] It would equally enable such decisions to be achieved more efficiently. This would in turn facilitate the effective progress of other claims through the system. Less time on each claim would enable the court to move the backlog of claims waiting to be heard through the system more quickly. As such, it would increase the prospect that those claims would result in a substantively just decision. Reducing delay would place substantive justice within the reach of more people, both through the resultant reduction in cost it would engender and through ensuring that claims did not founder prior to judgment through diminution of the quality of evidence or due to parties discontinuing or settling claims for delay-based reasons. Efficiency gains would enable more claims to progress to judgment. IT reform was not alone in its promotion of substantive justice.

The introduction of active case management by the court was another such example. Whilst it was intended to ensure the litigation process was carried on with greater emphasis on economy and efficiency, while also promoting consensual settlement,[46] it was equally intended to improve the court's ability to secure substantive justice. Active case management is the means by which the court implements the aim of dealing with cases justly.[47] It was the means by which the overriding objective was to be put into practice. Two of the express means by which case management was to do so, and which the Woolf Reforms identified as forming an aspect of dealing with cases justly,[48] was through ensuring that: (i) those issues that were properly in dispute were identified at an early stage; and (ii) then decided which of those issues needed full investigation at trial or which could be disposed of summarily.[49] Early identification of issues and appropriate summary resolution of some of them was entirely consistent with promoting economy, efficiency and proportionality. It was equally a means to increase the court's ability to secure substantive justice and the effective enforcement of such decisions. Proper identification of issues in dispute minimises the potential for judgments to rest on false premises. It also increases the prospect that they are based on true premises.

---

[45] H. Woolf (1995) at 82ff; H. Woolf (1996) at 284ff; R. Jackson (December 2009) at 434ff.
[46] H. Woolf (1995) at 5; H. Woolf (1996) at 107.
[47] CPR r. 1.4(1); see Introduction, n. 16.
[48] H. Woolf, 'A New Approach to Civil Justice', in *Law Lectures for Practitioners 1996* (*Hong Kong Law Journal* special edn) (Sweet & Maxwell Asia, 1996) at 4.
[49] CPR r. 1(4)(1)(b) and (c).

It ensures relevant evidence is obtained, and that relevant legal argument is put before the court. It explicitly requires those issues that need full investigation to go to trial, and hence, determined through the application of right fact to right law. And, finally, it ensures that such issues are determined expeditiously, leading the way to timeous enforcement.

In addition to this, case management served a broader purpose. One of the problems the Interim Report identified as stemming from the approach to litigation under the RSC was the lack of rule-compliance, the attendant growth in technical, procedural litigation and the misuse of the means to secure evidence, e.g. discovery and expert evidence.[50] This undermined the justice system's ability to secure substantive justice. Claims would founder on procedural points, evidence obtained would obscure the truth rather than be pursued 'in the interests of justice'[51] and across the board excess cost and delay would be generated, which would not only undermine the achievement of an accurate result, but would also tend to frustrate effective enforcement. Through curbing such satellite litigation, refocusing evidence, reducing procedural skirmishing and securing greater rule-compliance, active case management would increase the system's ability to ensure claims progressed to trial, judgment on the substantive merits and effective enforcement.

Improving IT and introducing case management as a means to improve the system's ability to secure substantive justice were not isolated reforms. They were aspects of a wider strategy to improve the justice system's ability to produce the 'right result' in litigation, to achieve substantively just decisions. The Interim and Final Reports may both have emphasised that substantive justice was no longer to be paramount, because in future it was to be balanced by an equivalent commitment to the various aspects of procedural justice, i.e. economy, efficiency, equality and proportionality, that it remained an object of the system.[52] In future, the justice system would treat procedural and substantive justice as equally important; and that which is equal is clearly still present even if its role is diminished.[53] As a consequence, the justice system would, as the Woolf Reports had it, operate so as to produce both a substantively

---

[50] H. Woolf (1995) at 7ff. Discovery would be renamed as disclosure.   [51] Ibid. at 8.

[52] Ibid. at 19; H. Woolf (1995) at 4, 216; F. Hayek, *Law, Legislation and Liberty* Vol. I (University of Chicago Press, 1978); M. Damaska, *The Faces of Justice and State Authority* (Yale University Press, 1986) at 27ff and 64ff; R. Dworkin, *A Matter of Principle* (Clarendon Press, 1985) at 11–12.

[53] H. Woolf (1995) at 216: 'Procedural justice is as important as substantive justice.'

just process and substantively just results.[54] The latter would be achieved through an application of the former. This was to be the basis of Woolf's new approach. That it was takes us back to the point made earlier: the overriding objective was intended to articulate a new approach where two subordinate policy aims were to be balanced against each other in order to secure effective access to the courts for all those who needed to resort to litigation to vindicate and enforce their rights. The two subordinate aims, one of which was the commitment to substantive justice, were now equal: 'to deal with cases justly', as the overriding objective required, was to ensure a substantively just process and a substantive just result. It was to give expression to the new theory of justice that the Woolf Reforms created the overriding objective. The term 'dealing with cases justly' represented that merger; a point that Laws LJ acknowledged in *Adoko* v. *Jemal*, when he explained that: 'The proper and proportionate use of court resources is now to be considered part of substantive justice itself.'[55] Those elements of procedural justice relating to economy, efficiency, equality and proportionality, specified in CPR r. 1.1(2), were part of what it meant to refer to substantive justice.[56] It had become a

---

[54] H. Woolf (1996) at 4.   [55] *Adoko* v. *Jemal* (CA 22 June 1999, unreported) at 8.

[56] The converse point can also be made: that substantive justice is inherent in the principles that make up procedural justice. As H. Brooke, 'The 'Overriding Objective', Procedural Sanctions and Appeals', in Andenas, Andrews and Nazzini, *The Future of Transnational Civil Litigation* at 54, explained it, the overriding objective through setting out a commitment to procedural justice articulated 'principles of fairness developed by . . . rule-makers and . . . judges . . . over the last 120 years'. Those principles are those set out in article 6 of the European Convention on Human Rights. Accuracy is one of those principles, as accepted by both the House of Lords and the Strasbourg Court: *Chahal* v. *United Kingdom* (1997) 23 EHRR 413; *Secretary of State for the Home Department* v. *MB* [2007] 3 WLR 681; *Brown* v. *Stott (Procurator Fiscal for Dunfermline)* [2001] 2 WLR 817; *Brandstetter* v. *Austria* (1993) 15 EHRR 378. It is inherent in a number of aspects of procedural justice: the right to proper notice of claims (*White* v. *Weston* [1968] 2 QB 647; *De Geouffre de la Pradelle* v. *France* A/253-B (1992 unreported)); the right to legal assistance for the impecunious (*Munro* v. *UK* [1987] 52 DR 158; *Airey* v. *Ireland* (1979–80) 2 EHRR 305; *Steel and Morris* v. *UK* (2005) 41 EHRR 22); the right to an adversarial hearing (*O'Reilly* v. *Mackman* [1983] 2 AC 237 at 276); the right to equality of arms (*Delcourt* v. *Belguim* (1969) 1 EHRR 355); the right to evidentiary disclosure and cross-examination of witnesses (*Kanda* v. *Government of Malaya* [1962] AC 322 at 337; *Re D (Minors)* [1996] AC 593 at 603; *R* v. *Thames Magistrates' Court ex parte Polemis* [1974] 1 WLR 1371; *Hadmor Productions Ltd* v. *Hamilton* [1983] 1 AC 191 at 233; *Feldbrugge* v. *The Netherlands* (1986) 8 EHRR; *X* v. *Austria* (1972) 42 CD 145); and the right to a reasoned judgment (*Ruiz Torija* v. *Spain* (1994) 19 EHRR 553 at [29]; *Garcia Ruiz* v. *Spain* (2001) 31 EHRR 589; *Ruiz-Mateos* v. *Spain* [1999] EHRLR 344; *Flannery* v. *Halifax Estate Agencies Ltd* [2000] 1 WLR 377; *English* v. *Emery Reimbold & Strick Ltd & Others* [2002] 1 WLR 2409 at [8]).

blended concept, articulated by CPR r. 1.1(1) and its imprecation that cases should be dealt with justly. One facet of the overriding objective, then, is the continuing commitment to securing substantive justice. It was not because, like the various elements of procedural justice articulated in CPR r. 1.1(2), it was referred to explicitly. It was because one aspect of the Woolf Reforms was to increase the justice system's ability to secure substantive justice, and the overriding objective was intended to give expression to the spirit of the reforms. It was not the case that, as Zuckerman and the draftsman both have it, a commitment to truth is absent from the overriding objective. It is patently present, even if it is so in a less than immediate way.

5.3   The promotion of economy, efficiency and expedition: minimising litigation cost

It is apparent from the historical outline of reform, set out in Chapters 1 and 2, that from the 1820s justice reform attempted to reduce litigation complexity, cost and delay in order to increase the justice system's ability to secure substantive justice.[57] The Woolf Reports did not demur. They started by acknowledging the adverse effects of excess cost and delay. They noted with approval Bingham MR's statement from *Rastin* v. *British Steel Plc*, how delay had 'long been recognised as the enemy of justice'.[58] They did so while discussing the adverse effects of delay in initiating the claim; delay in obtaining a hearing date; and delay in conducting the final hearing itself. Each of these effects, which the Woolf Reports identified as deriving from the party-control of litigation, contributed, as Bentham would have agreed, to reducing the court's ability to achieve a merits-based decision through increasing the possibility that evidence would deteriorate.[59] As the Beeching Report concluded correctly in 1969,

> It is a negation of justice if the legal system permits, when it does not actually cause, delays of such length that witnesses may have forgotten or refurbished their evidence to the point where it is unreliable; or of such

---

[57] May, 'The ALI/UNIDROIT Rules of Transnational Civil Procedure in the Perspective of the New English and Welsh Rules' at 44: 'economy is aimed at eliminating that which is intrinsically unnecessary'.

[58] [1994] 1 WLR 732, 739; H. Woolf (1995) at 12; *Purdy* v. *Cambran* [2000] CP Rep. 67 at [46].

[59] H. Woolf (1995) at 13.

length that there is a real probability that the plaintiff will die before the case is heard; or of such length that the residual life over which the benefit of damages received will be enjoyed is materially reduced.[60]

The Woolf Reports concurred, and noted other negative consequences that flowed from excess delay. For instance, how increased cost arising from delay, whether through poor management of actions or through the use of tactical procedural skirmishing that had nothing to do with the 'real substance of the case' was also a means by which substantive justice's achievement could be frustrated.

Just as Bentham had noted previously, the Interim Report also concluded that such cost increased the prospects of mis-decision through the non-initiation of proceedings. It acted as an improper denial of substantive justice, and thus the vindication of rights, through acting as a barrier to individuals bringing claims.[61] Even where claims were initiated, such cost had a negative effect. It acted to artificially and unnecessarily increase costs during the course of litigation. Again, in terms Bentham would have well understood, such costs could force litigants to withdraw their claim or otherwise settle it on unjust terms.[62] For Bentham, this would have undermined utility maximisation. For Woolf, it undermined effective access to justice.

Delay-induced excess cost was exacerbated by other factors that gave rise to unnecessary cost, each of which further undermined substantive justice's achievement. The Interim Report, as had Bentham, identified procedural complexity as a source of unnecessary litigation cost.[63] Too overly complex a system undermines the achievement of substantive justice as well as the effective enforcement of such decisions, because it tends to delay judgment or enforcement until it is of no genuine value. Equally, it results in litigation being disproportionately expensive.[64] It thereby acts as a disincentive to individuals to pursue claims, or denudes judgments of their practical utility by rendering them too expensive to achieve.[65] The Woolf Reports identified the misuse and lack of control over evidence, whether that be expert evidence, evidence obtained via witness statements or documentary discovery, and party-control of

---

[60] Chapter 1, n. 63; *The Report of the Royal Commission on Assizes and Quarter Sessions* (Cmd 4153, 1969) at 131.
[61] H. Woolf (1995) at 9.   [62] Ibid. at 7.   [63] Ibid. at 15.
[64] H. Friendly, 'Some Kind of Hearing' [1975] *University of Pennsylvania Law Review* 1267, 1275.
[65] H. Woolf (1995) 2–18 and 199.

procedure, as causing such complexity, unnecessary cost and delay. Cost was unnecessary here, as it did little or nothing to facilitate substantive justice's achievement and, as with delay-induced cost, it reduced the system's ability to achieve that aim in any event. Moreover, it too increased the prospect of non-initiation of proceedings and the improper conclusion of proceedings where they were commenced.[66] Justice bought at too great a cost is just as much a case of justice denied as justice too greatly delayed.

Having acknowledged the nature of the historical problem concerning cost and delay, the question was how the Woolf Reforms were to attempt to resolve it, so that it could be decreased to such an extent that it would no longer reduce the justice system's ability to secure substantive justice. They did so through giving greater prominence to efficiency, expedition and economy than had been the case under the RSC. The justice system was to be committed to them, just as Bentham's theory was committed to giving proper effect to the positive role he attributed to justice's collateral ends. This was to be achieved through both structural and procedural reforms, which were then implemented via the rules of court.

5.3.1   Structural and procedural reforms aimed at minimising cost and delay

The most obvious of the structural reforms aimed at minimising cost and delay was the abolition of separate procedural rules for the High and County Courts: a reform that had originally been canvassed in the Civil Justice Review.[67] To support this, pre-reform, pre-CPR authorities as they became, as a general rule were no longer to guide the application of individual rules.[68] Authorities that articulated, or were developed consistently with, the RSC's theory of justice, would have had a tendency to undermine the proper operation of the new approach to justice.[69] Procedural complexity that had developed under the RSC was not to undermine the reformed justice system's operation. Simplification was not, however, sufficient. Other steps were required if cost and delay were to be minimised. The most obvious change the reforms proposed was the introduction of judicial active case management, and the concomitant transfer of responsibility for the proper progress of litigation from the litigants to the court. The Civil Justice Review had also

---

[66] Ibid. at 9.   [67] Cmd 8205, 1981 at 50; H. Woolf (1995) at 207ff.

[68] Ibid. at 217; *Hashtroodi* v. *Hancock* [2004] 1 WLR 3206 at [11]–[16].

[69] *Garratt* v. *Saxby* [2004] 1 WLR 2152 at [18].

previously recommended this.[70] A central feature of the civil justice system, and its commitment to an adversarial approach to litigation, had been party-control of litigation. Just as parties dictated the terms of the dispute, they set the pace at which the claim progressed. Superficially, that should not have been problematic and should not have generated unnecessary cost or delay. That, however, assumed one thing: that both parties were willing and able to ensure their claim progressed expeditiously. That assumption was one the court could not depend upon, not least because of the perverse incentives that the RSC's theory created in terms of rule-compliance and procedural litigation arising from non-compliance. If, however, control of the litigation process was taken out of the parties' hands and given over to the court, the assumption could be rendered a reality. Court-controlled case management carried out consistently with the overriding objective could, in the first instance, be used to set reasonable procedural timetables that required parties to focus on the real issues. Party-induced delay, work on issues unnecessary to the proper resolution of claim, could be controlled properly and, with it, the cost of litigation could be brought under control. Secondly, it could be used to ensure that parties stuck to those timetables. Parties would be encouraged to do so, for instance, through the threat of effective sanctions, which would in time embed a culture of rule-compliance rather than the previous laissez-faire approach to case progression embedded by the RSC.[71] Increased use of sanction powers for procedural default would also ensure that the new rules would have the normative force the RSC's rule had lost as a consequence of *Tildesley* and *Birkett*. This would then lead to greater adherence to well-ordered, expeditious court-managed litigation timetables. It would reduce satellite litigation arising from non-compliance. Taken together, it would lead to substantive justice being achieved at minimal cost and in minimal time.[72] It was an approach that Bentham would have understood and seen as a practical means of implementing his theory's commitment to securing justice's direct end consistently with a commitment to the primary role played by its collateral ends.

---

[70] Cmd 8205, 1981 at 41; H. Woolf (1995) at 7ff; H. Woolf (1996) at 13ff.

[71] H. Woolf (1995) at 15, 208, 215; P. Middleton, *Report to the Lord Chancellor* (HMSO, 1997) at [2.35]; M. Zander, 'The Government's Plans on Civil Justice' 61 (1998) *Modern Law Review* 382, 388; *Sayers* v. *Clarke-Walker* [2002] 1 WLR 3095 at [23]; *Hashtroodi* v. *Hancock* at [36].

[72] H. Woolf (1995) at 7 and 20; H. Woolf (1996) at 72ff.

In addition to the increase in procedural economy, efficiency and expedition that rule-simplification was intended to herald[73] and case management was to implement in practice, the Woolf Reports proposed a number of discrete procedural reforms, each of which were intended to minimise cost and delay. These pervasive procedural reforms were complemented by specific ones, focused on discrete procedural rules that were identified as major causes of unnecessary and excess litigation cost and delay, i.e. discovery,[74] witness[75] and expert evidence.[76] Discovery, for instance had been identified as a major contributor to excess cost and delay, notwithstanding the fact that it was an essential means through which parties to litigation could obtain probative evidence. Unreflective discovery carried out consistently with the expansive test established in *Peruvian Guano*[77] at the time that the Victorian Court of Appeal was establishing the RSC's theory of justice was to be brought under control. The RSC-based test where discovery was 'virtually unlimited'[78] in scope was to be replaced with a more calibrated one that would limit discovery. Such control would not only bring the cost and delay associated with such wide-ranging, practically untrammelled discovery down, but it would also ensure that it did not undermine the court's ability to secure substantive justice. One of the problems associated with the RSC's approach to discovery was that it had a propensity to undermine the court's ability to find right fact. As Zuckerman put it:

> Large bodies of documentary material tended to increase costs by creating opportunities for calling evidence or cross-examining witnesses about matters that were not central to the issues in the case. Far from clarifying the facts, an excess of documents may tend to complicate and confuse the issues and undermine the court's ability to get to the truth. It is therefore not only in the interests of economy that the disclosure process needs to be controlled but also in the interest of truth finding.[79]

The problem was one that Bentham would have been only too familiar with: too much discovery could lead to claims being withdrawn through the cost and delay they generate, just as it could obfuscate where it should

---

[73] The simplification was not, however, achieved: *Collier* v. *Williams* [2006] EWCA Civ 20; [2006] WLR 1945 at [1].

[74] H. Woolf (1995) at 8.   [75] Ibid. at 176.

[76] Ibid. at 181: 'The need to engage experts was a source of excessive expense, delay and, in some cases, increased complexity through the excessive or inappropriate use of experts.'

[77] *Compagnie Financière du Pacifique* v. *Peruvian Guano Company* (1882) 11 QBD 55.

[78] H. Woolf (1995) at 166–7.   [79] Zuckerman, *Zuckerman on Civil Procedure* at 464.

illuminate. In both cases, rather than promote substantive justice, it undermined its very achievement. Introducing a more restrictive test, and placing it under court control, would eliminate these problems and thereby increase the court's ability to secure substantive justice.[80] It would because, again, this was a reform that was consistent with what for Bentham was the primary role of justice's collateral ends.[81] Delay and expense were to be minimised consistently with the need to ensure that substantive justice could be attained, i.e. it was not to be less than strictly necessary to achieve it. Discovery was to be no more than sufficient to enable the court to determine the claim justly. Minimisation was not, however, an absolute rule. More than strictly necessary expense and time on the discovery process could be expended, although this was subject to the requirement that it was to be kept within an absolute maximum beyond which further expenditure or delay would start to undermine the court's ability to achieve substantive justice. Reform was to facilitate substantive justice through minimising cost and delay.

The same approach was to be taken to witness evidence, and particularly, the court's approach to witness statements. The Woolf Reports' treatment of this was particularly telling. Witness statements were a relatively recent innovation into English civil procedure.[82] Since their introduction they had, however, been subject to a great deal of abuse and misuse, all of which generated unnecessary litigation cost and delay.[83] This was despite the express imprecation in the RSC that their purpose was 'to achieve the fair and expeditious disposal of proceedings and the saving of costs'.[84] Their misuse and abuse arose because courts adopted a strict approach to how they were to be used at trial. Litigants could not, subject to limited exceptions, elaborate on what was stated in them as part of oral examination-in-chief.[85] They thus became the only opportunity to set out such evidence. This approach was adopted in the name of saving time and cost, which was laudable. However, it had the reverse effect. To ensure that all possible evidence was before the court in as positive a fashion as possible, they became increasingly detailed, intricate and long documents. The more prolix the statement, the greater the unnecessary time and delay to the proceedings it generated, as each party ensured their own statement responded to the excessive points made in their opponent's. Prolixity could also divert both litigants and

---

[80] H. Woolf (1995) at 165–9; H. Woolf (1996) at 125–6; CPR r. 31.
[81] H. Woolf (1995) at 19–20 and 164ff.   [82] Ibid. at 175.   [83] Ibid. at 176.
[84] Ibid. at 175; RSC Ord. 38.   [85] CPR r. 32.6.

court from the real issues, whilst consequently requiring otherwise unnecessary time, and its attendant cost, to be expended at trial in order to deal with unnecessary points raised in the statements. In the light of this approach, what had been intended to save time and cost, had had the opposite effect.[86]

The Woolf Reports' proposals for witness statement reform were a paradigmatic example of a reform intended to facilitate the achievement of substantive justice whilst minimising cost and delay. The rules regarding them were to be simplified and the court's approach to their use was to become more flexible. Litigants were to be penalised in costs for producing statements that were too prolix. In this way, the same unnecessary costs and delays common to discovery were to be eliminated from the use of witness statements. Litigants were also to adopt a more cooperative manner in their production and treatment. In other words, a technical approach based in a culture that sought to secure success in litigation through taking procedural points unrelated to the substantive merits was now to be deprecated. In this way, the progress of litigation to a merits-based judgment would not be derailed by meretricious satellite litigation that simply rendered substantive justice, if achieved at all, unnecessarily expensive and untimely.[87]

The same approach was taken to expert evidence. The Woolf Reports accepted that party-control of litigation in a culture whose aim was to secure substantive justice, but which, due to its complexity, bred procedural litigation aimed at securing victory at all costs, bred excess cost and delay in this area too.[88] As Donaldson MR had previously noted in another context, while the court's

> only interest and duty ... [was] to do justice in accordance with the law. The interest of the parties is to seek a favourable decision and their duty is limited to complying with the rules of the court...[89]

In a culture bred by the congruence of the RSC's commitment to substantive justice and party-control of litigation, a favourable decision was one reached on procedural grounds, or grounds unrelated to the substantive merits of the real issue in dispute. Victory at all costs was victory on any

---

[86] H. Woolf (1995) at 175–80.

[87] CPR r. 32; H. Woolf (1995) at 176–8; H. Woolf (1996) at 129. Further revisions were made as a consequence of the Jackson Review, see CPR r. 32.2(3) in force from 1 April 2013.

[88] H. Woolf (1995) at 181–94.   [89] *Abse* v. *Smith* [1986] QB 536 at 545–546.

basis, whether procedural or substantive. In so far as expert evidence was concerned, this was embodied in the prevalence of party use of multiple experts on the same issue, of use of experts on issues that were unrelated to the real issue in dispute, and a failure to ensure that expert evidence was produced in a timely and cost-effective fashion. The Reports' solution to these problems maintained the commitment to substantive justice; but it gave greater emphasis to the need to achieve that end in such a way that the use of experts gave rise to no more than necessary litigation cost.[90] They proposed, for instance, measures to increase expert independence from parties as a means to increase their capacity to assist the court in its pursuit of true fact.[91] They also sought to reduce unnecessary litigation cost attendant on the use of experts in a number of ways.

The primary means by which cost and delay was to be minimised was through effective case management. Expert evidence was to be placed under effective court control. While control powers existed under the RSC, they had not been used adequately. The lax approach to control under RSC Ord. 38 r. 4 was to end.[92] Substantive justice's pre-eminence under the RSC had actively undermined its effective use.[93] With the overriding objective's introduction, control of expert evidence was to be subject to the aim of minimising cost and delay in the pursuit of substantive justice. Cost and delay were also to be minimised by limiting the number of experts litigants could instruct; a reform that went beyond minimising cost and delay, but also potentially reduced the court's ability to secure substantive justice.[94] Additionally, litigants were to be required to cooperate with each other over the appointments of experts. They were to do so in order to narrow the scope of their enquiries.[95] Finally, experts were to narrow issues rather than have them appointed to widen the scope of enquiry beyond the real issue in dispute.[96]

Each of these various procedural and structural reforms on their own would not, however, have been sufficient to ensure that cost and delay were minimised. On their own the various reforms to discovery, evidence and other areas of procedure, in so far as their scope was concerned, were traditional reform attempts. On their own, they did not go beyond answers to internal questions, carried out as exercises in normal science. This was

[90] H. Woolf (1995) at 181.   [91] CPR r. 35.3.   [92] CPR r. 35.7.
[93] W. Braithwaite, 'Single Joint Experts', *Personal and Medical Injuries Law Letter* (2003)
[94] See Chapter 6.
[95] Personal Injury Pre-Action Protocol at 2.4.
[96] H. Woolf (1995) at 185ff; H. Woolf (1996) at 137ff.

the case even where the introduction of case management was concerned. While it has been powerfully argued, for instance, by Turner that it was a revolutionary innovation, it was not.[97] It was a procedural device taken from the United States, where by the time the Woolf Reports alighted on it, it had long been in place and long subject to criticism as an inadequate vehicle for curing the crisis of civil justice.[98] At best, it was a device that, properly used, could produce some reduction in procedural delay. There was, however, no real evidence to support the assumption it would have a positive impact on litigation cost. This is unsurprising, not least where the United States is concerned. Case management there, particularly that under the Federal Rules, was subject to its traditional overriding objective. It was to be carried out consistently with the aim of securing substantive justice. Given a choice between, for instance, imposing a procedural sanction, refusing relief from one, granting or refusing permission to make a late amendment to pleadings, the answer was obvious: the same approach as predominated under the RSC, and which was adopted by the Court of Appeal in *Hannigan*, *Sayers* and *B* v. *B* would be adopted. Substantive justice would trump economy and efficiency. The supposed benefit of active case management would disappear.[99] At best, if case management and the other discrete procedural reforms had been introduced into a justice system still governed by the RSC's overriding objective, there would inevitably have been a temporary reduction in cost and delay as had happened in similar circumstances in the United States. The old ways would then have reasserted themselves. The system's aim directs how procedure is used, and that is as true for case management as it is for any other aspect of procedure. Something more than the introduction of case management was needed if there were to be any prospect that it, and the other procedural reforms, might be able to introduce a sustainable and proper reduction in cost and delay.

---

[97] Turner, '"Actively": The Word that Changed the Civil Courts' at 77–88.

[98] J. Resnick, 'Managerial Judges' 96 (1982) *Harvard Law Review* 374; S. Flanders, 'Blind Umpires—A Response to Prof Resnik' 35 (1984) *Hastings Law Journal* 505; R. Marcus, 'Déjà-vu All Over Again? An American Reaction to the Woolf Report', in Zuckerman and Cranston (eds), *Reform of Civil Procedure*; S. Flanders, 'Case Management: Failure in America? Success in England and Wales?' 17 (1998) *CJQ* 308; I. Scott, 'Caseflow Management in the Trial Court', in Zuckerman and Cranston (eds), *Reform of Civil Procedure*; Zander, 'The Woolf Report: Forwards or Backwards for the New Lord Chancellor?'.

[99] M. Rosenberg, 'Sanctions to Effectuate Pre-Trial Discovery' [1958] *Columbia Law Review* 480; D. Piggot, 'Relief from Sanctions and the Overriding Objective' 24 (2005) *CJQ* 104. See Chapter 6, n. 6 and Chapter 7, n. 10.

The something more was the incorporation of three aspects of procedural justice into the overriding objective: economy, efficiency and expedition.[100] If the court was to deal with a case justly, it had to operate the new rules, and within them active case management,[101] consistently with those elements of procedural justice which, as discussed earlier, the Woolf Reforms considered to be equal to the commitment to substantive justice in the new theory of justice that was to be effected by the overriding objective's introduction. Just as importantly, litigants were under a duty to assist the active management of litigation consistently with the overriding objective.[102] In all of this, Woolf's new theory differed from the US approach. The important point here is that these commitments were incorporated in the overriding objective for the same reason Bentham emphasised the primary role he ascribed to justice's collateral ends; a point Sir Anthony May emphasised when he stressed how procedural economy facilitated substantive justice.[103] It did so because it was to ensure that, to secure its achievement, no more than sufficient resources were expended in the course of litigation and, just as importantly, that sufficient resources to undermine its achievement were not expended during the course of litigation. The purposive nature of the overriding objective was to ensure that case management was conducted, and decisions regarding rule-compliance, discovery and other forms of evidence were taken, consistently with the new approach. It was to ensure that reforms aimed at reducing cost and delay did not in practice fail to do so because they were interpreted and applied in an environment where securing substantive justice was more important than minimising cost and delay and where any tension between the three would generally be resolved in favour of the former. Such an environment, which would do no more than replicate the primacy of substantive justice evident in *Tildesley* and *Birkett*, would do no more than replicate the situation that those decisions created under the RSC. The key to the reforms' success was not the discrete procedural reforms themselves, but the proper implementation of the purposive provision that would guide their use: the overriding objective.

---

[100] CPR r. 1.1(2)(b)–(d); H. Woolf (1995) at 20; H. Woolf (1996) at 16; May LJ in *Vinos* v. *Marks & Spencer* at [20]: 'one of the main aims of the CPR and their overriding objective is that civil litigation should be undertaken and pursued with proper expedition.'

[101] H. Woolf (1995) at 5; CPR r. 1.4(1).   [102] CPR r. 1.3.

[103] May, 'The ALI/UNIDROIT Rules of Transnational Civil Procedure in the Perspective of the New English and Welsh Rules' at 45.

5.3.2   The overriding objective's articulation of the commitment to minimising cost and delay

The commitment to minimising litigation cost and delay is easier to see within the overriding objective. Unlike the commitment to substantive justice, there is explicit reference to the need to secure economy and efficiency in it.[104] There is no need, therefore, to tease out how these principles of procedural justice are expressed within the idea of dealing with cases justly. They were explicitly present from the original draft of the, then, general objective, and remain so. They were clearly present to guide the manner in which the structural and specific procedural reforms were implemented in practice. There is nothing controversial about this.

The role played by the commitment to these aspects of procedural justice is not controversial either. It was intended to ensure that substantive justice was achieved at no greater litigation cost and delay than was necessary. As such, it was not intended to operate as a limit or break on the pursuit of that aim. It was a commitment limited by, and facilitative of, substantive justice. As such, it was a flexible commitment, and one that was intended to improve the court's ability to secure substantive justice. It was a moveable feast, a point on which the traditionalists would agree.[105] If mistakes were made, they could be rectified, even if that meant more time and expense than strictly necessary to achieve substantive justice had to be expended. It could be, because minimising cost and time was simply that, a commitment to minimise them. As the Interim Report put it in defining the civil justice system's objectives:

> The conduct of trials should be expeditious, with issues, evidence and argument presented in as economical a manner as justice permits.[106]

Justice, the need to secure substantive justice, is the limiting factor here. It is predominant, just as the traditionalists understood it to be. In this they were, and are, right. Because substantive justice is predominant, the overriding objective could properly permit more than necessary cost and time to be incurred in its pursuit. It could, for instance, permit procedural error or mistakes to be rectified, just as Bentham's theory allowed for that to occur, even though such rectification or relief took cost and delay beyond that which was strictly necessary to secure

---

[104] CPR r. 1.1(2)(b) and (d).
[105] J. Bentham (1834) PJP at 19; SR at 5; RJE at 335; H. Woolf (1995) at 19–21.
[106] H. Woolf (1995) at 28 and 214.

substantive justice. The problem with this, of course, is that it means that minimising cost and delay can all too easily become an aspiration which in practice is impossible to achieve. This becomes the case, as it did under the RSC, because it can always be set aside in order to give greater weight to securing substantive justice. The Woolf Reports, like Bentham before them, understood this limitation on the role that economy, efficiency and expedition could play in a theory of justice that was primarily committed to securing that aim. They both recognised that those principles were the means to an end and could not be relied on to undermine or limit it; they were to save expense and delay in the pursuit of justice. On their own, though, they could not rein in substantive justice.[107] They could not because, as Brooke LJ had it in *Sayers*, they were to be given less weight than that commitment.

5.4   Conclusion: securing substantive justice at minimum cost

This chapter has considered two uncontroversial elements of Woolf's new theory of justice: they are the elements it shares with the RSC's theory and Bentham's. Equally, they are elements that the traditionalist view of the overriding objective would have, and has, happily endorsed. They serve one purpose: to promote the court's constitutional purpose of vindicating rights, and thereby supporting the rule of law, by enabling it to achieve substantive justice in individual cases. They do so in two ways. First, and most obviously, through maintaining the commitment to reaching just decisions, without which rights cannot be vindicated. Secondly, they do so through promoting the minimisation of cost and delay. This, in turn, serves two purposes. It helps to promote the prospect that a substantively just decision is reached in each individual case. It does so through reducing the prospect that potential litigants will be put off seeking to enforce their rights due to a fear that to do so would be too costly or time-consuming. It also does so through reducing the prospect of mis-decision caused by, for instance, delay denuding evidence of its probative value. Equally, it does so through aiming to reduce procedural litigation, which, through unnecessarily increasing cost and delay, may result in claims being abandoned or settled at an inappropriately low level. More broadly than this, by requiring the justice system to operate more efficiently than previously through, for instance, aiming to reduce

---

[107] J. Bentham (1843) PJP at 30.

the number of procedural applications, it allows a broader distribution of the system's resources amongst more litigants. It serves to promote the interests of all potential litigants as, by reducing the time the court spends on each case, it increases the number of cases it can deal with. More cases can thus, efficiently proceed to judgment and the vindication of rights. It is in this way also an aspect of the more distributive form of justice that was a hallmark of Bentham's theory of justice. In the next chapter, the novel elements of Woolf's theory, the elements that are antagonistic to substantive justice, are discussed. These place a limit on the pursuit of that aim, and as such, take the Woolf Reforms beyond the traditional approach to civil justice reform. They transform what would otherwise be no more than an exercise in normal science into what for Kuhn would have been an extraordinary investigation.

Woolf's new theory of justice (II)

Ultimately the issue is whether the overriding objective of dealing with this case justly calls for us to bring these proceedings to an end.[1]

It is not the case that the administration of justice, alone among the services provided by the state, is exempt from any considerations of cost.[2]

6.1 Introduction

The RSC's theory of justice was one committed to an individualistic form of justice. It was predicated on securing substantive justice in each particular case; as Lord Brougham LC famously described it in the 1830s, it was concerned with arriving at 'justice between man and man'.[3] It took no account of the wider effect that any particular case had on other court users. For instance, it took no account of the effect that the amount of court time taken up by any one claim had on the ability of other court users to gain effective access to the courts, to justice. As a theory of justice it did not 'look beyond the case in hand'.[4] This was in stark contrast with Bentham's. It could not simply focus on the case in hand, and the need to do justice between the immediate parties to any particular claim. While securing substantive justice was the primary aim of his theory, it was only because it was the presumptive means by which utility was maximised. The question in dealing with any one claim was not simply how to secure substantive justice, but how to do so in a way that maximised utility. In assessing that question, the court had to consider whether utility might be maximised by denying substantive justice and effective enforcement of rights. In assessing this question, the court would necessarily have to look

---

[1] *Flaxman-Binns* v. *Lincolnshire County Council* (Practice Note) [2004] 1 WLR 2232 at [41].
[2] *Sutradhar* v. *Natural Environment Research Council* [2006] 4 All ER at [42].
[3] Speeches of Henry Brougham (1838) Vol. II at 324, cited in J. Jacob, *The Fabric of English Civil Justice* (Stevens & Co, 1987) at 1; *James* v. *United Kingdom* (1986) 8 EHHR 123.
[4] D. Piggot, 'Relief from Sanctions and the Overriding Objective' 24 (2005) *CJQ* 104, 104.

beyond the case in hand. It had to look at the needs of other litigants to gain effective access to the courts. In order to maximise utility it might have to take steps to reduce the possibility that substantive justice was achieved in any particular case or class of case through, for instance, rationing procedure. To enable the greatest possible number of litigants to have an opportunity to secure a judgment on the merits, it might be necessary to reduce the length of hearings, the amount of evidence led at trial and the amount of legal argument at trial. In this way, the justice system might then be able to maximise utility, even though it might as a consequence have to reduce the probability that substantive justice might be done. The reduction in the quality of judgment would, however, be justified through an appeal to utility. Bentham's theory also had to go beyond a consideration of the case in hand in another sense. The cost of securing substantive justice in any particular case might come at too great a price in terms of disutility. In that case, it would have to be denied. Justice would have to bend to the demands of utility. For Bentham, the individual justice of the RSC was subject to the distributive justice of his utilitarianism.

The Woolf Reports adopted Bentham's approach and developed a theory of justice that required the court 'to consider the effects of [its] decisions on the civil justice system as a whole'.[5] They did not do this because they adopted a form of utilitarianism, but rather, because they accepted that the RSC's theory of justice was not capable of securing the rule of law. They did not say this in bald terms, but rather, by criticising the litigation culture that had arisen under the RSC as one that was unable to secure effective access to justice for all court users. The RSC had, through its complexity, cost and delay, put the courts out of the reach of too many citizens.[6] Where access to justice is denied on these grounds, rights cannot be vindicated, public confidence in the law will decline, and as a consequence of both, the rule of law will fail. While the Reports did not do so, they could have drawn the conclusion that the RSC's theory was in fact based on a fallacy of composition, i.e. that what is true of one part of a whole is then true of the whole. It may be

---

[5] Ibid.; J. Sorabji, 'B v B: Forwards or Backwards for the Overriding Objective' 24 (2005) *CJQ* 414, 417: 'Because the Court is required to take account of such global considerations the manner in which the overriding objective must be applied cannot simply be confined to an assessment of the relative weight of a commitment to justice on the merits on the one hand and the prejudice to one party if relief is granted on the other hand.'

[6] H. Woolf (1995) at 7ff.

true, for example, that atoms are colourless, but it does not follow that anything constituted of atoms is equally colourless. What is true of the part is not true of the whole. The RSC's theory of justice took as its starting point the idea that securing substantive justice in the particular case, vindicated rights and consequently secured public confidence in the courts and upheld the rule of law. It was, and is true, that securing substantive justice in the particular case vindicates rights in that case. It is also true that doing so contributes to maintaining public confidence in the courts and, thus, upholds the rule of law. It is not, however, true that public confidence in the courts and the rule of law in general is secured through the RSC's commitment to substantive justice.

This can be illustrated by reference to the *Tildesley* test. Under it, the question of whether to grant relief from the consequences of non-compliance with procedural time limits, as was apparent from Chapter 2, focused to a significant extent on whether any prejudice caused by one litigant to another in a single claim could be compensated in costs. The question looked solely at the case in hand. It took no account of the consequences to other litigants of the manner in which the litigation had been conducted. It was a test for relief that took no account of the fact that the justice system's resources were limited, and that if any particular claim utilised more than an equitable share of them, other claims would suffer as a consequence. Greater resource allocation and use by one claim was detrimental to other court users' right of access to the courts. *Tildesley* looked solely at prejudice to the immediate parties and not to the justice system as a whole. This had two consequences. Focusing increasing amounts of the court's resources on securing substantive justice in those cases where the litigants' conduct gave rise to a substantial amount of procedural litigation could not but be prejudicial to other litigants. Court time that would have been expended on those litigants would not be available to them. Their claims would have been subject to otherwise avoidable delay. That delay might then have adversely affected the court's ability to secure substantive justice in their case. The complexity that arose from the accretion of procedural precedent caused by those litigants who did not get on with their cases and their procedural applications might act as a barrier to entry to the system for some. Its costs and delays might act as a barrier to judgment for others. And these points would simply add to the delay occasioned by the *Tildesley* parties and their applications using up the court's resources. Focusing on securing substantive justice in the particular case, as the RSC theory and its application via *Tildesley* required, meant that access to the court and substantive justice was denied to others. Substantive justice for some was the denial of justice for others, which is antagonistic to the rule of law. This problem was compounded by the fact that the *Tildesley* test bred complacency amongst litigants regarding compliance with court orders and rules. The greater the complacency, the greater the laissez-faire approach to compliance, and then the greater the number and length of applications for relief from sanction for non-compliance or to amend pleadings. As a consequence it bred, not least through its application in *Birkett*, ever-greater resource use by individual cases. Substantive justice was bought at a high price, both to litigants in individual cases, but due to the effect this had on the justice system's resources, to other litigants. Focusing on the individual case and the need to do justice between the parties to it, meant that that justice system was not in a position to secure an equitable distribution of its resources across all those who needed to call on it to vindicate their rights; it undermined the rule of law. It also meant that the system became ever-more complex, costly and riven with delay, which again undermined the rule of law. It was a theory that failed to achieve its stated aim in general because it was predicated on the false assumption that it would do so through achieving it in each individual case.

Bentham's theory did not generalise from the individual case, or treat maximising utility as a form of emergent property of a justice system that focused on securing substantive justice in the individual case, nor did Woolf's new theory of justice. Like Bentham's theory, Woolf's adopted an overarching policy aim, which stood above securing substantive justice. This aim was the need to secure equitable access to the justice system for all court users: the access principle. As a consequence of this it also adopted a second subordinate policy aim, equal to securing substantive justice: the principle of proportionality. This would play the same role as the reductive aspect of justice's collateral ends played in Bentham's theory. It is important here to note that as a consequence of this, within Woolf's theory the term 'justice' took on a different meaning to that which it had under the RSC. Just as for Bentham, for Woolf it was not synonymous with substantive justice. It was to mean proportionate justice. Proportionate because the need to secure equitable access to justice required the justice system to place a limit on the ability of individual claims to secure substantive justice. The individualised justice that was at the heart of the RSC's theory was to be subject to the more distributive needs of a justice system limited in its resources. Woolf's theory did this through incorporating three aspects of procedural justice into the overriding objective, the principles: of equality (CPR 1.1(2)(a)); of proportionality (CPR 1.1(2)(c)); and most importantly, of the fair distribution of the court's resource across all court users (CPR 1.1(2)(e)).[7] This chapter considers these aspects of what it means to deal with a case justly, and how they take Woolf's new theory of justice beyond the RSC's, and provide the basis for a new approach to litigation.

6.2   Equality, access and proportionality: a new primary policy aim and the reductive aspect of justice's collateral ends

The starting point for an analysis of how Woolf's theory incorporates a wider policy aim superior to substantive justice is the principle of equality. This principle is most commonly understood as focused on ensuring that, as far as possible, litigants in individual actions are treated equally as between themselves during the course of proceedings. Litigants have, for instance, the right to receive a fair trial. This right is one held and exercisable by both claimant and defendant equally. It is, as such, an indivisible right.[8] Consistently with this, the civil justice system operates so that neither claimants nor defendants in particular proceedings receive unjustifiably favourable treatment. Both parties should, for instance, be afforded the right to make submissions before judgment. They should both have access to the same evidence, and be able to challenge evidence submitted by the other party. Failure to secure these aspects of the right would reduce the court's ability to secure substantive justice, as only

---

[7] Ibid. at 26: 'The overall aim of my Inquiry is to improve access to justice by reducing the inequalities, cost, delay and complexity of civil litigation and to introduce greater certainty as to timescales and costs. My specific objectives are:

- to provide appropriate and proportionate means of resolving disputes;
- to establish "equality of arms" between the parties involved in civil cases;
- to assist the parties to resolve their disputes by agreement at the earliest possible date; and
- to ensure that the limited resources available to the courts can be deployed in the most effective manner for the benefit of everyone involved in civil litigation.'

Delcourt v. *Belgium* (1969) 1 EHRR 355; *Airey* v. *Ireland* (1979–80) 2 EHRR 305; *Golder* v. *UK* (1975) 1 EHRR 524; *H* v. *UK* (1985) 45 DR 28; *Feldbrugge* v. *The Netherlands* (1986) 8 EHRR; *X* v. *Austria* (1972) 42 CD 145; *Munro* v. *UK* [1987] 52 DR 158; *Ashingdane* v. *UK* (1995) 20 EHRR 442; *Tolstoy Miloslavsky* v. *UK* (1995) 20 EHRR 442; *Steel and Morris* v. *UK* (2005) 41 EHRR 22.

[8] *Dombo Beheer BV* v. *The Netherlands* (1994) 18 EHRR 213 at [33]; *Maltez* v. *Lewis* (27 April 1999, unreported); [1999] 4 All ER (D) 425; *Price* v. *Price (trading as Poppyland Headware)* [2003] EWCA Civ 888 at [35].

partial and unchallenged evidence would be before it. It would also infringe the procedural right to equality before the law.

Equality is not, however, limited to a consideration of the parties to any particular claim. It is not hermetically sealed, indivisible only between the parties to individual litigation. It is indivisible in another way. It has a collective aspect as well as a party-focused one. This other aspect of it arises from the fact that all citizens have an indivisible right of access to the justice system in order to vindicate, and if necessary, enforce their rights. As the Strasbourg court put it in *Nosal* v. *Ukraine*, in respect of the right of equality contained within article 6 ECHR, the State is under a positive obligation to put in place a justice system that is legally and practically effective for all those who need to have recourse to it.[9] It had previously made the same point in *Frydlender* v. *France*, when it held that it 'is for the Contracting States to organize their legal systems in such a way that their courts can guarantee to everyone the right to a final decision within a reasonable time.'[10] If the justice system simply focused on individual claims, it could not provide such a guarantee. It would not be able to ensure an equitable distribution of the court's limited resources to all those who needed to avail themselves of the right of access. A party-focused view, which ignored or was unable to take proper account of the collective view, could simply allow any particular claim to utilise large amounts of the justice system's resources. It could allow them to utilise resources that ought properly to have been available to other litigants, so that they could exercise their right of access effectively. If the justice system is to secure the collective aspect of equality, its processes and procedures have to take account of the needs of other litigants than those in any particular set of proceedings. It cannot simply operate to secure substantive justice in the particular case, as the RSC's theory required.

The Woolf Reports explicitly accepted that an effective justice system was one that treated access to justice as an indivisible right held by all court users. While discussing the rationale that lay behind the introduction of case management, the Final Report noted how, in order to,

> preserve access to justice for all users of the system it [was] necessary to ensure that individual users [did] not use more of the system's resources

---

[9] *Nosal* v. *Ukraine* [2005] ECHR 777 at [40].

[10] [2000] ECHR 353 at [45], citing *Caillot* v. *France* [1999] ECHR 32 (4 June 1999, French text only); *Attorney-General* v. *Times Newspapers Ltd* [1974] AC 273 at 307.

than their case require[d]. This mean[t] that the court must consider the effect of their choice on other users of the system.[11]

The Report accepted that the justice system had to consider the effect decisions in individual cases had on the justice system as a whole. The introduction of the principle of proportionality into the overriding objective was the means by which this was to be done, and the collective aspect of equality was properly implemented.[12]

Proportionality here had two aspects. First, it required that the cost and time expended on any single claim should be proportionate to the value of that claim: individual party costs should be proportionate.[13] A balance was to be struck between: the cost of finally determining cases by the application of true fact to right law; and the benefit to be derived from giving effect to substantive law as between the parties. This aspect of proportionality has been described as inward-looking proportionality[14] and as individual proportionality,[15] as it focuses on the immediate case before the court. The latter term is used here. It requires that the benefit derivable from pursuing substantive justice and effective enforcement does not outweigh the cost of its achievement in the individual case. Secondly, no single claim should utilise more than a proportionate share of the justice system's resources. A balance has to be struck between the positive value of pursuing any single claim to a merits-based determination and the requirement to facilitate the pursuit of such for other claims. This has been described as outward-looking[16] or collective proportionality,[17] because it focuses on the right of litigants beyond those in any particular case who need to pursue substantive justice. It requires no single claim or class of claim to utilise too great a share of court resources such that a negative impact on the need of other cases to gain

---

[11] H. Woolf (1996) at 24.

[12] Ibid. at 22; CPR r. 1.1(2)(b) and (e); A. Zuckerman, 'A Reform of Civil Procedure – Rationing Procedure rather than Access to Justice' 22 (1995) *Journal of Law and Society* 155, 160; A. Zuckerman, 'Civil Litigation: A Public Service for the Enforcement of Civil Rights' 26 (2007) *CJQ* 1, 3; A. Clarke and J. Sorabji, 'The Importance of Civil Justice' 41 (2009) *Bracton Law Journal* 32 at [22]–[24].

[13] CPR r. 1.1 (SI 1998/3132 as amended in 2013 by SI 262/2013); H. Woolf (1995) at 9, 27, 35; H. Woolf (1996) at 17, 46ff.

[14] J. Sorabji, 'The Road to New Street Station: fact, fiction and the overriding objective' [2012] *EBLR* 1–77, 86.

[15] *Marcotte c. Longueil(ville)* [2009] 3 RCS 65; see C. Piché, 'Figures, Space and Procedural Proportionality' 01 (2012) *IAPL-RIDP* 145 for a discussion.

[16] Sorabji, 'The Road to New Street Station'.

[17] *Marcotte c. Longueil(ville)*; see Piché, 'Figures, Space and Procedural Proportionality'.

effective access to justice arises.[18] Both forms of proportionality were present in Bentham's theory of justice. They formed the reductive aspect of justice's collateral ends, in that both are concerned with ensuring that the cost or disbenefit to be derived from securing substantive justice and its enforcement do not outweigh the benefit obtained from its achievement.[19] As the Jackson Review put it, whilst discussing the need to ensure the effective implementation of individual proportionality, a cost–benefit analysis had to be done during the course of litigation.[20] Did the cost of a particular step in litigation outweigh the benefit to be derived from it?

Giving effect to a commitment to achieve substantive justice whilst minimising litigation time and cost in the overriding objective furthered the commitment to both aspects of proportionality. Minimising resource use to as close to no more than necessary to secure substantive justice optimises the prospect of achieving a judgment whose positive value outweighs its cost in the individual case. Equally, it minimises the share of the justice system's resources each claim utilises. It thus minimises the resources, from which all litigants must draw, used by each individual claim. As pointed out in Chapter 5, prosecuting claims consistently with the aspect of Woolf's new theory that was akin to the positive role played by justice's collateral ends in Bentham's can only go so far to promote the proportionate use of resources by individual litigants. Minimising resource use in substantive justice and effective enforcement's pursuit, given limited resource availability and unlimited resource demand, is an insufficient means to ensure effective access to justice for all. Such a commitment must be supplemented by the imposition of limits on resource allocation to individual claims or classes of claims. Such limits can only be imposed by a commitment to the reductive role played by justice's collateral ends and the restriction it imposes on substantive justice's pursuit. Such limits require a compromise to be struck between the resources made available to each claim and

---

[18] H. Woolf (1995) at 2–3: 'In considering the problems of the civil justice system I have had in mind the basic principles which should be met by a civil justice system so that it ensures access to justice:

• It should be just in the results it delivers.
• It should be fair and be seen to be so by:
  - ensuring that litigants have an equal opportunity, regardless of their resources, to assert or defend their legal rights; . . .'

[19] See Chapter 3.7.   [20] R. Jackson (December 2009) at 38.

substantive justice's pursuit, a compromise that reduces the possibility that the court could achieve substantive justice and effective enforcement. In some cases, this will mean that claims have to be brought to an end before a substantively just decision is reached. In others, it means that the court must determine the claim in the light of less probative evidence than would have been available under the RSC. In both cases the nature of, and commitment to, substantive justice will necessarily have changed. It will be proportionate to the nature and value of the claim as between the parties in those cases where it can be achieved. It will be denied in those cases where it cannot be achieved at a proportionate cost to other court users' right to receive an equitable share of the court's resources. Facilitating overall access thus requires the justice system to give proper effect to both individual and collective proportionality. Only by doing so can a fair distribution of resources be secured for all court users so that they can obtain effective access to justice. Woolf's new theory of justice is committed to this through its endorsement of the idea that individual litigants were not to utilise more resources than their case required or justified, in the light of the effect such resource allocation had on all other litigants.[21] As Lord Clarke MR explained it:

> furthering the overriding objective ... calls for the case management power to be applied consistently with the duty under CPR 1.1(2)(e) which requires the court to take account of the needs of all litigants and the court in furthering the overriding objective; to further access to justice for all.[22]

Its central importance to the new theory of justice, contrary to the lack of emphasis given it by the overriding objective's traditionalist interpretation, has been affirmed on a number of occasions. A number of both pre- and post-CPR authorities have affirmed both individual and collective proportionality's role within the overriding objective, the limit it places on the commitment to substantive justice and its justification by reference to access to justice.

The first such decision was that given by the Court of Appeal in *Beachley Property Limited* v. *Edgar*; the decision the Court of Appeal in *Mortgage Corporation* held ought not to have been followed at first instance in its case.[23] In *Beachley*, Lord Woolf, who gave the leading decision, repudiated

---

[21] H. Woolf (1995) at 2 and 26; H. Woolf (1996) at 23.

[22] A. Clarke, *The Supercase – Problems and Solutions: Reflections on BCCI and Equitable Life* (29 March 2007) (KPMG Forensic's Annual Law Lecture) at [18].

[23] CA 21 June 1996, unreported. See Chapter 4, n. 28.

the *Tildesley* test, and consequently, the theory that underpinned it. He did so in the context of considering whether to permit a party to submit evidence that was not served within the prescribed time limit. He first acknowledged that the evidence in question was relevant to one of the most important issues in the case. If the plaintiff were refused permission to adduce the evidence, the court's ability to achieve substantive justice would be severely curtailed. Were the RSC's theory of justice to apply, as it should have done at the time, since the CPR had not yet been introduced, the *Tildesley* test should have determined how the court exercised its discretion. If it had, the application would have succeeded, and the plaintiff would have been permitted to adduce the evidence. Lord Woolf, however, decided the appeal as if the reforms set out in his Reports had already come into force. The application was refused. It was refused because the court had to go beyond the traditional test for relief. As he explained the position:

> It is no use the party coming forward and saying, 'The evidence will help our case ...' You have to consider the position not only from the plaintiff's point of view, but also from the point of view of the defendant, and with a view to doing justice between other litigants as well.[24]

The court, as it would when the Woolf Reforms came into effect formally, considered the consequential effect granting relief would have on other litigants. The grant of relief had to be considered by reference to proportionality, particularly collective proportionality. If the application were granted, there would be an adverse effect on the rights of other litigants to receive an equitable, a proportionate, share of the court's resources. By failing to act consistently with rules of court designed to ensure that all litigants had effective access to justice, the plaintiff had gone beyond their equitable resource allocation. Granting relief from the consequences of default might – in this case, would – enable substantive justice to be done in the immediate case. It would, however, undermine the justice system's ability to afford a fair process to other litigants, thus denying them a fair opportunity to secure substantive justice in their cases. To permit reliance on the evidence would have undermined the need to keep the litigation within the bounds required by collective proportionality. Substantive justice's achievement could justifiably be frustrated then because doing so furthered the wider policy aim of securing effective access to justice for all court users. In this way the justice system could, through denying

---

[24] CA 21 June 1996, unreported at (6).

substantive justice in a particular case due to the actions of the litigants, further it in others and thereby further the rule of law. Denying justice in one case secured justice as a public good in others, and in general.

Beachley's influence was, however, limited at the time due to its being determined whilst the RSC system was operative. Neuberger J attempted to apply it in *Letpak* v. *Harris*, just as it had been applied at first instance in *Mortgage Corporation*. His decision was set aside by the Court of Appeal, just as the decision in *Mortgage Corporation* was set aside. In setting it aside, Waller LJ noted that the approach taken in *Beachley* was one for the future: a wind of change was blowing, but at that time it had not blown aside the *Tildesley* test and the theory of justice that gave birth to it.[25] More significantly, Lord Woolf agreed with Waller LJ's assessment. In *Grovit* v. *Doctor* he, too, acknowledged that the time to adopt a new approach, and one consistent with the Woolf Reports' reforms, was when the CPR was implemented and not before.[26] His prior approach in *Beachley* was premature. He reiterated this point in *Arbuthnot Latham Bank Ltd* v. *Trafalgar Holdings Ltd*, where he discussed the nature of the change that the CPR was to effect, but had not yet done so.[27] As he put it, the new approach that the CPR would usher in would be one that required both litigants and their lawyers to:

> recognise that any delay which occurs from now on will be assessed not only from the point of view of the prejudice caused to the particular litigants whose case it is, but also in relation to the effect it can have on other litigants who are wishing to have their cases heard and the prejudice which is caused to the due administration of civil justice.[28]

While it would continue to take account of the elements of the *Tildesley* test, the court would also have to take account of 'the consequence to other litigants and to the courts of inordinate delay was not a consideration ... in issue'. Under the CPR the court would have to take account of the effect litigant behaviour in individual cases and its decisions in those cases had on 'other litigants who [wished] to have their cases heard and the prejudice which is caused to the due administration of civil justice [by decisions taken in individual cases]'.[29] When it came into

---

[25] CA 9 November 1996 at (8)–(13); TLR 6 December 1996; *Moy* v. *Pettman Smith* [2002] EWCA Civ 875 at [58]–[59]. See Chapter 4, n. 27.
[26] [1997] 1 WLR 640, 644.   [27] [1998] 1 WLR 1426.   [28] Ibid., 1436.
[29] Ibid. at 1433 and 1436; *Lace Co-Ordinates Ltd* v. *Nem Insurance Co. Ltd* (CA 19 November 1998) at (7).

force, the old approach to securing justice would no longer hold. In a rationed system, rationing had to be maintained.

The decisions in *Beachley*, *Letpak* and *Arbuthnot* outlined how Woolf's new theory was to apply in practice. They predated the CPR's introduction. The first post-CPR case to raise the question of the *Tildesley* tests and the RSC theory of justice's continued status was *Woods* v. *Chaleff & Ors.*[30] The issue was whether a late amendment should be allowed. The court – which included Waller LJ – allowed the appeal and set aside the amendment. It did so whilst acknowledging that to allow the amendment would be contrary to the spirit of the new regime; the one that Waller LJ had previously explained in *Letpak*. Notwithstanding its implicit endorsement of collective proportionality and the need to secure effective access for other court users, the judgment did not provide a clear exposition of the approach. It was not a Bramwell LJ explanation of the new approach. It went no further than an allusion to the new theory of justice and the new approach it required by a judge who had acknowledged it in a previous decision.

Shortly after this early decision, the Court of Appeal returned to the *Tildesley* test. In *Adoko* v. *Jemal*, the issue was relief from the consequences of a failure to apply for permission to appeal in time; the same question that the Court of Appeal would later consider in *Sayers*. The question thus focused on rule-compliance and the consequences of default. The Court of Appeal made it clear that such decisions were now subject to a wider consideration than the need to secure substantive justice in the sense that the RSC's theory of justice understood it. The discretion to grant relief now had to be considered by reference to the principles of individual and collective proportionality, and the need to secure effective access to justice to all court users. CPR 1.1(2)(c) and (e) applied. As May LJ explained it, the courts had to ensure that 'so far as is practicable, [they allotted] to individual cases an appropriate share of the court's resources while taking account of the need to allot resources to other cases'.[31] Laws LJ concurred; proportionality was now an aspect of justice.[32] The new approach was next explained by the Court of Appeal in *UCB Corporate Services Ltd (formerly UCB Bank Plc)* v. *Halifax (SW) Ltd (UCB)*, where it was held that it applied in cases where the court had to consider whether to give relief from the consequences of litigants failing to effectively prosecute claims. When considering such

---

[30] CA 28 May 1999, [1999] EWCA Civ 1522.   [31] CA 22 June 1999, unreported at (7).
[32] Ibid. at (8).

applications, the court was now required to 'take into account the effect of what has happened on the administration of justice generally'. This involved 'taking into account the effect of the courts [*sic.*] ability to hear other cases if such defaults are allowed to occur'.[33] Collective proportionality was key. The wind of change blowing from the Woolf Reports and noted in *Letpak*, *Grovit* and *Arbuthnot* was now shaking the bows, and in doing so, it was casting down *Tildesley*.

The difficulty with the first three Court of Appeal decisions however is that while they confirmed the importance of the access principle and collective proportionality they did not, as the Court of Appeal did in *Tildesley*, *Clarapede* and *Cropper*, also articulate how the new theory and its elements were to be applied. They endorsed change, but left open how it was to be interpreted and applied in practice. The first significant post-CPR decision to discuss the practical aspects of the change in approach was *Charlesworth* v. *Relay Road Ltd & Others* in 2000.[34] The issue was whether the court should exercise its jurisdiction to permit a statement of case to be amended following judgment but prior to the court order being drawn up. Granting the amendment would introduce a new argument and require fresh evidence to be adduced. It would necessarily require the trial to be reopened. It would increase litigation cost and time beyond what was necessary. It would, however, facilitate substantive justice's achievement, as it would enable the 'real substantial question' in the claim to be put before the court.[35] This was the type of issue that under the RSC, and its commitment to substantive justice, would have been decided straightforwardly by applying *Tildesley*. If the traditionalist approach to the overriding objective had been applied, the same approach would have been taken, albeit that it would have been put in the language of balancing substantive justice, economy and efficiency with the first of the three elements determining where the balance lay.

Charlesworth predates the traditionalist authorities, however, and Neuberger J took an approach consistent with that outlined in Woolf's Final Report and *Arbuthnot*, and which the Court of Appeal had approved in December 1999 in *UCB*. He accepted that in exercising its discretion under the CPR the court had to take account of and balance two conflicting principles. This was not the false and flawed balancing exercise that would be carried out in, for instance, *Sayers*. On the contrary, it was a balance between the need to secure substantive justice

---

[33] [1999] CPLR 691.   [34] [2000] 1 WLR 230.   [35] *Kurtz* v. *Spence* (1888) 36 ChD 774.

in the instant case and whether it should be denied due to the need to secure collective proportionality and, through it, a fair distribution of the justice system's resources to other court users. It was the same balance as had to be struck in Bentham's theory between justice's direct end and the reductive aspect of its collateral ends. It was struck between them and determined by reference to the wider policy aim. To do this, a two-stage approach to the question of amendment was adopted. First, Neuberger J identified the continuing importance of the *Tildesley* test and its focus on the instant case. He did so by reference to Brett MR's articulation of it in *Clarapede*.[36] He noted how its continuing importance had recently been affirmed by the Court of Appeal in *Gale* v. *Superdrug Stores Plc*, a pre-CPR decision.[37] Millett LJ in that decision had endorsed the *Tildesley* test's continued importance and explicitly criticised the Woolf Reforms' attempt to render litigation more economical and efficient. As he put it, such reforms, while laudable, could not be permitted to enter into conflict with the 'overriding need to ensure that justice is not sacrificed'. As he went on to state:

> It is easy to dispense injustice quickly and cheaply, but it is better to do justice even if it takes a little longer and costs a little more.[38]

That was the position under the RSC. It was a ringing endorsement of the view that procedural reform had to operate within the framework set by the RSC's theory of justice. Securing substantive justice was to remain the predominant policy aim, and economy and efficiency were to remain no more than the means to facilitate it. As Millett LJ noted, securing substantive justice was a principle that could not simply be 'brushed aside on the ground that [it] was laid down a century ago or [failed] to recognise the exigencies of the modern civil justice system'.[39] On the contrary, as he stated, it represented 'a fundamental assessment of the functions of a court of justice which has a universal and timeless validity'.[40] Just as in *Mortgage Coporation* and just as it would be case for the traditionalists, economy and efficiency were of little account and proportionality did not to any real degree enter the picure. Millett LJ's view was not, however, one that simply endorsed the traditionalist interpretation of the overriding objective. It was one that straightforwardly rejected any idea that the RSC's theory of justice could be revised or superseded. It was a rejectionist view of the reforms.[41]

---

[36] (1883) 32 WR 262, 263.   [37] [1996] 1 WLR 1089, 1098–1099.   [38] Ibid.
[39] Ibid.   [40] [2000] 1 WLR 230 at 235.   [41] See Chapter 7 for a discussion.

Neuberger J rejected Millett LJ's approach. He did so by endorsing what had been the dissenting judgment in *Gale*, that of Thorpe LJ, who had held that the CPR had in fact altered the position. As Thorpe LJ had put it, with explicit reference to Millett LJ's judgment, '(authority) as to the practice in the High Court more than a century ago cannot recognise the demands and exigencies of the civil justice system as it is today'. On the contrary, he noted the public interest following the Woolf Reforms required a more robust approach that excluded 'from the system unnecessary litigation'.[42] As he rightly understood it, the public interest now went wider than substantive justice's pursuit in each individual case. He, too, rejected Millett LJ's rejectionist approach to reform. Following the approach indicated by Thorpe LJ, and in the light of the fact that the CPR was in force, Neuberger J explained that applications, such as those that had arisen in *Gale* and *Charlesworth*, had to be decided by the overriding objective and not by the simple application of the *Tildesley* test.[43] The Court of Appeal in *Purdy* v. *Cambran* would later concur with this assessment, when it held that the court had to consider the 'intrinsic justice of a particular case in the light of the overriding objective'[44] when considering questions that previously would have been dealt with simply by applying *Tildesley*. As May LJ noted in *Purdy*, it was an approach entirely consistent with that taken by the Court of Appeal previously in *UCB*. Neuberger J's approach thus was not only consistent with prior Court of Appeal authority (*UCB*), but also confirmed by that Court in *Purdy*. It was an approach, as all three judgments noted by reference to the overriding objective, which required all relevant issues to be taken account of before the court exercised its discretion. Two of those issues were set out in CPR 1.1(2)(c) and (e), i.e. individual and collective proportionality, the need to take account of overall resource allocation. They were because the issue for the court was not simply the need to facilitate substantive justice's achievement in the individual case, but to consider how best to secure equitable access to justice for all court users, so they had a fair opportunity to seek justice in their cases.

The upshot of this was that in addition to the *Tildesley* test, which remained relevant due to the commitment to substantive justice expressed in the overriding objective, Neuberger J held that a second test had to be applied. This test focused on both aspects of proportionality.[45]

---

[42] [1996] 1 WLR 1089, 1101.   [43] [2000] 1 WLR 230, 235.
[44] [2000] CP Rep. 67 at [51].   [45] [2000] 1 WLR 230, 235–236 and 239.

As he put it, the court had to approach the question of amendment not just in terms of the interests of the individual parties, as

> even where, in purely financial terms, the other party can be said to be compensated for a late amendment or late evidence by an appropriate award of costs, *it can often be unfair in terms of the strain of litigation, legitimate expectation, the efficient conduct of the case in question, and the interests of other litigants whose cases are waiting to be heard,* if such an application succeeds.[46]

Even if the *Tildesley* test was satisfied, relief could properly be denied if it would infringe either aspect of proportionality to do so. Substantive justice was thus tempered by wider considerations. This interpretation of the effect of the overriding objective did not stand alone. As Neuberger J noted, there was a body of pre-1999 Court of Appeal authorities that emphasised that the court's approach was to change when the CPR was introduced. He noted, for instance, how on the eve of the CPR's introduction, Waller LJ in the Court of Appeal in *Worldwide Corporation Limited* v. *GPT Ltd* elaborated and approved the same interpretation of it that he had placed on the overriding objective.[47] Rejecting an approach that simply relied on Bowen LJ's statement of the *Tildesley* approach from *Cropper*, Waller LJ, consistently with the approach he had previously taken in *Letpak* and the approach he would apply in *Woods* v. *Chaleff* when the CPR came into force, had stated how:

> the courts are now much more conscious that in assessing the justice of a particular case the disruption caused to other litigants by last minute adjournments and last minute applications have also to be brought into the scales.[48]

He had gone on to describe how the court was now and in future to ensure that no more than proportionate resources could justifiably be expended on any single action. What was proportionate was assessed by reference not simply to the nature of the immediate case, but crucially, by reference to the needs of all litigants: in other words, both individual and collective proportionality had to be accounted for. He went on to note that this approach, which was to be articulated in the (at that time soon-to-be-introduced) overriding objective, was one that Bingham MR had approved in *Thermaware* v. *Linton*. In that case, Bingham MR held that the Practice Direction on Case Management (1995)[49] and the stricter

---

[46] Ibid., 235. Emphasis added.   [47] CA 2 December 1998, unreported.
[48] Ibid. at (10).   [49] Practice Direction (Case Management) [1995] 1 WLR 262.

approach to ensuring the efficient and economic pursuit of substantive justice that had been advocated in both *Ketteman* v. *Hansel Properties*[50] and *Ashmore* v. *Corporation of Lloyds*[51] had to:

> be read against growing recognition that the luxurious approach to the expenditure of court time which was indulged in in the past is something which, in the interests of litigants as a whole, simply cannot be any longer afforded.[52]

The stricter approach developed in the RSC's latter years was to be read against a background that went further than looking at the benefits to be gained by ensuring substantive justice was achieved economically and efficiently in the individual case. It went further; and this was something that, as Waller LJ had noted in *Worldwide Corporation*, Millett LJ had simply failed to appreciate in *Gale*.[53] Reform was not simply a question of yet one more attempt at reform as an exercise of normal science. The growing recognition, which the Woolf Reforms and the overriding objective embodied and articulated, was that substantive justice's achievement could now be denied in the instant case where to permit its pursuit to continue would have a detrimental effect on the effective operation of the justice system and its ability to secure equitable access to justice for litigants as a whole. As Waller LJ had explained it in *Worldwide Corporation*:

> We share Millett LJ's concern that justice must not be sacrificed, but we believe his view does not give sufficient regard to the fact that the courts are concerned to do justice to all litigants, and that it may be necessary to take decisions vis-à-vis one litigant who may, despite all the opportunity he or his advisers have had to plead his case properly, feel some sense of personal injustice, for the sake of doing justice both to his opponent and to other litigants.
>
> . . .
>
> The court is concerned with doing justice, but justice to all litigants, and thus where a last minute amendment is sought with the consequences indicated, the onus will be a heavy one on the amending party to show the strength of the new case and why justice both to him, his opponent and other litigants, requires him to be able to pursue it.[54]

Justice must not be sacrificed. But it must not be sacrificed for all litigants rather than for the individual litigant who seeks relief from sanction,

---

[50] [1987] AC 189, 220.   [51] [1992] 1 WLR 446.   [52] CA 17 October 1995 at (16).
[53] Ibid. at (17).   [54] CA 2 December 1998 at (19), cited in [2000] 1 WLR 230, 236–237.

or a late amendment. Justice, once the preserve of substantive justice between the immediate parties, of 'justice between man and man' was now 'justice to all litigants'. As a consequence, it was substantive justice tempered by proportionality – proportionate justice – in the service of securing equitable access for all court users. Individual justice was thus subject to the need to secure distributive justice. Neuberger J endorsed this approach.

The Court of Appeal did not simply endorse Neuberger J's in *Purdy*, it affirmed it again in *Arrow Nominees Inc & Another* v. *Blackledge & Others*. It acknowledged substantive justice's change in status and access to justice's importance as the justice system's new substantive aim.[55] The appeal itself was from a decision concerning the question whether to strike out a claim for non-compliance with a disclosure obligation. Absent disclosure, a fair trial was not possible, i.e. substantive justice could not be achieved. The Court of Appeal allowed the appeal and struck out the claim. In reaching its decision, the Court assessed what the concept of a fair trial meant. Consistently with the approach taken by the Strasbourg court, Ward LJ in his judgment emphasised how a fair trial was one conducted without the undue use of temporal or financial resources. While this could have meant no more than the traditional approach to resource use, i.e. one that required it to be kept to a minimum as between the parties consistent with a commitment to the positive aspect of justice's collateral ends, Ward LJ went further. He emphasised that in assessing appropriate resource use, the interests of litigants other than those involved in the immediate litigation had to be taken account of as per CPR r. 1.1(2)(c) and (e). Resource use was not simply a matter of taking the RSC's approach to it. It was a question of proportionality in order to secure access to justice for all litigants. He said this:

> [The judge erred because he] did not appear to allot to the case an appropriate share of the court's resources while taking into account the need to allot resources to other cases. In this day and age they are elements of case management which must not only be seen to have been placed in the scales but also given due and proper weight when assessing how justice is to be done to the parties and to other litigants.[56]

This new approach was one he then noted had been articulated in both *Arbuthnot* and *Lace Co-Ordinates* v. *NEM Insurance Co Limited*.[57]

---

[55] [2000] CP Rep. 59; [2001] BCC 591.   [56] Ibid. at [73].
[57] CA 19 November 1998, unreported.

He approved, for instance, Hirst LJ's statement that decisions such as *Arbuthnot* had laid down guidelines for the future. Those guidelines, which expressed the 'overall interests of justice and fairness' now included, and emphasised, the importance of ensuring effective access to justice for all litigants.[58] By approving Hirst LJ's statement, the court in *Arrow Nominees* also approved Lord Woolf's statement of principle from *Arbuthnot*, that when the CPR was introduced, justice would require the court to take account of the interest of all litigants in having effective access to justice. Ward LJ put it this way:

> The trend of the authorities before C.P.R. was increasingly to support the notion that as the court became more pro-active, so greater importance was given to the need to emphasise and protect the court's interest in administering justice fairly not only as between the parties before the court but to all other others using the court service. Access to the courts was open to all but the time of the courts was a precious resource which needed to be managed rigorously in order to be fair to all. The C.P.R. is the apotheosis of those ideals.[59]

This approach is in stark contrast to the traditionalist view of the overriding objective, not least the one given in *B* v. *B. Arrow Nominees* is accordingly important for two reasons. First, it confirmed the approach taken by Neuberger J (an approach later affirmed by the Court of Appeal in *Daniels* v. *Thompson*, which in turn had relied on *Worldwide Corporation*, when it disallowed an amendment on the grounds that to permit it would infringe individual proportionality even though the amendment would arguably not have infringed collective proportionality).[60] It affirmed that acting consistently with the overriding objective required the court not only to assess the justice of the immediate case as per *Tildesley*, but also the wider interests of all litigants.[61] Secondly, it affirmed and applied the approach advocated by Lord Woolf in *Arbuthnot* and explained by him again when he had given the Court of Appeal's principal judgment in *Biguzzi*. In that latter case, he had stated that in assessing whether a case had been dealt with justly under the CPR:

---

[58] Ibid. at (10), cited in [2000] CP Rep 59; [2001] BCC 591 at [69].   [59] Ibid.

[60] [2004] EWCA Civ 307; [2004] PNLR 33 at [52]–[53]. In reaching the decision on collective proportionality, Dyson LJ also adverted to another post-CPR Court of Appeal decision that attempted, less successfully than others, to outline the change effected by the overriding objective's introduction; see *Cobbold* v. *London Borough of Greenwich* (CA, 9 August 1999, unreported).

[61] [2004] EWCA Civ 307; [2004] PNLR 33 at [69]–[72].

the courts are not confined to considering the relative positions of the parties [viz. the *Tildesley* test]. They have to take into account the effect of what has happened on the administration of justice generally. That involves taking into account the effect of the court's ability to hear other cases if such defaults are allowed to occur [viz. collective proportionality].[62]

Arrow Nominees thus confirmed, again, that under the CPR, the pre-CPR line of authority, explained and applied in *Biguzzi* and *Charlesworth*, which articulated the nature of what would become the CPR 1.1(2)(e) commitment to collective proportionality, was binding. The Court of Appeal in *Securum Finance Ltd* v. *Ashton* would again endorse this approach.[63] The message was, or ought to have been clear; justice was no longer hermetically sealed. Substantive justice in the individual case could now legitimately be sacrificed where its achievement would undermine the court's ability to satisfy the obligation to ensure equitable access to justice for all. Substantive justice was now subject to a wider goal. A claim could be dealt with in a manner that left an individual litigant with, as Waller LJ put it in *Worldwide Corporation*, a sense of personal injustice because substantive justice had not, or was perceived not to have been, achieved in their case because wider considerations had required the court to etiolate its commitment to it.[64] Perceived injustice in the individual case was, however, just when considered against the wider public interest of securing equitable access to justice for all court users. These same points would finally be reiterated once more in *Savings & Investment Bank Ltd* v. *Fincken*, where Rix LJ explained how all aspects of the overriding objective, including the need to ensure proper resource allocation across all court users, had to be taken account of in determining applications to amend. Again the point was made that the decision in *Worldwide Corporation*, while being a pre-CPR decision, showed the trend towards the approach that the CPR was to introduce and go beyond.[65]

This line of authority, and its acceptance of the role individual and collective proportionality were to play once the CPR was introduced is not confined to a series of Court of Appeal decisions. The House of Lords approved it in *Sutradhar* v. *Natural Environment Research Council*.[66]

---

[62] [1999] 1 WLR 1926, 1933.

[63] [2001] 1 Ch 291 at [34]; applied in *Overseas Development Ltd* v. *Cox* [2002] EWCA Civ 635 at [28]–[34].

[64] CA 2 December 1998, unreported.   [65] [2003] EWCA Civ 1630 at [78]–[79].

[66] [2006] 4 All ER 490; Sorabji, '*B v B*' at 87–8.

In that decision, Lord Hoffmann emphasised two aspects of the Bentham-like nature of Woolf's theory. First, he noted how conflict could arise between the need to secure substantive justice and individual proportionality. The cost and time of litigation might be too great as between the parties to permit a claim to proceed to judgment. On the facts of *Sutradhar*, it was.[67] As Bentham would have put it, the disutility generated by the cost of achieving justice's direct end consistently with the positive role played by its collateral ends outweighed the utility value of giving proper effect to substantive law. Secondly, he noted that substantive justice's pursuit could also impose too great a cost on the public purse and other litigants' right of access. It would, in other words, run contrary to the need to ensure that the proper administration of justice is carried out in the confines placed on it by limited resource allocation. To permit the claim to continue would infringe a commitment to collective proportionality, and the access principle. Justice thus required the court to refuse to permit the claim to continue to judgment. To do otherwise would undermine the ability to secure justice for other litigants due to the excessive resource use required to determine the immediate claim on its merits.[68] There was thus an absolute limit on substantive justice's pursuit and one that arose because of the need to preserve a wider public interest.

This decision in *Sutradhar*, like the Court of Appeal authorities, is in stark contrast to the RSC approach and the overriding objective's traditionalist interpretation. What is clear from it, and the Court of Appeal authorities, is that individual, substantive, justice was no longer to be the reference point for what it meant to refer to justice. There had been a paradigm shift: one theory of justice had been replaced by another. As Lord Hobhouse had put it in *Three Rivers*, it was no longer the case under the CPR that litigants were entitled to their day in court: justice no longer required it. Litigants were not entitled, as they were under the RSC, to substantive justice as of right. They would now only be entitled to a proportionate share of resources in order to pursue substantive justice. Proportionality was the touchstone. Contrary to the traditionalist view of the overriding objective, which *Sutradhar* impliedly disapproved, justice was no longer synonymous with substantive justice. Saving cost and time was no longer a matter of minimising them in the pursuit of substantive justice. As Lord Hoffmann had it, conflict and compromise

---

[67] [2006] 4 All ER 490 at [42].
[68] Ibid. Clarke and Sorabji, 'The Importance of Civil Justice' at [2]–[5].

could now arise between resource use and substantive justice. Bentham's conflict between justice's direct end and its collateral end was now a feature of the civil justice system. It was one that arose due to the need to secure fair resource allocation for all court users; to provide a more distributive form of justice than was previously the case.

6.3   Institutionalising proportionate justice through structural change

Proportionality and the access principle were not just introduced via the overriding objective. Like the commitments to economy, efficiency and expedition, they were also realised through structural changes to the justice system,[69] through structural proportionality. In order to secure this, the justice system had to be designed so that it was capable of producing two related results. It would have to be structured to maximise the prospect that individual claims could result in the effective enforcement of substantively just decisions not just at minimum cost and in minimum time, but at proportionate cost. This might mean, for instance, in simple low value claims, that a basic form of procedure was to apply. This would minimise cost and time to judgment. It would also reduce the prospect that substantive justice was capable of being achieved, as it would not, for instance, permit certain types of probative evidence to be put before the court. By reducing the extent of process available to a class of claims in order to ensure that they were prosecuted consistently with both individual and collective aspects of proportionality, it would institutionalise the risk – or perhaps likelihood – that in those classes of claim an approximation of substantive justice was the best that litigants could hope to achieve. Such a prospect would, however, be justified on a cost–benefit analysis focused on producing the optimum chance of securing substantive justice at a reduced resource allocation, so that all court users could obtain an equitable distribution of the justice system's resources. The system and its procedures would also have to be structured so that no single claim or class of claim produced too great a quantity of cost, either to the litigants or to the justice system as a whole, in the pursuit of substantive justice. The justice system would thus have to be structured in the same way that one designed in order to be consistent with Bentham's theory would have had to be structured. The consequences

---

[69] Davies, cited in C. Hanycz, 'More Access to Less Justice: Efficiency, Proportionality and Costs in Canadian Civil Justice Reform' 27 (2008) CJQ 98, 105ff.

of Woolf's theory for institutional design were the same as for Bentham's. Both systems would have to be designed so as to ensure that benefit derived from its processes neither outweighed the cost to individual litigants nor the cost to the justice system, and through it, wider society. The system would consequently have to be designed so that:

- Its structures and procedures were capable of securing substantive justice at minimal cost and time, but in a way such that that was tempered by the need to ensure they could not generate disproportionality on an individual or collective basis.
- Those structures and procedures would have to be designed so that as many litigants as possible could gain effective access to the system. This might then mean that some claims would be afforded only the most summary and rudimentary procedures, procedures that offered only a slight, or at best, poor prospect of achieving substantive justice and effective enforcement, while other claims were simply denied an opportunity to secure substantive justice.

Consistently with the principles articulated through the overriding objective, civil procedure was to be designed in this way so as to strike a balance between substantive justice and its limitation or denial on proportionality grounds in order to secure equitable resources for all court users. Resource use was to be matched to the nature of the dispute so as to ensure that all litigants have effective access to justice. In other words, it justified distinctions being drawn between different types of cases and the level of resources that could be afforded to them, i.e. which linked resource use to claim value and complexity and the need to provide an equitable distribution of those resources to all court users as specified in CPR r. 1.1(2)(b), (c) and (e).[70] It justified, for instance, the creation of procedural case tracks that matched resource allocation to claim value and complexity: that embodied the commitment to ensuring litigation is carried out consistently with individual and collective proportionality.[71] Equally, it justified limits being placed on opening speeches; on evidence (court control of disclosure and expert evidence);[72] and on hearing length, through active case management designed to ensure that litigants could no longer subvert the justice system by an approach that generated 'expense [that was often excessive, disproportionate and unpredictable; and delay [that was] frequently

---

[70] Clarke and Sorabji, 'The Importance of Civil Justice' at [22].
[71] H. Woolf (1995) at 19–22, 41–56.   [72] Ibid. at 153 and 175.

unreasonable'.[73] It is not possible to detail all aspects of the Woolf Reports' structural reforms, which implemented the new theory of justice through institutional design, therefore the two most significant ones are considered: active case management and the creation of procedural case tracks.

6.3.1   Active case management

The introduction of active case management, coupled with the introduction of a positive obligation on litigants to assist the court in achieving the overriding objective rather than substantive justice, was perhaps the most significant structural change implemented as a consequence of the Woolf Reforms.[74] The court was now able to control litigation so as to ensure that it was conducted consistently with the new theory of justice.[75] Litigants were also, due to the duty imposed on them to ensure that their conduct during the course of litigation was not only carried out to ensure that their claim was prosecuted so as to secure substantive justice at minimal and proportionate cost, but equally so as not to breach the requirements imposed by collective proportionality.[76] It would be, or ought to be, impermissible for parties to conduct litigation in a spirit that was inconsistent with this express duty.[77] They would, as Best CJ had put it in 1830, be under an explicit obligation that required those who came to justice to do justice, albeit it was to be a more distributed form of justice.[78]

These two structural changes were specifically intended to facilitate implementation of Woolf's new theory of justice in a number of ways. First, they were intended to assist the achievement of substantive justice economically and efficiently, i.e. at minimal cost and time. They were thus intended to ensure that what for Bentham was justice's direct end was achieved consistently with the primary role of its collateral ends.

---

[73] Ibid. at 7 and 26–41; R. Aikens, *Report and Recommendations of the Commercial Court Long Trials Working Party* (Judiciary of England and Wales, 2007) at 6–12.

[74] CPR rr. 1.2, 1.3 and 1.4. The introduction of costs management and docketing as a consequence of the Jackson Reforms is no more than an extrapolation of case management on the one hand and the final implementation of a previously unimplemented aspect of the Woolf Reforms' approach to case management on the other.

[75] H. Woolf (1995) at 18 and 52.   [76] *Kesslar* v. *Moore & Tibbits* [2005] PNLR 17 at (27).

[77] H. Woolf (1996) at 72; *Gregson* v. *Channel Four Television Corp* [2000] CP Rep. 60 at [23]; *Hertsmere Primary Care Trust & Others* v. *Rabindra-Anandh* [2005] 2 All ER 274.

[78] The 1830 Report at Appendix B (49).

They would do so through ensuring parties identified the real issues in dispute at an early stage; that court timetables were abided by; and that procedural tactical litigation was avoided.[79] Early identification of issues can limit the scope for a dilatoriness on the part of the parties not only in respect of its ascertaining the true nature of the case that must be brought and defended, but it also focuses early attention on what evidence will be needed and from whom and requires the parties to cooperate with each other to some extent through that identification process. It can thus also promote the minimisation of litigation cost to no more than necessary to achieve substantive justice through, for instance, narrowing the issues and reducing the degree and extent of evidence gathering required. Equally, it can facilitate early instruction of expert witnesses, if necessary, and the instruction of only such witnesses as are truly necessary to the real issues. Less evidence on fewer issues not only has cost benefits, but also facilitates earlier readiness for trial, thus reducing the length of time taken to final judgment. Equally, early identification of issues and early disclosure as a consequence of active case management, and parties acting consistently with their duty to the court, can also facilitate the prospect of settlement, thus enabling resources to be allocated to those court users who truly need access to the system in order to secure substantive justice and vindicate their rights.[80]

This aspect of the Woolf Reforms also demonstrates the commitment to the new theory of justice in another way. One of the fundamental problems that arose as a consequence of the RSC's theory was that party-control of litigation conducted ostensibly to achieve substantive justice, but actually pursued to achieve success whether that was based on a merits-based judgment or on technical, procedural grounds, engendered the growth of an excessively adversarial litigation culture. As the Interim Report described the situation under the RSC:

> The key problems facing civil justice today are cost, delay and complexity. These three are interrelated and stem from the uncontrolled nature of the litigation process...
>
> By tradition the conduct of civil litigation in England and Wales, as in other common law jurisdictions, is adversarial. Within a framework of substantive and procedural law established by the state for the resolution of civil disputes, the main responsibility for the initiation and conduct of proceedings rests with the parties to each individual case, and it is

[79] H. Woolf (1995) at 10; H. Woolf (1996) at 62.
[80] *Shirayama Shokusan Co. Ltd* v. *Danovo Ltd* [2004] 1 WLR 2985, 2989.

normally the plaintiff who sets the pace. The role of the judge is to adjudicate on issues selected by the parties when they choose to present them to the court.

Without effective judicial control, however, the adversarial process is likely to encourage an adversarial culture and to degenerate into an environment in which the litigation process is too often seen as a battlefield where no rules apply. In this environment, questions of expense, delay, compromise and fairness may have only low priority. The consequence is that expense is often excessive, disproportionate and unpredictable; and delay is frequently unreasonable.

This situation arises precisely because the conduct, pace and extent of litigation are left almost completely to the parties.[81]

Party-control created a culture characterised by aggressive, confrontational behaviour on the part of litigants that rendered it more akin to a form of warfare rather than the means to achieve substantive justice.[82] Every tactic was deployed to secure success, irrespective of substantive justice or its achievement. Litigants would seek to exploit any technical default by the other party, increase costs and delay in order to force an unfavourable settlement or secure a premature end to the litigation. In this way it complemented the laissez-faire attitude to compliance generated by *Tildesley* and *Birkett*. As the Woolf Reports noted, this overtly adversarial attitude to litigation was one of the major causes of unnecessary and excessive litigation complexity, cost and delay.[83] Along with lack of procedural discipline, it not only undermined the RSC's efficacy, but if permitted to continue there would have been a realistic expectation that it would go on to undermine the Woolf Reforms' efficacy.[84] As the Jackson Review confirmed, that expectation was unfortunately realised due to the courts' failure to properly articulate a consistent view of what the overriding objective meant.[85] These issues are considered further in Chapter 7.

The introduction of effective case management and the duty to the court, if used properly, was to be a necessary condition of effective reform; necessary because it was the means by which the court could give effect to the overriding objective, and through it, procedural proportionality. By introducing discipline and greater inter-party cooperation in the conduct of litigation, unnecessary litigation cost was to be reduced. Rendering the judicial process more consensual and less confrontational was intended to

---

[81] H. Woolf (1995) at 7.   [82] *Davis* v. *Eli Lilly & Co* [1987] 1 All ER 801, 804.
[83] H. Woolf (1995) at 207.   [84] See Chapter 4, n. 44.
[85] R. Jackson (May 2009) Vol. II at 416ff; R. Jackson (December 2009) at 386–400.

render the pursuit of substantive justice more economical and efficient. Equally, through requiring parties to cooperate with each other in the progress of litigation from an early stage, to identify issues early, or appoint experts early,[86] the court was to ensure that both substantive justice's achievement economically and efficiently was promoted as well as, in those cases that warranted it on proportionality grounds, its denial. Its achievement was promoted in those cases that continued to trial. Its denial was promoted by creating the conditions for consensual settlement. A consequence of both was the promotion of proportionate justice: economic and efficient substantive justice in individual cases ensured that resources were not unnecessarily used and were thus available to other litigants; substantive justice's denial through its consensual denial ensured that resources that would otherwise be used were available to other litigants. No longer were litigants to be able to conduct litigation in a laissez-faire, yet aggressive, manner in 'their own self-interest' as was the case under the RSC. They would now have to conduct litigation so as to facilitate its determination 'either through judgment or settlement, efficiently and economically, in the interests of both parties to the litigation, litigants generally and the court'.[87] Parties would have to manage cases, as would the court, with a view not just to achieving substantive justice at minimal cost. Taken together, these two structural reforms operating consistently with the new theory would also, as Lord Clarke MR confirmed, form the basis on which the post-Woolf justice system was to

> ensure that each case [was] afforded no more than a proportionate amount of judicial and party resources, that the real issues in dispute are identified early and concentrated on by the court and the parties, and that the claim is dealt with expeditiously. Taken together they enable a simple and straightforward procedural system to be tailored effectively to the needs of the court, the parties and to litigants in general so that justice in the individual case can be achieved at a reasonable cost and within a reasonable timeframe.[88]

In this way they were therefore to embody the structural commitment to the new theory of justice.

---

[86] H. Woolf (1995) at 11 and 19; H. Woolf (1996) at 107ff.

[87] J. Sorabji, 'Costs – Unreasonable Conduct within a Mediation – *Carleton v Strutt & Parker (a partnership)*' 27 (2008) *CJQ* 288, 293; *Hertsmere Primary Care Trust & Others* v. *Rabindra-Anandh*; *Hoddinott v. Persimmon Homes Wessex Ltd* [2007] EWCA Civ 1203, [2008] 1 WLR 806; *Carleton v. Strutt & Parker (a partnership)* [2008] EWHC 616 (QB).

[88] Clarke, *The Supercase – Problems and Solutions* at (7).

6.3.2 Procedural case tracks

The introduction of procedural case tracks was also intended to give concrete structural effect to proportionality. As the Final Report noted, 'Proportionality underlies the whole concept of the fast track.'[89] Through the case tracks, the justice system was to ensure that it would not, as the RSC and its predecessors had done, apply 'the same procedures to all cases regardless of financial weight, complexity or importance'. Resource use was to be matched to the nature of the case.[90] In order to secure an equitable distribution of the courts resources, different cases would be treated differently and similar cases would be treated similarly.[91] No longer would all cases have access to the same form of procedure, nor could they expect the justice system to offer them the same degree of commitment to achieving substantive justice. Each case was to be afforded a form of process that was consistent with the need to secure substantive justice subject to the new commitment to both individual and collective proportionality.

Three procedural tracks were recommended within the Interim and Final Reports: the small claims track, which was to replace County Court arbitrations, for claims up to £5,000 in value (£1,000 for personal injury claims); the fast track, for claims of £5,000–£15,000 (personal injury claims over £1,000 up to £15,000); and the multi-track for claims over £15,000 in value.[92] Claims were to be allocated to a track after service of the statements of case and the filing of allocation questionnaires.[93] They were, however, to be allocated not just on value, albeit that was to be the single most significant factor,[94] but also by taking account of factors such as the nature of the remedy sought, the complexity of the facts, law or

---

[89] H. Woolf (1995) at 28.   [90] Ibid. at 19.

[91] M. Rosenberg, 'The Federal Rules after half a century' [1984] *Maine Law Review* 243, 247; *Joyce* v. *Liverpool City Council* [1996] QB 252.

[92] H. Woolf (1996) at 20–72. See Ministry of Justice, *Solving disputes in the county courts: creating a simpler, quicker and more proportionate system: A consultation on reforming civil justice in England and Wales* (CP6/2011), (March 2011), for proposals to change their financial boundaries.

[93] CPR r. 26.5 (pre-April 2013). Allocation questionnaires were replaced by Directions questionnaires in April 2013, as a consequence of the Jackson Reforms. This was predicated on the fact that allocation hearings were understood to generate disproportionate cost, as a large number of them were simply perfunctory hearings where standard directions were made. As a consequence of further proportionality the hearings were replaced by an administrative track allocation exercise: see R. Jackson (December 2009) at 469 and CPR r. 26.3(1) (post-April 2013)

[94] H. Woolf (1996) at 19.

evidence, the number of parties involved, the importance of the claim generally, the parties' views and, consistently with CPR r. 1.1(2)(c)(iv), the parties' circumstances.[95] The small claims track was intended to provide a limited form of procedure denuded of many of the procedural mechanisms otherwise available. As such, disclosure was limited to such material as a litigant wished to rely upon. The prospect of substantive justice's achievement being reached was thus reduced, given that parties were not required to disclose material adverse to their case. Trials were to be informal, listed for less than half a day, and were intended to be conducted by the litigants in person with the judge taking a more inquisitorial and investigative role than is otherwise permissible. Less expert legal involvement, less time for cross-examination, and limits on the presentation of evidence thus further reduced the court's ability to ascertain true fact and to apply it to right law. Finally, it was to permit no more than limited, fixed, cost recovery; thus limiting the scope of work that a litigant might be prepared for a lawyer to do on their behalf.[96] The fast track was to provide a more traditional approach for intermediate, albeit still straightforward claims.[97] As such, it was structured so that parties could expect to achieve decisions that reasonably tracked substantive justice relatively quickly, at reasonable – and to a degree, certain – recoverable cost.[98] This intention was given form through, for instance, restricting disclosure to standard disclosure;[99] and minimising the pre-trial time period.[100] Furthermore, fast track trials were generally to take no more than a day. Expert evidence was generally to be limited to a single, jointly instructed, expert.[101] Again, the prospect of substantive justice being achieved was reduced due to the limits placed on evidence and trial length. Conversely, those very limits ensured that more trials than previously could be heard. Thus, effective access had been increased; albeit access was to a more proportionate form of justice. Only on the multi-track, which was to be reserved for the highest value and most complex cases, was the whole panoply of procedure, in principle at least, available to litigants.[102] Even there, though, the court, consistently with its duty to actively manage cases, was to tailor procedure so that resource

---

[95] CPR r. 26.7 and 8.   [96] CPR r. 27.   [97] CPR r. 28.

[98] H. Woolf (1995) at 21, 35, 41–5; CPR r. 46.2 (pre-April 2013), see CPR PD 47.19 (post-April 2013).

[99] CPR r. 31.6 (pre-April 2013); R. Jackson (December 2009) at 364; CPR r. 31.5 (post-April 2013).

[100] H. Woolf (1995) at 43.   [101] *Daniels* v. *Walker* [2000] 1 WLR 1381.

[102] H. Woolf (1995) at 48; CPR r. 29.

allocation matched the requirements of the claim; as the Interim Report put it, there had to be 'an approach which is proportionate to the weight of the case applies throughout the system'.[103] Disclosure, for instance, would remain subject to standard disclosure and, following the Jackson Reforms, would be further tailored consistently with the need to secure proportionality.[104] Expert evidence was also to be limited, as a general rule, to that given by a single, jointly instructed expert.[105] Opening speeches and cross-examination were also to be subject to control, so as to ensure that no more than proportionate resources were used during trials. Litigation on the multi-track was consequently still to be subject to limits imposed consistently with substantive justice's denial and the aim of furthering effective access to justice for all, as the Aikens Report into the excesses of the *BCCI* and *Equitable Life* actions and the Jackson Report both affirmed.[106]

Given the differential approach they take to the nature and extent of procedure available to individual claims, the case tracks can clearly be seen to give structural form to the commitment contained within CPR r. 1.1(2)(b), (c) and (e) to deal with cases proportionately and ensure each claim received no more than equitable resource allocation. As the Interim Report described the position by reference to the small claims track, the case tracks were intended to eliminate the 'excessive and disproportionate cost' that the RSC's one-size-fits-all form of process married with its commitment to substantive justice created.[107] On the contrary, they were 'designed to provide appropriate ways of handling cases from the simplest and least expensive to the most complex, important and financially weighty'. By appropriate ways, the Report refers to the fact that they would enable the justice system 'to achieve a just and timely resolution of

---

[103] H. Woolf (1995) at 36.

[104] CPR r. 31.5 (pre-April 2013); R Jackson (December 2009) at 364ff; CPR r. 31.5 (post-April 2013).

[105] CPR r. 35.7. The Jackson Reforms further narrowed use of expert evidence through requiring early identification of issues, cost estimates of expert evidence and the introduction of concurrent expert evidence; see R. Jackson (December 2009) at 375ff; CPR r. 35.4, CPR PD 11.1–11.4 (post-April 2013).

[106] Aikens, *Report and Recommendations of the Commercial Court Long Trials Working Party*; Clarke, *The Supercase – Problems and Solutions*; *Three Rivers DC* v. *Bank of England (No 3)* [2003] 2 AC 1; *Equitable Life Assurance Society* v. *Ernst & Young (A Firm)* [2003] PNLR 23; *Equitable Life Assurance Society* v. *Hyman* [2002] 1 AC 408; R Jackson (December 2009 at 469; CPR r. 29.120 (post-April 2013).

[107] H. Woolf (1995) at 35.

the dispute at a cost which is proportionate to the nature of the issues involved and the means of the parties'.[108]

This explanation regarding the purpose of procedural tracks mirrors the Report's explanation of the justice system's altered purpose; both are predicated on facilitating the 'just and timely resolution' of disputes. As is clear from the Report's reference to the equal importance procedural and substantive justice are to be afforded under the reformed system and the Final Report's confirmation of procedural justice's increased importance so as to ensure the justice system is able to deliver substantively just results through substantively just processes, this was a reference to substantive justice's achievement consistently with the need to minimise cost and time in the pursuit of substantive justice and the need to ensure it is pursued consistently with a commitment to both individual and collective proportionality.[109]

That the procedural tracks were intended to provide the structural means to properly effect the commitment to substantive justice, its denial through the introduction of proportionality and the new predominant policy aim of securing effective access to justice for all court users, is most clearly seen through the Woolf Reports' discussion of concerns raised by the Association of Personal Injury Lawyers (APIL) regarding their introduction. APIL's concern was that the introduction of case tracks went further than simply ensuring that substantive justice could be achieved at minimal litigation cost. It had the same concern as Dehn.[110] It anticipated that the reforms intended the case tracks to go further than this and were to introduce a fetter on the justice system's ability to achieve substantive justice. For APIL, track allocation really would give rise to rough justice rather than substantive justice. As it understood it, the commitment to proportionality, and its structural consequences, amounted to a denial of individual justice, which it clearly and intentionally did, albeit it did so in the wider public interest.[111]

APIL's particular concern arose in respect of the fast track. It argued that in so far as personal injury claims were concerned, the reduced form of procedure it was to provide was insufficient, as it did not enable the court to arrive at substantive justice. In particular, it feared that the introduction of standard disclosure, one-day trials and the use of single joint experts rather than multiple party-specific experts would ensure that this was the case.[112] Substantive justice's achievement, as

---

[108] Ibid. at 35–6.   [109] Ibid. at 216; H. Woolf (1996) at 4 and 274.
[110] See Chapter 5, n. 2.   [111] H. Woolf (1996) at 192.   [112] H. Woolf (1995) at 14.

far as APIL was concerned, was being sacrificed.[113] The limitation placed
on the nature and availability of expert evidence was a particular cause
of concern in this regard. The fewer the number of experts available in
a claim, the greater the risk that true fact would not be determined.[114]
Its stance in the face of this was the same as would be adopted by
the litigants in *Sutradhar*: i.e. that there was no need to limit procedure
or the attendant costs because we, the litigants, can afford to pay substantive justice's price.[115] As in *Sutradhar*, APIL's position was one that
took no account of the effect that granting an unfettered right of access
to substantive justice would have on either the justice system as a whole
or other litigants and their right of access. It treated all claims as
hermetically sealed: individual substantive justice was the only proper
form of justice on this view. It is an approach that would require an
assessment of resource allocation (*pace* CPR r. 1.1(2)(c) and (e)) by sole
reference to what is necessary to achieve substantive justice in each and
any individual case. Such a stance would have been reasonable *if* the
Woolf Reforms maintained the commitment to the traditional theory of
justice. Even then, it would only have been reasonable in a world of
infinite resource availability, and one where the fallacy of composition
at the heart of the RSC's theory and the fact that from a practical
perspective it was self-defeating in any event, as *Birkett* showed, did
not hold true.

If substantive justice's achievement, assessed solely by reference to the
individual and immediate case before the court, remained justice's aim,
APIL would have had a strong case. If the Woolf Reforms had accepted
its position, it would be difficult to justify the claim that the new theory of
justice went further than traditionalist interpretation of the overriding
objective. APIL's argument, however, missed the point. Its concern that
proportionality under CPR r. 1.1(2)(c) and (e) as embodied in the case
tracks went beyond simply ensuring that no more than minimal
resources were expended on achieving substantive justice was correct.
The conclusion it drew as to the adverse effect the Woolf Reforms would
have on substantive justice's achievement was correct: proportionality

---

[113] H. Woolf (1996) at 24 and 137.

[114] W. Braithwaite, 'Single Joint Experts', *Personal and Medical Injuries Law Letter* (2003);
Clarke, *The Supercase – Problems and Solutions* at [30]–[31].

[115] H. Woolf (1996) at 25; S. Issacharoff, 'Too Much Lawyering, Too Little Law: Comments
on "Access to Justice"' in A. Zuckerman and R. Cranston, *Reform of Civil Procedure –
Essays on 'Access to Justice'* (Clarendon Press, 1995) at 245ff.

was inconsistent with the pre-eminence of a commitment to substantive justice. APIL was right to express those concerns. And those concerns foreshadowed a question that Hanycz would raise. With reference to what she understood to be Woolf's focus on efficiency as the driving force of the reforms, she rhetorically asked 'whether the same procedure, in light of its reduced processes, retains the ability to deliver just, accurate outcomes?'[116] APIL's answer in 1995 was a resounding no: substantive justice was being sacrificed as a consequence of reduced procedure. While both APIL's and Hanycz's concerns and conclusions were valid, neither engages their target, as Kuhn understood was the case where normal science is rejected in favour of a paradigm shift. Their positions are predicated on the false assumption that substantive justice remained, in so far as the Woolf Reforms were concerned, justice's substantive aim.

Reforms' actual position and the introduction of procedural tracks that structurally institutionalised reduced procedure were intended to produce the very result of which APIL complained. It was intended to institutionalise the risk that some final decisions might well not see the application of true fact to right to law. Introducing structures and procedures that restrict resource use according to the value and importance of a claim, in order to secure equitable resource allocation across all court users, cannot but place an absolute limit on the justice system's ability to achieve substantive justice. While there would be some cases, perhaps many cases, where the fast-track procedure would remain capable of arriving at substantive justice to the same standard as prevailed under the RSC, it was understood that in some cases the quality of decision-making at trial would be reduced as a consequence of the newly limited procedure. Such a system was and is, of course, consistent with the incorporation of a commitment to proportionality. It is not one that can properly be said to be committed to substantive justice as its substantive aim. The Woolf Reforms were not just alive to this possibility; it was their aim. It was the inevitable consequence of the increase in procedural justice's importance and its focus on the needs of all court users.[117]

The Woolf Reports responded to APIL's concerns in two ways. First, they emphasised the continued importance of substantive justice. They did so by arguing that the reforms would encourage lawyers to become

---

[116] Hanycz, 'More Access to Less Justice' at 103.   [117] H. Woolf (1996) at 2.

more efficient. They would become better able to prosecute claims at minimal cost. Greater efficiency would undermine APIL's concern that less than necessary resources were available on the fast track. By placing a limit upon the availability of resources, especially financial ones, which could be expended on claims, a brake was to be imposed on systemic inefficiency. This would not reduce the court's ability to achieve substantive justice because the time and expense that it sought to reduce, in fact, made no contribution to the achievement of substantive justice.[118] Efficiency here, as under the primary role played for Bentham by justice's collateral ends, supports substantive justice's achievement. It does so here for two reasons.

First, it increases the prospect of substantive justice's achievement in the instant case through, for instance, ensuring that unnecessary expense and delay did not increase the prospect of non-initiation, discontinuation before judgment, or a less than substantively accurate final determination. It would limit the prospect of degradation of witness evidence and the adverse effect that had on substantive justice's achievement. It would equally facilitate substantive justice through reducing the opportunities for satellite litigation. It would also therefore facilitate the achievement of both individual and collective proportionality. Secondly, inefficiency and expense reduction reduced the call each claim would have on the totality of court resources. It would thus ensure that no more than minimal judicial time and expense was expended on each claim and thus increase equitable resource allocation across all court users. This would increase the prospect that substantive justice would be achieved. There is undoubtedly some truth in this. As a response it did not, however, meet APIL's concerns, which centred on the fear that even if optimal efficiency were achieved court control of a limited, proportionate process would not in fact permit substantive justice's achievement. Efficiency gains obtained through, as the Woolf Reports put it, better working practices on the part of lawyers would not, for instance, answer the problem, as later put by Braithwaite, that a single joint expert could not be relied upon to assist the court in reaching a proper determination of a claim on its substantive merits.[119] For APIL, the Woolf Reports' answer misses the point. Issacharoff noted this when he commented critically on this aspect of the reforms. He said:

> Rough justice is exactly that. There is every reason to believe that with less
> resources devoted to any particular case, with less discovery in particular

---

[118] Ibid. at 24–6.   [119] Braithwaite, 'Single Joint Experts'.

and lawyering in general, the outcomes of cases are more likely to be erroneous ... The [Interim] Report, perhaps for reasons of diplomacy, or perhaps for limited desire to invoke the wrath of litigants, pretends that the alternatives to full process are equally good.[120]

For APIL, Hanycz and Issacharoff, the underlying issue is that the Woolf Reports assumed, and assumed wrongly, that increased efficiency would give rise to a system that could still achieve substantive justice and still aimed to do so. For Issacharoff, the failure to engage APIL is pretence on the Interim Report's part, as it is unable straightforwardly to admit that substantive justice is no longer justice's sole aim. While this is right, the Reports' position is not exactly opaque, even if the initial response to APIL is disingenuous. The commitment to both aspects of proportionality, the increase in procedural justice's importance generally embodied in the overriding objective and the structural reforms they proposed and which were implemented, all spoke with one voice: substantive justice is no longer the sole aim. While it can still be achieved and is still an aim, it is no longer the justice system's predominant aim. For APIL, the Woolf Reforms ought simply to have sought to increase the court's ability to achieve substantive justice, as all previous reforms had attempted to do. They did not. Nor were they intended to. Normal science was not the objective.

It is through this, though, that the Woolf Reports' second response to APIL arises; a response which also met Issacharoff's critique. Describing the procedural case tracks' purpose, a number of points were made in the Interim Report.[121] It emphasised the importance of a number of aspects of procedural justice. Equality of arms was promoted, for instance, through changing the costs regime and reducing the prospect that wealthier litigants could utilise procedural tactics designed to wear down their opponents. Individual access to justice would thus be increased through a reduction in litigation conducted as Fabian war. The procedural case tracks, by reducing litigation cost and time, would also increase access to justice for those who previously could not have afforded to litigate. Such individuals would previously have been denied justice where, post-Woolf, they would have access to proportionate justice.[122] In all of this, it was clear from the outset that the reforms were to sacrifice the traditional commitment to substantive justice; that access to justice

---

[120] Issacharoff, 'Too Much Lawyering, Too Little Law' at 251.
[121] H. Woolf (1995) at 78.   [122] H. Woolf (1996) at 23–4.

was to be rationed.[123] There is no real suggestion, as Issacharoff implied, that the Woolf Reports avoided stating this explicitly. They did so. They did so through the overriding objective. They did so through the introduction of procedural case tracks and court control of litigation.[124] They did so through the reform of expert evidence, so that post-reform, the expert witness industry would cease to be a singularly effective means of undermining effective access to justice through acting as a substantial cause of non-initiation and mis-decision.[125] The same points could be made for discovery, just as they could for non-compliance with procedural obligations.[126]

Through the totality of reform, the Woolf Reports made it quite clear that the commitment to increasing access to justice for all through rationing procedure and reducing the commitment to substantive justice was reform's explicit intention. The procedural case tracks, as a systematic filter aimed at promoting access to justice by reducing litigation time and cost so that a proper balance was struck between the need to secure equitable resource allocation and the value that giving proper effect to substantive law had, were one part of that process.[127] Through them, the Reports articulated how the justice system was to restrict process and lower the prospect that substantive justice would be achieved. APIL's criticism of the effect of Woolf's reforms was an accurate one. Unfortunately, as Kuhn would have pointed out, it was a criticism that missed its mark. It was one that only had any value if the reforms maintained a commitment to the traditional, RSC, theory of justice. In rejecting that theory, the criticism sails past its target. It was criticism predicated on a false assumption; that substantive justice was still to be the justice system's substantive aim.

---

[123] A. Zuckerman, 'A Reform of Civil Procedure – Rationing Procedure rather than Access to Justice' 22 (1995) *Journal of Law and Society* 155, 158.

[124] E.g., H. Woolf (1995) at 164ff and 181ff; Heilbron–Hodge Report at 44.

[125] H. Woolf (1996) at 137.

[126] *Compagnie Financière du Pacifique* v. *Peruvian Guano Company* (1882) 11 QBD 55 at 59–60; *Jones* v. *Monte Video Gas Company* (1880) 5 QBD 556; H. Woolf (1995) at 8, 13, 19–20; N. Andrews, *English Civil Procedure* (Oxford University Press, 2003) at 601; D. Mackie, 'Discovery in Commercial Litigation', in Zuckerman and Cranston, *Reform of Civil Procedure* at 144.

[127] Such a system is in its way consistent with Bentham's imprecation to legislators to devise a justice system best suited to promote utility-maximisation: J. Bentham in Mill, *Utilitarianism* at 59ff and 64ff.

6.4   Conclusion: a theory of proportionate justice

The Woolf Review undertook an examination of the civil justice system from first principles. It considered the system's purpose and how its procedural rules and structures were to achieve that purpose. In doing so, it required the introduction into the rules of court of a purposive provision of the type utilised in other common law jurisdictions: an overriding objective. In those jurisdictions, their overriding objectives expressed the justice system and its rules' purpose in traditional terms. The common law overriding objectives, present in the United States, South Australia and Ontario, all articulated the same overriding objective that had implicitly governed the RSC since its adoption of equity's approach to securing substantive justice. In its early characterisation of the overriding objective the Interim Report offers some support to the view that the fundamental reappraisal of the justice system's purpose resulted in the conclusion that it was not to change. There is some support for this in the line of Court of Appeal authorities that read the overriding objective as an English version of the pre-established common law overriding objectives: as an explicit version of the RSC's implicit overriding objective and the theory of justice that expressed. Over this and the previous chapter the non-traditionalist reading of the overriding objective and its theory of justice has been examined. It can seen from both Woolf Reports, the structural and procedural changes they effected to the justice system, and through an examination of the overriding objective itself and the manner in which it has been interpreted by a distinct line of Court of Appeal authorities that have focused on its emphasis on the need to take account of the rights of all court users to secure effective access to justice where decisions are taken in particular cases. The case for downgrading the RSC's commitment to securing substantive justice has been made, so that, despite Lord Woolf maintaining that the 'overriding objective is that the courts should do justice', what it meant was something different.[128] Just as for Bentham, for whom justice meant utility, for the Woolf Reforms, which adopted a theory of justice structured in the same way as his utilitarian theory, justice was no longer synonymous with securing substantive justice.

Justice was to be proportionate. It was no longer to be pursued at all or any cost, as was the case under the RSC. It was to be achieved through seeking substantive justice subject to limits. First, it was not to be pursued

---

[128] *Clarkson v. Gilbert (Rights of Audience)* [2000] 2 FLR 839 at [17].

if to do so, economically and efficiently, would give rise to too great a cost
to the individual litigants. It was not to be pursued if to do so would be
disproportionate as between the immediate parties to litigation. Secondly,
it was not to be pursued where its achievement would give rise to too
great a cost to the justice system as a whole and its ability to provide an
equitable distribution of the justice system's limited resources to all court
users. It was not to be pursued if to do so was disproportionate as
between the immediate parties to litigation and litigants as a whole. As
the Supreme Court of Canada has been said to have described it, substantive justice was to be limited by the need to secure both individual
and collective proportionality.[129] These limitations were incorporated
into Woolf's theory through its commitment to two particular aspects
of procedural justice: equality and proportionality. Through incorporating these considerations, as well as those of procedural economy,
efficiency and expedition, Woolf's new theory of justice is one that can,
in the wider public interest, require claims that could otherwise secure
substantive justice at minimal cost and time, be denied a judgment on the
substantive merits. As for Bentham's theory of justice, it could do so,
when to permit a claim to continue to trial and judgment would infringe
a wider policy aim than securing substantive justice, even if ordinarily the
primary means by which that wider aim was realised was through
achieving substantive justice. Unlike the RSC's theory of justice, Woolf's
new theory required the court in certain circumstances, where it could
justifiably be said that individual or collective proportionality might be
infringed so as to undermine equitable resource allocation, to consider
'... whether the overriding objective of dealing with this case justly calls
for [the court] to bring ... proceedings to an end ....'.[130] It was a theory
that required the court, as Waller LJ put it in *Worldwide Corporation*, to
do 'justice to all litigants' rather than simply justice in the individual
case.[131] It was also, for the same reason, a theory that justified a relative
reduction in the commitment to substantive justice. In some cases and
classes of case, the system could, consistently with the new theory and the
overriding objective, reduce the courts' ability to determine true fact and
apply it to right law. By rationing access to procedure, by managing
cases and allocating them to procedural case tracks that limited use of

---

[129] *Marcotte c. Longueil(ville)*; see Chapter 7, n. 101.
[130] *Flaxman-Binns* v. *Lincolnshire County Council* (Practice Note) [2004] 1 WLR 2232 at
[41].
[131] CA 2 December 1998, unreported; *Vinos* v. *Marks & Spencer* [2001] 3 All ER 784 at [26].

procedural mechanisms that facilitated fact-finding and legal argument, the court could properly reduce the prospect that substantive justice would be achieved. Procedure would become proportionate to the value and nature of a claim. In doing so, there could justifiably be a reduction in the quality of substantive justice. That this could properly occur would, however, be justified through the new theory's elevation of the principles of procedural justice to substantive justice's equal in the pursuit of the wider public policy aim of securing equitable access to justice for all. That was the theory. As with any new theory, as the traditionalist view of the overriding objective shows, its implementation was not straightforward, nor was it successful. Its articulation in the Woolf Reports, and authorities, such as those that attempted to lay to rest the *Tildesley* and the RSC's theory of justice which it gave life to show, was not enough to fully establish it. Articulation needs to be followed by understanding and effective implementation.

PART III

Introduction: Implementation

Over the last decade there have been mounting concerns about the costs of civil justice.[1]

The Woolf Reforms were introduced on 26 April 1999. By 3 November 2008, when Sir Rupert Jackson was appointed to carry out another fundamental review of litigation costs, they were officially deemed a failure.[2] Just as Zander and others had predicted, they had apparently failed to cure the crisis in civil justice.[3] Litigation was as expensive as ever, if not more so. On the face of it, nothing had changed. Reform had been tried. It had failed again. Yet more reform was, once again, necessary. The Jackson Review's findings were, however, telling. The post-Woolf crisis in civil justice had been both overstated and had a unique and clearly identifiable cause. In the first instance it was apparent, and this has neither been widely accepted nor understood, that the Review concluded that in the vast majority of cases there was no evidence to support the claim that there was a continuing, systemic costs crisis.[4] The Review described the actual position in these terms:

---

[1] R. Jackson, (May 2009) Vol. I at 2.   [2] Ibid.

[3] M. Zander, 'Why Woolf's Reforms Should be Rejected', in A. Zuckerman and R. Cranston (eds), *Reform of Civil Procedure: Essays on 'Access to Justice'* (Clarendon Press, 1995); M. Zander, 'The Woolf Reforms: What's the Verdict?', in D. Dwyer (ed.), *The Civil Procedure Rules Ten Years On* (Oxford University Press, 2009) at 342: 'the main problems of cost, delay and complexity remain either much the same or worse than when the reforms were introduced'. Cook, 'A Simple Solution to the Ludicrous Lottery of Litigation Costs', *The Times* (26 February 2002), cited in M. Zander, 'Will the Revolution in the Funding of Civil Litigation in England eventually lead to Contingency Fees?' 52 (2002) *DePaul Law Review* 259 at 290; R. Jackson, (May 2009) Vol. I at 2.

[4] A. Zuckerman, 'The Jackson Final Report – Plastering over the Cracks to Shore Up a Dysfunctional System' 3 (2010) *CJQ* 263; J. Sorabji, 'Prospects for Proportionality: Jackson Implementation' 32 (2012) *CJQ* 213, 227.

A fair overall summary of civil litigation in 2007 may run as follows: approximately 2.1 million civil cases were launched, of which at least 95% were brought in the county courts. *Approximately 90% of all civil cases were concluded without any prolonged contest and at costs proportionate to the issues at stake.* The remaining 10% of cases were contested (whether or not settled before trial) and potentially gave rise to significant costs liabilities.[5]

The costs crisis that the Woolf Reforms had seemingly failed to cure existed in no more than ten per cent of all civil claims. There was no general crisis. Just as significantly, the cause of excess cost in the ten per cent was identified as arising from the abolition of legal aid for personal injury claims and the consequent reform of conditional fee agreements made via 1999's Access to Justice Act. As Sir Rupert Jackson explained it, 'the CFA regime [was] the largest single cause of disproportionate costs'.[6] The continuing crisis was in reality, then, one predominantly caused by litigation funding reforms that arose independently of the Woolf Reforms. It would accordingly be eliminated by reforms to those provisions.[7] The Jackson Review thus proposed fundamental reform of the CFA and wider litigation-funding regime. Those reforms were broadly accepted and implemented via the Legal Aid, Sentencing and Punishment of Offenders Act 2012.

This is not to say that the Woolf Reforms had been an unalloyed success. The CFA regime may have been the primary cause of the continuing costs crisis, but it was not the only one. A number of discrete aspects of the CPR were properly identified as being in need of remedial work, e.g. disclosure, the use of witness statements, expert evidence. The Woolf Reforms to these and other areas had not gone far enough. They remained a significant cause of excess litigation cost. In order to properly implement proportionality, and secure the equitable distribution of the justice system's resources across all court users, further reform of those and other aspects of procedure were to be effected.[8] However, the most significant area where problems were identified was case management, the vehicle through which Woolf's new theory of justice ought to have

---

[5] R. Jackson (May 2009) Vol. I at 53. Emphasis added.

[6] R. Jackson, 'The Review of Civil Litigation Costs in England and Wales', in G. Meggitt (ed.), *Civil Justice Reform – What has it achieved?* (Sweet & Maxwell, 2010) at 137.

[7] R. Jackson (December 2009) at 71–134; Legal Aid, Sentencing and Punishment of Offenders Act 2012, part 2.

[8] For an outline of the reforms as enacted in these areas, see S. Sime and D. French, *Blackstone's Guide to The Civil Justice Reforms 2013* (Oxford University Press, 2013).

been implemented. The courts had failed to utilise it properly and it had not realised the improvements the Woolf Reforms anticipated. At a prosaic level, this ought to have been anticipated. Case management, notwithstanding the early attempt to implement it through the Practice Direction on Case Management (1995), as Zander noted, was a new skill.[9] It would take time to learn and then to be applied consistently with the overriding objective's requirements.[10] The central failing of case management post-1999 was that the courts had failed to eradicate the previous lax approach to rule compliance and the liberal approach to procedural default that had characterised the RSC.[11] A new means of managing litigation had been introduced, but the process of management had not in fact changed. All that had in reality changed was that the court now, through primarily failing to enforce compliance with procedural obligations, managed litigation in the same way that in Woolf's view lawyers had prior to 1999, i.e. in a laissez-faire way. This ought to have been unsurprising for a number of reasons.

First, for a stricter approach to rule compliance and relief from sanction to take hold, it would have to have been clearly accepted that the overriding objective was no longer, as it was under the RSC, to do substantive justice. The overriding objective would have had to be understood for what it actually was: the expression of a new theory of justice. That the Court of Appeal, in those cases highlighted in Chapter 5, had given it a traditionalist interpretation, made that practically impossible to achieve, notwithstanding the line of authority detailed in Chapter 7. Secondly, and compounding the problem caused by the traditionalists, some authorities went further than the traditionalists. They recognised the overriding objective as it was intended to be and simply rejected the idea that it could properly set out a commitment that was no longer committed to the RSC's theory. For those who took the rejectionist line, the only proper way to approach case management was to apply it so as to achieve substantive justice. They took the approach favoured by the pre-existing common law overriding objectives and by Millett LJ in *Gale*. That this would be the case for some members of the judiciary ought to have been expected. Zander predicted in 1997 that a rejectionist approach would arise. As he put it, forty years of experience of case

---

[9] Practice Direction (Case Management) [1995] 1 WLR 262.
[10] M. Zander, 'The Woolf Report: Forwards or Backwards for the New Lord Chancellor?' 16 (1997) *CJQ* 20 at 11.
[11] *Fred Perry (Holdings) Ltd* v. *Brands Plaza Trading Ltd* [2012] EWCA 224 at [1].

management in the United States demonstrated that where the judiciary were required to manage cases in a way that privileged efficiency and economy over justice, the former would be given precedence. They would reject the attempt to alter the status quo and would either tacitly or actively reject the idea that substantive justice should not be given precedence.[12] The consequence of this approach in the United States was that case management did not produce cost savings.[13] It did not matter who managed the proceedings, party or court: they were being managed to the same traditional purpose. As long as this remained, and remains, the case, the experience seen in the United States would be replicated in England. Thirdly, even in those who accepted that a new theory of justice had been put in place, it takes time to properly effect cultural change, as the nineteenth-century reforms so clearly demonstrate. Fundamental reform takes time and concerted effort.[14] It is not an overnight phenomenon. The short period from 1999 to 2009 was simply not long enough to properly implement the new approach to litigation required by the overriding objective's introduction, nor was sufficiently concerted effort put into the task of doing so. Finally, by the time the Woolf Reforms were implemented, the RSC had been in place for 126 years. The theory of justice that underpinned it had long since ceased to be a new approach to doing justice. It was the established paradigm, and it was one that intuitively expressed what was described by one of the rejectionist authorities as a timeless and universal principle of justice: securing substantive justice between litigants. At an intuitive level which links back to Zander's comment regarding case management's failure in the United States, the suggestion that the court should no longer give precedence to securing substantive justice simply appears to be a denial of the very essence of what it means to be a court of justice. It was one thing for Lord Devlin, and Lord Woolf, to suggest that only an idealist would cavil at an approach that was anything but committed to achieving substantive justice at any cost. It is another thing entirely to replace that ideal with something less than individualised substantive justice, not least

---

[12] Zander, 'The Woolf Report' at 11.

[13] J. Leubsdorf, 'The Myth of Civil Procedure Reform', in A. Zuckerman (ed.), *Civil Justice in Crisis: Comparative Perspectives of Civil Procedure* (Oxford University Press, 1999) at 65.

[14] Zander, 'The Woolf Report' at 11: 'profound changes of culture are extremely difficult to achieve and changes of legal culture especially so'.

when the replacement can in some cases require courts to deny litigants an opportunity to achieve it at all.

Taken together, these four factors could not but have led to the failure to properly implement Woolf's new theory through the case management process. This in turn could not but then have had an adverse impact on the operation of the other elements of procedure. If the manner in which case management was to be carried out was not properly understood or implemented, the likelihood that a consistently proportionate approach to disclosure, the use of witness statements, expert evidence, control of the trial process to limit witness evidence and so on would be taken, would be limited. Given this, the Jackson Review's recommendation of further reform to implement a stricter, more effective, approach to procedural compliance, one that was more consistent with the overriding objective, was inevitable as was its recommendation that case management should be bolstered by active costs management.[15] Such consequences were inevitable, because neither the Woolf Reports nor the Court of Appeal had properly explained the new theory's necessary theoretical underpinning. Nor had the latter taken as rigorous an approach as the Victorian Court of Appeal had done in the 1870s–90s to ensure that its explanation of its new approach was accepted and followed by traditionalists and rejectionists alike. If Woolf's new theory and case management were to be implemented effectively from 1999, the same approach that saw substantive justice replace common law formalism in the nineteenth century ought to have been taken. It was not. Implementation of the Jackson Review's recommendations on 1 April 2013 marked the second attempt to introduce Woolf's new approach to justice. The issues surrounding the problems of implementing the overriding objective's commitment to proportionate justice that will need to be addressed to ensure that this second attempt works successfully, are explored in Chapter 7. If these issues are not resolved successfully, there is little prospect that the Woolf Reforms and their refinement through the Jackson Reforms will succeed. They will fail because the paradigm shift that underpins them itself has failed.

---

[15] R. Jackson (December 2009) at 400–20; CPR r. 3.12(1), rr. 3.15–3.19 (post-April 2013).

Problems of proportionate justice

Proportionality... a 'chameleon' principle.[1]

The essence of proportionality is that the ends do not necessarily justify the means. The law facilitates the pursuit of lawful objectives, but only to the extent that those objectives warrant the burdens thereby imposed upon others.[2]

7.1 Introduction

Four fundamental problems undermined the effective implementation of Woolf's new theory of justice. If left unrectified, they will equally undermine the Jackson Reforms, their emphasis on robust case and costs management, and their attempt to build on the Woolf Reforms and finally render litigation cost proportionate.[3] Three of the problems are ones Kuhn would have been well aware of. They are typical of all scientific revolutions. The fourth stems from the nature of Woolf's new theory itself; it is a problem of normal science and is one that Woolf's theory shares with Bentham's. Due to that, it may prove to be the most intractable of the four.

The first problem is one of understanding. In order for any paradigm shift to take effect, what is being proposed has to be understood to be a rejection of the established approach. It has to be recognised as a revolutionary new approach. It ought to be evident from Chapters 4 to 6

---

[1] P. Munzi, cited in C. Piché, 'Figures, Space and Procedural Proportionality' 1 (2012) *IAPL-RIDP* 145 at 148.

[2] R. Jackson (December 2009) at 36.

[3] R. Jackson (May 2009) Vol. II at 416ff. The growth of satellite costs litigation generated by challenges to CFAs was a fifth such reason. It was not, however, a fundamental reason for failure, as it was a contingent matter arising from the nature of the CFA regime introduced in 2000: D. Neuberger, *Docketing: Completing Case Management's Unfinished Revolution* (9th Lecture in the Implementation Programme, Solicitors' Costs Conference, 9 February 2012) at [3] <http://www.judiciary.gov.uk/Resources/JCO/Documents/Speeches/mor-speech-solicitors-cost-conference-lecture-feb2012.pdf>.

that Woolf's new theory has a significant difficulty in this regard. While it has been readily accepted that his reforms, and the overriding objective that synthesised them, required greater weight to be placed on various procedural principles, not least proportionality, there is no one single view as to what that really meant or how it was to be achieved. The traditionalists understand the reforms as drawing no more than greater attention to principles of economy and efficiency that were present under the RSC and which remain subordinate to the predominant aim of securing substantive justice. The revolutionary view is that the reforms effected a Bentham-style reform, which rendered substantive justice subordinate to a wider policy aim and in doing so rendered securing individual justice subject to the need to secure a more distributive form of justice. In a sense, from 1999 to 2013 the English civil justice system experienced the same problem that the common law faced from the 1850s to the 1870s. A new theory was on the books, but it was not properly understood: some judges understood it in the way intended, others carried on as if nothing had happened. The first problem then, that will need to be overcome, is one of understanding. The traditionalist view will need to be laid to rest. In the first part of this chapter the manner in which the Jackson Reforms, and particularly the so-called Mark II overriding objective introduced as a consequence of those reforms, seek to do so is examined.[4]

If the first problem is one of lack of understanding, the second is the opposite. It is a problem of recognition and rejection. It understands that the Woolf Reforms intended to do something revolutionary. It then rejects them on principled grounds. As Kuhn had it, scientific revolutions need to be understood as such and then accepted. If not, they fail and the established paradigm remains in place. This rejectionist approach underpinned a number of decisions, e.g. the House of Lords' decision in *Moy* v. *Pettman Smith*,[5] Millett LJ's decision in *Gale* v. *Superdrug* and the tension between the first instance and Court of Appeal decisions in *Swain-Mason & Others* v. *Mills & Reeve LLP*.[6] It is also exemplified by Woolf-inspired civil justice reforms in Hong Kong. Just as with the first problem, if the new theory is to take hold the principled rejection of it will need to be tackled and laid to rest. The question is how, post-Jackson, this is to be accomplished.

---

[4] J. Dyson, *The Application of the Amendments to the Civil Procedure Rules* (18th Lecture in the Implementation Programme, 22 March 2013) at [7] <http://www.judiciary.gov.uk/Resources/JCO/Documents/Speeches/mr-speech-judicial-college-lecture-2013.pdf>.

[5] *Moy* v. *Pettman Smith (a firm)* [2005] 1 WLR 581.

[6] *Swain-Mason & Others* v. *Mills & Reeve LLP* [2011] 1 WLR 2735.

The third problem is a practical one, which stems from the first two. It is the court's failure to manage cases post-1999 consistently with the new theory's requirements. This failure has, for instance, undermined the court's ability to secure a greater degree of normativity for the rules of procedure than was apparent under the RSC. It is most evident, as Zuckerman has consistently argued, in the failure to secure compliance with procedural obligations.[7] The court has, in his words, demonstrated a 'weakness of will' in this regard. It has failed to take a properly hard line to procedural non-compliance, to relief from sanctions and applications to amend. It has carried on effectively as it did under the RSC.[8] That this was the case from 1999 was, however, inevitable, given the first and second problems of implementation. Those members of the judiciary who took the traditionalist view had no reason to adopt a different approach than was taken under the RSC. They may have, as occurred in the early years of the CPR, emphasised the need to take greater account of the need to secure efficiency, economy and, even proportionality, but substantive justice was still of greater account. The former were merely the means to better secure the latter, and subordinate to it.[9] Those judges who took the rejectionist line would have equally done the same. Ascribing the failure to secure a stricter approach to rule-compliance and a less forgiving attitude to relief from the consequences of default to weakness of will misattributes the nature of the problem. It suggests that the courts understand that they have to take a more hard-headed approach but cannot quite bring themselves to do so. The reality is different, as the use of sanctions for non-compliance with discovery obligations in the United States demonstrates. Since the 1950s, the US Federal Courts have tried and failed to implement a stricter approach to the use of sanctions on at least three occasions. Initial bursts of rigour immediately after reforms were introduced were then followed by a lapse back into a more liberal approach akin to that which Zuckerman has observed and the Jackson Review accepted was the case in England post-Woolf.[10] This problem had nothing to do with

---

[7] R. Jackson (December 2009) at 386–400.

[8] A. Zuckerman, *Weakness of Will – The Exercise of Case Management Discretion under the CPR* (unpublished paper presented at Atlantic Chambers, 24 May 2007); A. Zuckerman, 'The Revised CPR 3.9: a coded message demanding articulation' 32 (2013) *CJQ* 123.

[9] *JSC BTA Bank* v. *Ablyazov* [2012] EWCA Civ 1551 at [65].

[10] M. Rosenberg, 'Sanctions to Effectuate Pre-Trial Discovery' [1958] *Columbia Law Review* 480; D. Piggot, 'Relief from Sanctions and the Overriding Objective' 24 (2005) *CJQ* 104, 117.

weakness of will, however. It stemmed from the fact that the Federal Rules of Procedure's overriding objective was to secure substantive justice.[11] As Rosenberg explained, 'the difficulty with literal adherence to the reach-the-merits philosophy is that it dulls the cutting edge of sanctions intended to enforce compliance with procedural rules.'[12] Sanctions for non-compliance frustrate justice on the merits; judges are reluctant to use them for that reason, and litigants expect discretion to be exercised to enable a merits hearing to take place. The US system was designed, and due to its overriding objective operated, to favour substantive justice. Just as occurred under the RSC, that then undermined any normative value that sanctions for non-compliance might otherwise have had.[13] Attempts to introduce a stricter approach to compliance could not but fail. The system was designed so that it would do so. Substantive justice demanded it. In a similar way, an attempt to introduce proportionality into the Federal Rules' discovery process in 1983 also failed.[14] The intention was to reduce the scope of discovery and its attendant litigation cost and delay. It was frustrated, however, because proportionate discovery does not promote substantive justice as well as an unfettered, merits-tracking approach does. Consequently, the proportionality requirement, as the various attempts to impose a more rigorous approach to the use of the sanctions power, was more honoured in the breach.[15] That it was, was entirely foreseeable. Discovery was subject to proportionality, but proportionality was subject to the Federal Rules' overriding objective just as the sanctions power was. Proportionality could gain no generally applicable normative force because it was inconsistent with, and limited by, the commitment to securing substantive justice. The upshot of this in the United States is the recent realisation that if discovery is to be brought under control, then rule 1 of the Federal Rules needs to be revised; proportionality has to be introduced into it so that it becomes a general principle against which substantive justice has to be balanced, just as it is in Woolf's new theory of justice.[16] The

---

[11] See Chapter 4, n. 11.   [12] Rosenberg, 'Sanctions to Effectuate Pre-Trial Discovery' 480.
[13] See Chapter 2, n. 169.
[14] Federal Rules of Procedure, rule 26; J. Carroll, 'Proportionality in Discovery: A Cautionary Tale' 32 (2010) *Campbell Law Review* 455.
[15] Ibid. 458.
[16] J. Koeltl, 'Progress in the Spirit of Rule 1' 60 (2010) *Duke Law Journal* 537, 542; Institute for the Advancement of the American Legal System, *21st Century Civil Justice System – A Roadmap for Reform* (University of Denver); Institute for the Advancement of the American Legal System, *Pilot Rules Project* (University of Denver), at 2, proposed revised

practical problem evidenced in the United States' Federal Rules was not one of weakness of will, although that no doubted played a part. It was a systemic problem caused by its overriding objective.

The post-Woolf traditionalists and rejectionists hold the same view as was prevalent in the United States. They both, for different reasons, maintain the view that the CPR's aim is the same as the RSC's, and accordingly, of the Federal Rules of Procedure. It is unsurprising, then, that a similar approach to the imposition of sanctions under the CPR has been taken to that applied under the RSC and in the United States and that, for instance, the Woolf Reforms did not bring the costs of disclosure under control.[17] Holding to the same fundamental aim produces the same results. It does so because judicial will is being directed towards securing substantive rather than proportionate justice. The problem is not one of weakness of will, but of misdirected will. Remedying this problem will require a twin-track approach. The first two problems, detailed above, will have to be overcome. The traditionalists will need to be educated and the rejectionist approach laid to rest. The court will then have to take an approach to rule-compliance and relief from sanction consistent with Woolf's new theory, which ought then to develop as 'a coherent principle of practice'.[18] This is unlikely to happen in the absence of a coherent understanding of that principle, which in turn will rest on the need to ensure that Woolf's new theory is accepted as such. Then, and only then, as Kuhn well knew, will the struggle to implement it properly take place. It will not simply have to be a coherent principle, however. It will also have to be capable of practical application, which leads to the fourth problem.

Federal Rules of Procedure rule 1: '1.1 These Rules govern the procedure in all actions that are part of the pilot project. They must be construed and administered to secure the just, timely, efficient, and cost-effective determination of such actions. 1.2. At all times, the court and the parties must address the action in ways designed to assure that the process and the costs are proportionate to the amount in controversy and the complexity and importance of the issues. The factors to be considered by the court in making a proportionality assessment include, without limitation: needs of the case, amount in controversy, parties' resources, and complexity and importance of the issues at stake in the litigation. This proportionality rule is fully applicable to all discovery, including the discovery of electronically stored information.'

[17] R. Jackson (December 2009) at 364ff; R. Jackson, *Controlling the Costs of Disclosure* (7th Lecture in the Implementation Programme) (Lexis Nexis Conference on Avoiding and Resolving Construction Disputes, 24 November 2011) <http://www.judiciary.gov.uk/Resources/JCO/Documents/Speeches/controlling-costs-disclosure.pdf>.

[18] Zuckerman, 'The Revised CPR 3.9' at 138.

The fourth problem is perhaps the most intractable, as it stems from the very nature of Woolf's new theory, and its incorporation of a consequentialism that is also inherent in Bentham's theory. It is the felicific fallacy. Bentham's theory of justice required judges to apply his felicific calculus in assessing the utility value of their decisions.[19] There were two problems with this. The elements of the calculus were open-textured, leaving them open to multiple interpretations. As a consequence, it was simply not possible, in practical terms, to assess the utility value of any action by reference to them. The RSC's theory of justice suffered from no such problems. It had a straightforward, easily understandable predominant aim, in the form of substantive justice. Efficiency and economy were facilitative of that aim. They could not come into conflict with it, nor were they to be balanced against it. Court rules were to be applied so as to secure substantive justice. Where there was procedural non-compliance the court had at heart one question to ask: would exercising its discretion to cure the error enable the claim to progress to a trial and merits-based determination? If yes, then assuming the non-defaulting party could be compensated in costs for the inconvenience and prejudice the defaulting party had caused it, the cure should be administered. If no, or the prejudice to the other party could not be cured, then the cure could not properly be given. The RSC's theory was simple to understand and straightforward to apply. It was also, perhaps most importantly, intuitively right, given its focus on securing substantive justice. As Malcolm Gladwell, the American theorist, might put it given all this: the RSC's theory of justice, unlike Bentham's, was a sticky idea.[20] Once properly explained, it was capable of easily taking hold and of being widely accepted. It is, also, consequently necessarily difficult to shake loose.

Woolf's new theory of justice is more akin to Bentham's theory than the RSC's. It is not a sticky idea. It lacks the explanatory elegance and simplicity of the RSC. It lacks its intuitive validity, given its commitment to proportionality and the idea that justice in the individual case can be sacrificed for the greater good. These problems are compounded by the difficulty in effecting its practical application. Like Bentham's theory, it relies on the application of a number of open-textured concepts, each of which have to be weighed in the balance in order to further a wider public policy objective. It is easy to understand that through

---

[19] See Chapter 3, n. 63.   [20] M. Gladwell, *The Tipping Point* (Abacus, 2000).

the application of true fact to right law, substantive justice is achieved. While differences of opinion can arise as to the level of accuracy in decision-making that is necessary to achieve it, what is to be achieved is still easily understood. The same is not true of the principles of economy, efficiency, expedition and particularly, proportionality. One judge's inefficiency in the management of a claim is another's efficiency; and the same applies for the other principles. Matters have not been helped in this regard by the consistent failure by the courts to give any real guidance on how courts and litigants are to deal with these concepts. Here, as far as proportionality is concerned, the problem is further compounded. It requires courts to consider two questions: one is concerning individual proportionality, the other, its collective aspect. The latter is particularly problematic, as it raises the same question that faced Bentham's utilitarian judges: how are the wider consequences of decisions made in individual cases to be calculated? At what stage, for instance, does the conduct of litigation in a single case reach the point where it becomes disproportionate in so far as other court users are considered? In comparison with the straightforward application of Bramwell LJ's test from *Tildesley*, Neuberger J's reformulation of it in *Charlesworth* in the light of the overriding objective is not.[21] How exactly is the court to apply its reformulated version of the *Tildesley* test to give any real consideration of the consequences of granting relief in any one individual claim to other court users?[22] What exactly is the effect of any single decision; what effect does any one decision have on the ability of all other court users to secure effective access to justice? Just as Bentham's theory foundered, amongst other things, on the problem of utility aggregation, so does Woolf's in so far as assessing proportionality is concerned. The practical question is how to render Woolf's theory of practical application. If it cannot be applied as simply and straightforwardly as the RSC's theory, it is one that will fail either explicitly because it will ultimately be rejected, or implicitly, as in practice while lip service will be paid to it the traditionalist interpretation of it and the overriding objective will be adopted and applied.

This chapter examines how the four problems of implementation could be resolved in some instances through the effective application of

---

[21] See Chapter 6, n. 42.

[22] A. Higgins, 'The Costs of Case Management: what should be done post-Jackson?' 29 (2010) *CJQ* 317, 333: 'How much resources are too much for the system to bear as opposed to the parties to the dispute?'

the Jackson Reforms, in others by means suggested by reforms in other jurisdictions, and in others again, by novel means.

7.2 The Mark II overriding objective: educating the traditionalists

The first problem that must be tackled if the new theory of justice is to properly take hold post-Jackson is one of understanding. Education is needed. On 1 April 2013, the CPR's overriding objective was revised for the first time.[23] This reform was unheralded. It had neither been recommended in the Jackson Review, nor had it been suggested as being necessary during the Jackson Implementation Lectures.[24] The revision was intended to be educative. It was to emphasise the importance of individual and collective proportionality. This was to be achieved through the introduction of an express reference to proportionate cost into CPR r. 1.1(1), as well as a new sub-clause in CPR r. 1.1(2) that emphasised the need to enforce rule-compliance, such that it would specify that:

> (1) These Rules are a new procedural code with the overriding objective of enabling the court to deal with cases justly *and at proportionate cost.*
>
> (2) Dealing with a case justly *and at proportionate cost* includes, so far as is practicable
>
> . . .
>
> *(f) enforcing compliance with rules, practice directions and orders.*[25]

In one sense, the revision was unnecessary. The idea that dealing with cases justly did not already include a reference to proportionate cost and rule-compliance is one that stands no scrutiny. The Woolf Reports went out of their way to emphasise how the overriding objective expressed a commitment to proportionality, and particularly proportionate cost: that, amongst other things, was exactly what to deal with cases justly and CPR r. 1.2(c)(i) required.[26] Equally, while the original version of the overriding objective had not made it explicit that enforcing compliance with procedural obligations was an aspect of dealing with

---

[23] SI 262/2013.

[24] The series of lectures given by Sir Rupert Jackson and other judges aimed at explaining the nature of the Jackson Reforms <http://www.judiciary.gov.uk/publications-and-reports/review-of-civil-litigation-costs/lectures/?wbc_purpose=Basic&WBCMODE=PresentationUn.rss>.

[25] Post-April 2013 CPR 1, revisions in italics.

[26] CPR r. 1.1(2)(c), both pre- and post-April 2013.

cases justly, it should have been obvious that it was.[27] Securing effective rule-compliance is the optimum means through which a rationed system, with limited resources, can ensure that all those who need to use it are afforded a fair and equitable share of such resources. The reforms' necessity was, however, properly acknowledged when the rationale lying behind them was explained. The addition of explicit references to proportionate cost and rule-compliance was intended to render that which was already present in the overriding objective explicit. The reform was not an exercise in superfluity, but in fact served an unavoidable purpose: to launch a second attempt at implementing Woolf's new approach through explaining the nature of the reform they were intended to effect.[28] It was, as such, an acknowledgement of the fact that the nature of the overriding objective and its practical application had not been properly appreciated.[29] It thus had an educative role, one that would show that the traditionalist view of the overriding object-ive was flawed.

The initial reason given why the revisions were made was that they were intended to emphasise that the overriding objective was intended to secure an equitable distribution of the justice system's resources across all court users. Rather than explain this, though, by reference to promot-ing access to justice for all court users, as had previously been done by reference to CPR r. 1.1(2)(e) and its imprecation to take account of the needs of all court users when dealing with cases justly, a different tack was taken.[30] It was put in terms of the 'wider public interest', which was explained in the following way:

> Doing the proper administration of justice goes beyond the immediate parties to litigation. It requires the court to consider the needs of all litigants, all court-users. This idea finds expression in the overriding objective ... We have a managed system. That system must be managed for the needs of all litigants. The new emphasis in the overriding objective on proportionate cost and compliance is intended to make sure the wider public interest remains at the forefront of all our minds.[31]

---

[27] H. Woolf (1995) at 216.
[28] Dyson, *The Application of the Amendments to the Civil Procedure Rules* at [2]–[18].
[29] Zuckerman, 'The Revised CPR 3.9'.
[30] D. Neuberger, 'A New Approach to Civil Justice: from Woolf to Jackson', in *Civil Justice Reform – What has it achieved?* (Meggitt, ed.) (Sweet & Maxwell, 2010) 11, 15–16.
[31] Dyson, *The Application of the Amendments to the Civil Procedure Rules* at [17]–[18].

The overriding objective, as the Woolf Reports intended, articulated a commitment to securing equitable access to justice.[32] The reforms were intended to make this clearer. They did so first of all by demonstrating that the traditionalists' claim that substantive justice was in some sense outwith and superior to the overriding objective was wrong. Not only was the point made that dealing with cases justly did not mean securing substantive justice,[33] but the wider point that the relationship between substantive justice and procedure had changed as a consequence of the Woolf Reforms was reiterated. While this was not explained in the terms used in the Interim Report. i.e. that substantive justice was to be equal to procedural justice, it was put in clear terms.[34] The overriding objective, now more clearly given the Mark II revisions, set out how:

> doing justice was not something distinct from, and superior to, the overriding objective. Doing justice in each set of proceedings is to ensure that proceedings are dealt with justly and at proportionate cost. Justice in the individual case is now only achievable through the proper application of the CPR consistently with the overriding objective.[35]

The idea that CPR r. 1.1 somehow represented a commitment to substantive justice and the procedural aims set out in CPR r. 1.2 were subordinate to it, a point that is central to the traditionalist account, was simply wrong.[36] Individual justice was, it was clear, subject to the needs of distributive justice. In addition to this, the consequence of the introduction of the new wider public policy aim and its facilitator, proportionality, was explained in terms that Bentham would readily have understood. The emphasis on rule-compliance in the newly introduced CPR r. 1.1(2)(f) served a specific purpose. It and the renewed emphasis on taking a strict approach to rule-compliance was intended to ensure that litigation was conducted proportionately. This had two aspects. As the Woolf Reports intended, it was to ensure that parties did not expend a more than proportionate amount of their own resources. It was to give effect to individual proportionality. It was also intended to secure the

---

[32] See Chapters 5 and 6.

[33] Dyson, *The Application of the Amendments to the Civil Procedure Rules* at [15]: 'Dealing with a case justly does not simply mean ensuring that a decision is reached on the merits. It is a mistake to assume that it does.'

[34] H. Woolf (1995) at 216.

[35] Dyson, *The Application of the Amendments to the Civil Procedure Rules* at [26]; as endorsed and approved by the Court of Appeal in *Mitchell* v. *News Group Newspapers Ltd* [2013] EWCA Civ 1537 at [38]–[39].

[36] See Chapter 4, nn. 31–2.

wider public interest by ensuring that the pursuit of substantive justice in individual cases did not consume more than a proportionate amount of the court's resources.[37] It was to give effect to collective proportionality. The Mark II overriding objective and rule-compliance served 'the wider public interest of ensuring that other litigants can obtain justice efficiently and proportionately, and that the court enables them to do so'.[38]

While the Mark II overriding objective was not explained in terms of being drafted to guide the justice system's operation so as to secure equitable access to justice for all, the structure and approach is apparent. In particular, the replacement of the Woolf Reports' reference to access to justice by reference to the wider public interest is an important advance. It removes the possibility of potential ambiguity that reference to access to justice carried with it. In one sense it is a more honest expression because it eschews that ambiguity, and the possibility that it could be interpreted as saying the justice system is still dedicated to the RSC's theory and substantive justice. As such, it deals with the criticism that Issacharoff made of the Woolf Reforms: that they avoided telling the truth about the reforms' consequences.[39] By removing the potential ambiguity over what access to justice means, reference to the wider public interest clarifies the fact that the old theory no longer holds. The new theory now takes shape as one where the justice system fulfils its constitutional duty of vindicating rights through acting in the wider public interest. The justice system is not to continue with its fallacy of composition. It is now more clear to see that securing the rule of law through rights vindication arises through securing all court-users with an equitable allocation of the system's resources. Through that the court fulfils its constitutional duty, not through taking a myopic view focused solely on the immediate claim before it at any one time.

---

[37] J. Sorabji, 'The Road to New Street Station: fact, fiction and the overriding objective' [2012] *EBLR* 1–77.

[38] Dyson, *The Application of the Amendments to the Civil Procedure Rules* at 27, and see [31]: 'the revisions to both the overriding objective and rule 3.9 are designed to ensure that the courts, at all levels, take a more robust approach to ensuring that proceedings are managed so that no more than proportionate costs are incurred by the parties to those proceedings. They do so because proceedings must be managed in the public interest to ensure that individual parties do not expend more than is proportionate on their own claims; but as importantly, that they do not, through being permitted to expend more than a proportionate amount of the court's time and resources, impinge on the rights of other litigants to have fair access to the courts...'

[39] See Chapter 6, n. 128.

One note of caution, however, needs to be struck. If history teaches nothing else, as ought to be clear by now, it is that in the field of civil justice reform the transition from one theory of justice to another is never easy. The risk is always present that the new will be stifled by the old. The Mark II overriding objective leaves itself open to such a risk, as it could, in principle, still be interpreted along traditionalist lines. It does so because of the way in which explicit reference to proportionate cost was introduced into CPR r. 1.1. Rather than introducing it as part of an obviously composite concept through drafting, such as 'These Rules are a new procedural code with the overriding objective of enabling the court to deal with cases justly, *which includes* at proportionate cost', which would make it clear that the latter was, as it is, an aspect of dealing with cases justly, the Civil Procedure Rule Committee took a different approach. In order to emphasise the previously missed importance of securing proportionate cost as an aspect of the overriding objective, it was added to CPR r. 1.1 as an additional criterion. By taking the latter rather than the former approach, it might be said that the overriding objective is a binary objective, with two potentially conflicting aims: dealing with cases justly and dealing with them at proportionate cost. Here the traditionalist view that dealing with cases justly was no more than an express reference to securing substantive justice could find a new lease of life. It could be said that prior to the revision, dealing with cases justly simply made explicit the RSC's overriding objective. It was thus necessary to introduce a reference to proportionate cost because it was not there previously. Rather than make explicit what was implicit, the revision, the traditionalists might suggest, introduced a novel addition to the rule. This line of argument could then take a further step, one that would seek to reassert the traditionalists' approach to the relationship between substantive justice and principles of procedural justice contained within the overriding objective. As the revision, it could be said, introduced a second commitment into the overriding objective, the question would arise as to which of the two was the predominant criterion and which must give way when they, as inevitably they must, came into conflict? The answer the traditionalists' would then give to their question is patent: substantive justice, in the guise of dealing with cases justly, must take precedence over proportionate cost. If such a reading of the Mark II overriding objective were to take hold, it would be disastrous. Nothing would change; claims would continue to be managed without any real reference to individual proportionality or to the wider public interest. Faced with questions whether to grant relief from sanctions or whether to take decisions that emphasised the need to comply with procedural obligations, courts would revert to the *Tildesley* approach. The primary aim of the overriding objective would once more be treated as if it were to secure substantive justice. Just as the Court of Appeal held economy and efficiency to be of little account in *Sayers* when they conflicted with the need to secure that aim, the need to secure proportionate cost would be set aside. It would be of little account. Like economy and efficiency, it would be an aspiration to guide the civil process, but not an aim that could be relied upon to undermine or limit substantive justice.

The prospect that a traditionalist reading of the Mark II overriding objective might take hold ought to have been minimised, however, by the way in which its rationale was explained by Lord Dyson MR as a reform that simply made explicit something that was implicit to the overriding objective as originally drafted. The revision to CPR r. 1.1(1) thus did not introduce a new, second criterion, but simply emphasised a specific aspect of what it meant to deal with cases justly. It also ought to have been minimised as a consequence of a weakness in the traditionalist account and its reliance on the RSC's theory of justice. The risk remains, nevertheless. It is one that the Jackson Reforms, if they are to secure the aim that was set them, will need to guard against.[40] How this could be done effectively, not least through drawing out the fallacy at the heart of the RSC's theory, is an issue that is discussed in what follows concerning how the rejectionists' objection to Woolf's new theory (not least because the rejectionist and traditionalist accounts have a shared premise: that the RSC lives on) can be laid to rest.

Reform to the wording of the overriding objective and explaining its rationale in an extra-curial lecture on its own, even if it was one of the series of explanatory lectures intended to explain the nature of the Jackson Reforms ahead of their implementation, and one that was subsequently endorsed by the Court of Appeal in *Mitchell* v. *News Group Newspapers Ltd*[41] is, on its own, unlikely to produce the desired effect. It is a starting point, and a necessary one, to educating the traditionalists. The overriding objective's introduction in 1999 and the degree of explanation that was given prior to its introduction amounted to the same starting point. On its own, the pre-1999 explanatory effort was not sufficient to secure a proper understanding of the fact that a new theory

---

[40] See Introduction, n. 4.   [41] [2013] EWCA Civ 1537.

of justice had been introduced. It did not stop a traditionalist interpretation arising. While there is perhaps less chance of history repeating itself
when the revisions made are expressly said to emphasise a cultural
change in approach to litigation and the operation of the justice system,
there remains a chance, and undoubtedly a strong one, that more will be
needed. It is one thing for a ringing endorsement of a new approach to be
given;[42] it is another for it to be heeded, and another still, if it is heeded,
for it then to become the norm. There will need to be practical application of the new approach. There will therefore need to be a proper answer
to the third of the four problems of effective implementation.

7.3   The rejectionist approach: substantive justice an idea with a universal, timeless validity

The traditionalists failed to appreciate that a paradigm shift in justice had
occurred and carried on as if the RSC was still place; hence the need for
an educative effort. The second problem of implementation does not,
however, arise from a misunderstanding. On the contrary, it arises
because the overriding objective is understood properly and then rejected
on principled grounds. The principled objection is, as Conrad Dehn QC
put it, that the Woolf Reforms were an attempt to ensure that 'the
ascertainment of truth and achieving justice is no longer the overriding
objective of the system'.[43] That aim is viewed as improper, and as a
consequence, is to be rejected. The educative role played by the Mark II
overriding objective is irrelevant to such a rejectionist view. It simply
makes clear that which was already obvious to those who held that view.
If the rejectionist view is to be tackled successfully following the Jackson
Reforms' introduction, something more than education will be
required.[44] In order to properly tackle the rejectionists' approach it is

---

[42] A point that had, ironically, previously been acknowledged by the Evershed Committee in
1953, when it noted how it realised that 'exhortations will be likely to fail of their best
effect without the impetus of some practical suggestion': (Cmd 8878, 1953) at 9. Education is not enough.

[43] See C. Dehn, 'The Woolf Report: Against the Public Interest?', in A. Zuckerman and
R. Cranston, *Reform of Civil Procedure – Essays on 'Access to Justice'* (Clarendon Press,
1995) at 167; *Civil Justice Reform Final Report* (Chief Justice's Working Party on Civil
Justice Reform, Hong Kong Special Administrative Region, People's Republic of China,
2004) at 46–57; also see *Report of the Scottish Civil Courts Review* (2009) Vol. I at 200.

[44] J. Sorabji, 'Late Amendment and Jackson's Commitment to Woolf: Another attempt to
implement a new approach to civil justice' 31 (2012) *CJQ* 393, 411.

first necessary to gain an understanding of its nature. This can be fleshed out through an examination of the way that the Woolf Reforms have been understood internationally, and in a number of English authorities, both pre-1999 and post-1999. The former flesh out the nature of the objection, while the latter illustrate why, when combined with a traditionalist view of the reforms, there have been problems in embedding Woolf's new theory into English civil justice.

Turning first to the international reception of the Woolf Reforms. In a number of jurisdictions, not least within Canada and Australia, they have been understood as effecting a radical change to the nature of justice and have inspired similar reforms.[45] They have been understood correctly and embraced on those terms. In Hong Kong, however, the reforms were received differently. Shortly after the Woolf Reforms were introduced in England, Hong Kong embarked upon a similar reform exercise, during the course of which the question was raised whether a Woolf-style overriding objective ought to be introduced into Hong Kong's civil procedure rules.[46] It rejected such an innovation. Rather than an overriding objective, it recommended the introduction of 'underlying objectives', which, while similar to the individual elements of the CPR's overriding objective, would play a markedly different role. Reform would simply make explicit principles, such as procedural economy and efficiency, which previously had been implicit to and had informed the development of individual rules of court. In other words, a traditional common law overriding objective was to be introduced. Moreover, the reforms were not to introduce any commitment to proportionality akin to that which the CPR's overriding objective contained. That was rejected as too uncertain in scope and application.[47] All that was needed was 'a reminder that commonsense [*sic.*] notions of reasonableness and a sense of proportion should inform' judicial discretion; common sense notions that equally had informed rule 1 of the US Federal Rules of

---

[45] E.g., *Civil Justice Reform Project: Summary of Findings & Recommendations* (Attorney General's Office, Ontario, Canada) <http://www.attorneygeneral.jus.gov.on.ca/english/about/pubs/cjrp/>; *Civil Justice Review Report* (Victorian Law Commission Report, Victoria, Australia, March 2008) <http://www.lawreform.vic.gov.au/wps/wcm/connect/Law±Reform/resources/file/eb408e074f4eca1/VLRC%20Civil%20Justice%20Review%20-%20Report.pdf>.

[46] For a discussion, see G. Meggitt and F. Aslam, 'Civil Justice Reform in Hong Kong – A Critical Appraisal' 28 (2009) *CJQ* 111.

[47] Hong Kong Review (Final) at 48; Meggitt and Aslam, 'Civil Justice Reform in Hong Kong – A Critical Appraisal' at 120–2.

Procedure and were subordinate to the aim of securing substantive justice.[48] The Hong Kong Review took the approach the traditionalists in England understood the Woolf Reforms to have taken. The new underlying objectives were simply there to help 'manage rather than replace the adversarial system'.[49] They were to render the court process more efficient and effective in its pursuit of substantive justice. It was business as usual: an exercise in normal science.

In reaching the conclusion it did though, the Hong Kong Review held a very different view from the traditionalists of the Woolf Reports' intentions and the CPR's overriding objective's meaning. It noted, rightly, that the overriding objective was intended to introduce a 'new methodology' into the English civil justice system, i.e. a new approach or theory of justice.[50] It recognised the real nature of the enterprise and it rejected it. It did so for two reasons. First, it drew the conclusion that the CPR's overriding objective was too open-textured and gave rise to too great, and uncertain, a degree of judicial discretion. It thus posed too great a risk, if implemented of giving rise to palm tree justice and erratic judicial decision-making.[51] The same concerns had been expressed in England at the time the overriding objective was introduced, but had come to nothing.[52] Secondly, and more significantly, the Review concluded the new methodology had to be rejected because it did not maintain a commitment to securing substantive justice, and as such, it '... might divert the court from deciding cases in accordance with their substantive merits'.[53] It recognised that Woolf's new theory, expressed in the overriding objective, was one that no longer gave pre-eminence to securing substantive justice in particular cases and could, in some cases, legitimately see litigants denied its achievement. The Review drew the very conclusion regarding the Woolf Reports' aim as Conrad Dehn QC had done in 1995. It rejected Woolf's new approach encapsulated in the overriding objective because it took the view that it rejected the idea that

---

[48] Hong Kong Review (Final) at 54; Meggitt and Aslam, 'Civil Justice Reform in Hong Kong – A Critical Appraisal' at 120–2.

[49] Ibid. at 121.

[50] Ibid. at 118; *Chief Justice's Working Party On Civil Justice Reform, Civil Justice Reform – Interim Report and Consultative Paper* (2002) at 89.

[51] Hong Kong Review (Final) at 46 and 48–9, cf. *Civil Procedure 2009* (M. Waller, ed.) (Sweet & Maxwell) Vol. I at 1.3.2; D. Dwyer, 'What is the Meaning of CPR r 1.1(1)?' in D. Dwyer (ed.), *Civil Procedure Rules Ten Years On* (Oxford University Press, 2009).

[52] *Civil Procedure 2013* (R. Jackson, ed.) (Sweet & Maxwell) Vol. II at 11.7.

[53] Hong Kong Review (Final) at 46 and 48–9.

courts should aim at anything other than securing justice.[54] In order to ensure that its new underlying objectives could not be interpreted or applied in such a way, the Review recommended that a clear commitment to securing substantive justice had to be included in the rules. The underlying objectives were then to be made subordinate to it. That rule was introduced when the Hong Kong Reforms came into force in 2008. It states that 'the primary aim of case management [is] to secure the just resolution of the parties' dispute in accordance with their substantive rights'.[55] The Review thus required, and secured, the introduction of a rule that stood outside and above the underlying objectives; a rule which the traditionalists understood implicitly to stand above the CPR's overriding objective and which its Mark II version is intended to make clear is not the case.

The Hong Kong Review took a principled stand against Woolf's new theory. It rightly understood its intention, but held that limits could not properly be placed on the aim of securing substantive justice in particular cases. A similar principled rejection, which rests on the belief that it cannot be correct to deny substantive justice to litigants on grounds of proportionality, has unfortunately also been evidenced in England. The first indication of such a principled rejection of the new theory of justice arose shortly prior to the CPR's introduction in *Gale* v. *Superdrug*. As discussed in Chapter 6, in that case Millett LJ set out how the policy objective of achieving substantive justice could not simply be 'brushed aside on the ground that [it] was laid down a century ago or [failed] to recognise the exigencies of the modern civil justice system'.[56] On the contrary, it was 'a fundamental assessment of the functions of a court of justice which [had] a universal and timeless validity'.[57] Millett LJ's rejection of any suggestion that the aim of doing substantive justice could in some way be sacrificed on the altar of economy, efficiency or proportionality might have been no more than an historical curiosity; a last cry of the *ancien regime* on the eve of revolution. At the least, it ought to have been consigned to history, given the line of post-CPR Court of Appeal

---

[54] See n. 40 above.

[55] Hong Kong Review (Final) at 50 and 56–7, see Order 1A(2) of the Rules of the High Court (Amendment) Rules 2008 (Hong Kong), 'In giving effect to the underlying objectives of these rules, the Court shall always recognize that the primary aim in exercising the powers of the Court is to secure the just resolution of disputes in accordance with the substantive rights of the parties.'

[56] [1996] 1 WLR 1889.   [57] Ibid.

authorities that rejected it.[58] The rejectionist line did not, however, die with *Gale*. Following the Court of Appeal authorities that ended with *Finken*, and which were also discussed in Chapter 6, the House of Lords supported it in one of its few forays into the development of civil procedure in *Moy* v. *Pettman Smith (a firm)*.[59] In *Moy*, the Lords allowed an appeal from the Court of Appeal and, in doing so, criticised an approach to case management by a district judge which was entirely consistent with that articulated in the *Worldwide Corporation* to *Finken* line of Court of Appeal authorities and the new philosophy of justice Lords Hope and Hobhouse adverted to in *Three Rivers*.[60] Giving the principal judgment, Lord Carswell criticised the district judge for placing too great a weight on efficiency and economy and too little on securing truth.[61] The judge had erred because the former two aims had been relied upon to frustrate the court's real aim of securing substantive justice. According to Lord Carswell, the *Tildesley* test ought to have governed the case management decision.[62] The RSC's theory of justice lived on and the attempt to fetter or limit it was to be brushed aside. The decision has, unsurprisingly, been subject to criticism on a number of grounds.[63] It failed, for instance, to refer to the overriding objective. It failed to consider any of the Court of Appeal authorities that dealt with the nature of the test to be applied to case management decisions where, as in the immediate case, there had been a failure to comply with procedural obligations. Moreover, it failed, as Zuckerman has rightly pointed out, to consider the effect the case management decision would have had on the 'administration of justice as a whole'.[64] It thereby failed to consider the distributive nature of justice that is central to the Woolf Reforms by focusing its attention, as the RSC's theory required, solely on questions of individual justice. It was a decision that took no account of the need for the administration of justice to be a rationed and rationale system if it was to secure the rule of law. It simply proceeded on the basis that the right approach, and the one the district judge ought to have taken, was the one Millett LJ described as of universal and timeless validity: that substantive justice was the

[58] See the discussion of *Worldwide Corporation* authorities in Chapter 6; and see Chapter 5, n. 4.
[59] [2005] 1 WLR 581.   [60] [2003] 2 AC 1 at [106] and [153].
[61] [2005] 1 WLR 581 at [42].   [62] Ibid.
[63] Zuckerman, *Weakness of Will – The Exercise of Case Management Discretion under the CPR* at [58].
[64] Ibid.

predominant aim and could not properly be fettered by any need to promote efficiency and economy. Proportionality once more did not enter the equation and was ignored in its entirety.[65] As Lord Carswell put it:

> The decisions of the deputy district judge and circuit judge appear to have been largely driven by listing necessities and the need for enforcing a greater degree of efficiency and promptness on the part of practitioners. In the process the imperative of doing justice to the parties was subordinated, and Miss Perry may not unreasonably have felt that the trial judge would pay rather more regard to that imperative and be receptive to her application to be allowed to adduce the vital further evidence.[66]

The district judge's decisions were to be rejected because they improperly placed greater weight on listing, i.e. the need to ensure that all litigants had access to an appropriate and timely share of the court's limited resources as required by the wider public interest requirement set out in CPR r. 1.1(2)(e), and the need to secure greater economy and efficiency, both of which were to be promoted to facilitate substantive justice's achievement as well as ensure that both individual and collective proportionality were achieved, as required by all aspects of the overriding objective. They were simply dismissed as captious issues that ought not to have entered the equation. The imperative of doing justice in the individual case was superior to these considerations, rather than, as Woolf and the overriding objective had it, their equal. It was not something capable of being subordinated. Six years and a line of Court of Appeal authorities had done nothing to shake the belief that doing substantive justice remained the system's aim, and decisions that departed from that principle were to be rejected; *a fortiori* so was any theory of justice upon which such decisions depended for their justification. It is perhaps simply a coincidence that the sudden halt to Court of Appeal decisions, noted in 2011 in *Swain-Mason & Others* v. *Mills & Reeve LLP*,[67] which explained the post-Woolf approach to applications for relief from the consequences of procedural non-compliance, occurred after *Moy*.

Moy was not, however, the last word from the rejectionist camp. It underpins a series of decisions that followed the Jackson Review's completion and its identification of post-CPR failure by the courts to give

---

[65] See the discussion of *Sayers* in Chapter 4.   [66] [2005] 1 WLR 581 at [61].

[67] [2011] 1 WLR 2735, see discussion of *Worldwide Corporation* authorities in Chapter 6.

proper effect to the stricter approach to rule compliance which the Woolf Reforms required. It therefore post-dates the Jackson Review's endorsement of the fact that the laissez-faire approach to rule compliance justified by and arising from the RSC's theory of justice was no longer a valid approach in a system that was supposed to be committed to achieving proportionate justice.[68] The starting point of those decisions was an innocuous point that arose in Peter Smith J's first instance decision in *Swain-Mason*.[69] The issue in the case was not whether the approach to relief from sanctions had changed post-Woolf. It was accepted at that stage that it had. Peter Smith J relied on Peter Gibson LJ's flawed formulation of the position from *Cobbold*. The Court of Appeal rejected that approach: *Cobbold* did not set out the test properly. A series of other Court of Appeal decisions did, and ought to have been followed. In particular, the Court of Appeal emphasised, the proper approach and the one that ought to have been followed was that which it had previously endorsed in its pre-CPR decision in *Worldwide Corporation Limited* v. *GPT Ltd*. That approach should have been followed rather than *Cobbold*, because it properly set out the stricter approach to relief from sanctions required by the CPR.[70] Through endorsing *Worldwide Corporation Limited*, the Court of Appeal in *Swain* did not simply specify that its approach should be followed, however. It also endorsed *Worldwide Corporation Limited*'s rejection of Millett LJ's rejectionist approach.[71] That might have been the end of the matter, and the rejectionist line might have been laid to rest. However, its analysis has subsequently been rejected twice by the High Court. The point arose initially in *The Nottinghamshire and City of Nottingham Fire Authority* v. *Gladman Commercial Properties & Another* in 2011, where Peter Smith J considered the Court of Appeal's criticism of his first instance decision in *Swain-Mason*.[72] He then considered it again in an unreported first instance decision: *JSC BTA Bank* v. *Solodchenko*.[73]

An analysis of the position taken in the *Nottingham Fire* decision is instructive for the way it clearly articulates the rejectionist approach to

---

[68] R. Jackson (December 2009) at 397; D. Neuberger, *Docketing: Completing Case Management's Unfinished Revolution* (9th Lecture in the Implementation Programme, Solicitors' Costs Conference, 9 February 2012) at [19].

[69] *Swain-Mason & Others v Mills & Reeve LLP* [2010] EWHC 3198 (Ch).

[70] CA 2 December 1998, unreported.   [71] [2011] 1 WLR 2735 at [72].

[72] [2011] EWHC 1918 (Ch).

[73] ChD, 2 May 2012, discussed in Sorabji, 'Late Amendment and Jackson's Commitment to Woolf'.

Woolf, and by implication, Jackson. It first rejected an argument that the CPR was intended to introduce a stricter approach to granting relief from sanctions than had been in place under the RSC. In doing so, it wrongly assumed that such an approach would be one that sought to punish parties for non-compliance by refusing relief: the stricter approach has nothing to do with punishment, as the Woolf Reforms had made clear. It was to deter breaches and was intended to ensure that parties did not utilise more than a proportionate amount of the court's resources in the wider public interest.[74] It was thus to promote both individual and collective proportionality, as well as economy and efficiency, in the pursuit of substantive justice. That a strict approach to compliance breeds compliance through its deterrent effect is widely understood to succeed in those jurisdictions that have adopted it. Punishment does not tend to arise as a general issue in those jurisdictions due to the rules of court gaining a normative force that was unknown under the RSC.[75] Secondly, it focused on the issue of relief from sanctions solely on the question of prejudice as between the parties. It thus endorsed the *Tildesley* approach: could relief from the effects of non-compliance be granted 'without causing injustice to the other party'?[76] Questions of proportionality were of no significance, and the wider public interest was missing from the equation. It then went on to a discussion of the relationship between *Worldwide Corporation* and *Cobbold*. In this respect it made two significant points. First, it interpreted the two decisions as saying the same thing. The Court of Appeal in *Swain-Mason* was thus wrong to see a difference in approach between them. Given that the latter decision post-dated the CPR's introduction, it was, again contrary to the Court of Appeal's view, perfectly appropriate for it to have been relied upon and for the former to have dropped from the fossil record. Secondly, neither of the two decisions did anything radical in any event. They both simply gave expression to the approach the court had to take to late amendment prior to the Woolf Reforms. In other words, the Woolf Reforms had done nothing more than codify the RSC approach to late amendment.[77] They had thus codified the *Tildesley* test. From these two points a third then arose. Not only was it wrong to say that the CPR required a stricter

---

[74] H. Woolf (1996) at 77: 'As part of a case-managed system, sanctions should be designed to prevent, rather than punish, non-compliance with rules and timetables.'

[75] R. Fox, *Justice in the Twenty-First Century* (Cavendish) (2000) at 29ff; L. Leo, 'Case Management – Learning from the Singapore Experience' 30 (2011) *CJQ* 143, 158.

[76] [2011] EWHC 1918 (Ch) at [33].   [77] Ibid. at [42]–[55].

approach to relief from sanction applications, but such an approach was wrong in principle. It was, because the overriding objective was simply designed to ensure that litigants were granted the optimum means to proceed to a merits-based trial. Entirely in keeping with the overriding objective's traditionalist interpretation, Peter Smith J explained the position as follows:

> The whole purpose of the CPR was to grant Judges a flexible approach in dealing with the application of the rules, failing to comply with the rules and any matters that were necessary to perpetuate the overriding objective. That objective is plainly designed to ensure trials proceed on a merit basis so that every party has the fullest and fairest opportunity to present its case.[78]

This was the case, however, not simply on traditionalist grounds. It was because it was impermissible to interpret it another way. As he went on to explain:

> One must never lose sight of the fact that it is the overriding duty of the courts to come to a just and correct result and if for one reason or another because of the creation of a gloss or an over technical approach to pleadings a party is unable to deploy a case or give evidence which justice requires it to be able to deploy then that is not an appropriate exercise of a discretion. I say that of course that in allowing late amendments and late introduction of evidence the position of all parties has to be taken into account. If there is no prejudice (and there was none identified or made out by the Defendants in the *Mills & Reeves* case) it is difficult to see how an application to amend late should be disallowed because of the super imposition of a higher onus to justify. As the *Gale* case said people should not be punished for mistakes. The consequence of disallowance of an amendment like this if the trial is subsequently lost when there was a case that could have been run if it had been re-pleaded simply denies justice and even worse potentially transfers the compensation to the disappointed party's lawyers.[79]

The stricter approach was to be rejected, not because of any traditionalist reading of the overriding objective; it was to be rejected because taking such an approach would amount to a denial of justice. It would frustrate the court's ability – its duty – to secure substantive justice in the particular case. An approach that placed a limit on the *Tildesley* test

---

[78] Ibid. at [57].

[79] Ibid. at [62]. For a similar approach, albeit one that is concerned with procedure in the Employment Tribunal rather than under the CPR, see *Abercrombie and Others* v. *Aga Rangemaster Ltd* [2013] EWCA Civ 1148, esp. at [49] where Bowen LJ's *dicta* is endorsed.

was inimical to doing justice. It would in effect punish parties for procedural error, as Millett LJ had explained in *Gale*, just as Bowen LJ had done in *Cropper*. As such, it would, as Millett LJ had it, or as Lord Carswell had it in *Moy*, place considerations of economy and efficiency – mere procedural matters – over and above the aim of doing justice. That was impermissible; as Peter Smith J would go on to explain in *JSC BTA Bank* v. *Solodchenko*.[80] Relying on the UK Supreme Court's decision in *NML Capital Ltd* v. *Argentina*,[81] he held that the analysis in *Swain-Mason* was plainly wrong and could not survive. He took the same approach as that articulated by the *White Book*, which was discussed in Chapter 4.[82] The Supreme Court's decision had reiterated, in terms with which Esher MR would have been familiar, that procedural rules were the servant and not the master of the rule of law.[83] The approach taken in *Swain-Mason*, as it endorsed a stricter approach to rule-compliance and a more limited approach to relief from sanctions for non-compliance, was impermissible because it rendered doing justice subordinate to rule following. It was thus to be rejected. By necessary implication, so was any interpretation of the overriding objective that went beyond the traditionalist account, as Woolf's new theory of justice was also to be rejected. Mere matters of procedural justice could not trump those of substantive justice.

7.4 Practical steps to effective implementation

The rejectionist and traditionalist approaches to the overriding objective share a common premise. They maintain the view that the justice system's predominant aim is to achieve substantive justice. In a sense, they both adhere to the fallacy of composition that underscores the RSC's theory of justice. While an educative effort will go some way towards undoing the traditionalists' false understanding of the overriding objective, on its own it will not be sufficient to secure the acceptance of the new theory of justice it articulates. Moreover, it will do little to overcome the rejectionist view. If proportionate justice is to be both properly understood and properly applied following the implementation of the Jackson Reforms, more than education will be needed.[84] Equally, it will not be

---

[80] ChD, 2 May 2012, discussed in Sorabji, 'Late Amendment and Jackson's Commitment to Woolf'.
[81] [2011] 2 AC 495.   [82] See Chapter 4, n. 32.   [83] [2011] 2 AC 495 at [74].
[84] Zuckerman, 'The Revised CPR 3.9' at 135.

enough for the Court of Appeal simply to carry on issuing statements bemoaning the fact that case management is not being carried out with the necessary degree of rigour, while stating how the Jackson Reforms will, once more, bring with them a stricter approach as it has done in, for instance, *Fred Perry (Holdings) Ltd* v. *Brands Plaza Trading Ltd* (2012),[85] *Guntrip* v. *Cheney Coaches Ltd* (2012),[86] *Deripaska* v. *Cherney* (2012),[87] *Mannion* v. *Ginty* (2012),[88] and *Stokers SA* v. *IG Markets Ltd* (2012).[89] Exhortation, like education, achieves little on its own, as its repeated failure to bring about any lasting or meaningful change in behaviour since 1999 has all too clearly demonstrated.[90] If the traditionalist and rejectionist approaches to the overriding objective are to be overcome, and the proper basis on which case and post-Jackson costs management is to take hold, more will be needed.

The first thing that will have to be done is for the courts to acknowledge that cultural change takes time and concerted effort and act accordingly. It took almost half-a-century to finally eliminate common law formalism from the civil justice system. The 1870 reforms did not succeed overnight. They succeeded because they were the culmination of four decades of past reform. Their aim was well understood because of that and because the theory of substantive justice they were committed to was drawn from long-established equity procedure; a fact emphasised by the *Annual Practice*'s explanation of the correct approach to relief from the consequences of procedural non-compliance by reference to *Ferrand* v. *The Mayor, Alderman and Burgesses of Bradford* and its articulation of equity's commitment to doing, as it put it, complete justice.[91] Most importantly, following the RSC's introduction in the 1870s, the Court of Appeal, over a twenty-year period, developed a consistent line of authority, explaining and implementing its theory of justice. This can be contrasted with the approach taken following the CPR's introduction. It attempted to introduce a theoretical shift in approach of the same magnitude as the 1870 reforms. It did not, however,

---

[85] [2012] EWCA Civ 224.   [86] [2012] EWCA Civ 392.   [87] [2012] EWCA Civ 1235.
[88] [2012] EWCA Civ 1667.   [89] [2012] EWCA Civ 1706.
[90] See, for instance, *Biguzzi* v. *Rank Leisure* [1999] 1 WLR 1926; *Thomson* v. *O'Connor* [2005] EWCA Civ 1533 at [17]; R. Jackson (December 2009) at 397; Jackson, *Achieving a Culture Change in Case Management* (5th Lecture in the Implementation Programme) (22 November 2011) (http://www.judiciary.gov.uk/Resources/JCO/Documents/Speeches/lj-jackson-speech-achieving-culture-change-case-management.pdf); *Swain-Mason & Others* v. *Mills & Reeve LLP* [2011] 1 WLR 2735 at [72].
[91] 8 De G M & G 93, 44 ER 324 at 95, 325; see Chapter 2, n. 134.

do so as the culmination of a long period of similar reforms, all of which had the same aim. Unlike the RSC, the new theory of justice it attempted to introduce was a novel one. If the CPR could properly be compared to the nineteenth-century reforms, it was the equivalent of the 1834 Hilary Term Rules: the first attempt at its new approach. Its aim, as the differing views on its meaning shows, was not clearly understood. Most significantly, the Court of Appeal took a far too short-term approach to providing authoritative guidance regarding the practical application and effect of the CPR's introduction. The decisions from *Beachley* to *Finken*, for instance, may have attempted to explain the new approach to procedural compliance and amendment required by the overriding objective, but there were not enough of them over a sufficiently long period of time. It took over twenty years to fully establish the *Tildesley* test after it was first set out in the 1870s, and that was in the circumstances of the long background to those reforms. There was simply insufficient time and effort given to implementing the Woolf Reforms. The question for the Jackson Reforms is whether they are to play the part of the 1850 common law reforms or the 1870 reforms. Are they a staging post to successful reform? Given an understanding of the nineteenth-century reform process, there is a real possibility that they could play the part of the latter. To do so, though, the post-Jackson Court of Appeal will have to adopt the approach taken by its Victorian predecessor. It will need to dedicate a similar period of time and number of authoritative decisions to establishing the new theory of justice and the manner in which it is to be applied. It will also have to ensure that its decisions are consistent with each other, both where they deal with the same issue, such as relief from the consequences of non-compliance, or different issues, such as the approach to late amendment, disclosure, or the use of expert evidence. It cannot afford one line of authority akin to that in *Hannigan*, *Thurrock*, *Sayers* and *B* v. *B* to develop alongside another such as the *Worldwide Corporation Limited* to *Finken* line of authority. The same principles and approach will need to inform all its guidance. The decision to implement the Jackson Review's recommendation that a limited number of Court of Appeal judges, of whom Sir Rupert Jackson is one, should deal with reform-related appeals, ought to provide a proper basis for the Victorian approach to be replicated.[92] It ought to provide the basis for a consistent approach to be taken; one that was missing

---

[92] R. Jackson (December 2009) at 397; *Appointment of Appeal Judges for Costs and Case Management Appeals* (29 May 2013) http://www.judiciary.gov.uk/media/media-releases/

post-1999 due to the general lack of consistency amongst judicial per-
sonnel hearing Woolf-related appeals. It also, through utilising Sir Rupert
Jackson's expertise, ought to replicate the position the Victorian Court of
Appeal in respect of Bramwell LJ.[93]

Consistency over a significant period of time, like educative efforts
regarding the nature of the new theory of justice and its application,
while it is necessary, will still not be sufficient. The ultimate success of the
Victorian reforms was not simply a product of time, consistency and a
long line of authorities. It was also a product of the manner in which the
post-1870 authorities approached the implementation of substantive
justice. Rather than simply express dissatisfaction that the new approach
had not taken hold, they did two things. They started by giving a clear
explanation of the rationale underpinning the new approach to justice.[94]
They explained that civil procedure was to be carried out with one aim
in mind: to bring all the issues in dispute before the court and to
secure their determination on the substantive merits. They then went
further. They also made it clear that this new aim was the antithesis of
common law formalism; a point most clearly made by Bowen LJ in
Cropper in his rejection of the view that procedural rules operated to
discipline parties,[95] or as tripwires for the unwary.[96] In this, they took the
same approach that the High Court of Australia would take in *Aon Risk
Services Australia Ltd* v. *Australian National University.*[97]

The particular issue in *Aon* was whether, after Woolf-style reforms, the
Tildesley test, and the theory of justice it gave life to, remained valid in so
far as an application to amend pleadings was concerned. Previous High
Court of Australia authority had held, in keeping with *Tildesley*, that the
'paramount consideration' in such an application was the need to do
justice between the parties. The court's 'ultimate aim' was 'the attainment
of justice and no principle of case management [could] be allowed to

---

2013/appointment-appeal-judges-costs-judges>. The judges being: Lord Dyson MR,
Richards, Jackson, Davis and Lewison LLJ.

[93] It also replicates the position the Court of Appeal was in when the CPR was introduced in
1999, as both Lord Woolf, then Master of the Rolls, and Scott V-C, then deputy Head of
Civil Justice and the judge principally responsible for implementation of the Woolf
Reforms, were both able to sit on appeals concerning the new rules.

[94] See the discussion of *Tildesley* authorities, Chapter 2.

[95] *Cropper* v. *Smith* (1883) 32 WR 262 at 263.

[96] J. Jacob in *Report of the Committee on Personal Injuries Litigation* (Cmd 3691, 1968) at
151–2, [2], cited in R. Jackson (December 2009) at 391.

[97] [2009] HCA 27.

supplant that aim'.[98] Its previous authority was thus entirely in keeping with the RSC's approach, and was, as the court acknowledged, derived from it and the decisions in *Tildesley, Clarapede* and *Cropper*.[99] It was also entirely in keeping with Millett LJ's and Lord Carswell's rejectionist approach to Woolf's new theory. Substantive justice was the predominant aim and could not be set aside for mere procedural and managerial concerns. In *Aon*, the High Court of Australia put an end to this idea. Heydon J, for instance, was clear: the previous approach was no longer authoritative.[100] The idea that costs were a panacea that cured all ills, as Bowen LJ had established in *Cropper*, was no longer valid.[101] The very idea that justice was a matter only between the immediate litigants to any dispute was rejected. What might look like injustice when considered solely by reference to the consequences of, for instance, a refusal to grant an amendment or relief from sanctions was, when looked at in the wider context, nothing of the sort. Justice was a wider concept than one focused on the interests of the immediate parties to litigation. It was one that properly encompassed the wider public interest, the need to secure all litigants with an effective and equitable share of the court's resources so as to enable them to achieve access to justice as well as maintain public confidence in the courts.[102] Individualised justice was to give way to distributive justice.[103] It was, moreover, a concept of justice, the High

---

[98] *Queensland v. JL Holdings Pty Ltd* (1997) 189 CLR 146 at 154–5.

[99] See *Queensland v. JL Holdings Pty Ltd* [1997] HCA 1; (1997) 189 CLR 146; *Aon Risk Services Australia Ltd v. Australian National University* [2009] HCA 27 at [2].

[100] [2009] HCA 27 at 156 *per* Heydon J: 'The presentation and adjudication of the case in the courts below do cause it to merit a place in the precedent books. The reasons for placing it there turn on the numerous examples it affords of how litigation should not be conducted or dealt with. The proceedings reveal a strange alliance. A party which has a duty to assist the court in achieving certain objectives fails to do so. A court which has a duty to achieve those objectives does not achieve them. The torpid languor of one hand washes the drowsy procrastination of the other. Are these phenomena indications of something chronic in the modern state of litigation? Or are they merely acute and atypical breakdowns in an otherwise functional system? Are they signs of a trend, or do they reveal only an anomaly? One hopes for one set of answers. One fears that, in reality, there must be another'.

[101] [2009] HCA 27; (2009) 239 CLR 175 at [18]–[22], [73]–[79].

[102] Ibid., endorsing *Sali v. SPC Ltd* (1993) 67 ALJR 841; 116 ALR 625 at [64]: 'What might be perceived as an injustice to a party when considered only in the context of an action between parties may not be so when considered in a context which includes the claims of other litigants and the public interest in achieving the most efficient use of court resources.'

[103] A. Lyons, 'Recasting the Landscape of Interlocutory Applications: *Aon Risk Services Australia Ltd v Australian National University*' [2010] *Sydney Law Review* 549, 573.

Court of Australia noted, that the English Court of Appeal had given expression to in *Worldwide Corporation*, and one which went beyond that articulated by Millett LJ in *Gale*. Most importantly, though, it was an idea of justice that the High Court endorsed while clearly rejecting the previously established one. It rejected the rejectionist view of Woolf's new theory. The High Court, in tackling the issue of the continued status of a version of the RSC's theory of justice, could not have been clearer: the old theory and the means in which it was applied in practice were no longer valid. It had been replaced. Having made this clear, as the Victorian Court of Appeal had done in England, it then went on to explain why the old theory of justice had been replaced. Reform and rationale were clearly set out. That decision, since it was handed down, has been affirmed and followed. It has been applied consistently, even if in some cases it has been developed.[104]

While authorities such as *Biguzzi* v. *Rank Leisure*,[105] *Holmes* v. *SGB*,[106] and those discussed in Chapter 6, to a certain extent articulated Woolf's new theory, and the House of Lords in *Three Rivers* correctly characterised the CPR as marking a revolutionary new approach to doing justice, the English Court of Appeal has not given as clear and consistent an articulation in the post-1999 authorities of the nature and rationale over as extended a period as was the case in the nineteenth century. Nor has there been as emphatic and detailed an examination of it and the fact that it marks a rejection of the RSC's theory of justice as the Australian High Court's decision in *Aon*. There was, post-1999, a failure to grasp the nettle, provide a definitive articulation of the new theory and explain its underlying rationale. What statements there were in, for instance, *Woods* v. *Chaleff*, *Cobbold*, *Finken*, were insufficiently articulated. They were equally not continued in a sufficient number of authorities. Hence the critical comment in *Swain-Mason* that the very position and authorities that were relied on in *Aon* had fallen from view in England. They had fallen from view, as had the theory they sought to articulate and implement. If the Mark II overriding objective is to stand a better chance of effecting necessary change, the Victorian and Australian approaches will need to be taken. If the post-1999 English approach is replicated following the Jackson Reforms' introduction, there is little chance that Woolf's new theory will properly establish itself the second time round. The Jackson Reforms would consequently play the role of the 1850

---

[104] For a discussion of those authorities, see Lyons, ibid.   [105] [1999] 1 WLR 1926.
[106] [2001] EWCA Civ 354 at [38].

reforms, and case and costs management will be conducted consistently with the need to secure substantive justice. As such, they will do no good.

However, more still will need to be done than education and the production of a series of well-articulated judgments that explain that the old theory of justice no longer holds good, while also setting out the new theory and its rationale. The Victorian authorities did something more, as did the Australian High Court in *Aon*.[107] They both articulated the practical means by which the new theory of justice was to be implemented. It is one thing articulating a theory, it is another to transform what might otherwise be no more than nebulous concepts into something that a court and litigants can actually act upon and implement. This is particularly important where Woolf's new theory of justice is concerned. Ideas such as proportionality, which includes the need to take account of the interest of other court users to attain their proper share in the court's limited resources, are less than clear when it comes to practical implementation. They are open-textured and the English authorities – and the same criticism can be levelled at the Jackson Reforms here – do not even go as far as the Supreme Court of Canada, which in *Marcotte c. Longueil(ville)* has been understood to draw a clear distinction between the two different types of proportionality that exist within the overriding objective.[108] It made the point that Woolf-inspired reforms in Quebec's civil procedural code had introduced both individual and collective proportionality into its overriding objective.[109] Moreover, ideas such as what level of costs are proportionate in so far as individual litigation is concerned are not immediately obvious. What is needed is practical guidance from the Court of Appeal or via Practice Direction as to how the new theory, and particularly the application of both aspects of proportionality are to be implemented in practice so as to secure equitable access to justice for all court users. The Victorians took this approach by articulating the *Tildesley* test. It set out the practical means

---

[107] [2009] HCA 27; (2009) 239 CLR 175 *passim*.

[108] [2009] 3 RCS 65 at [43]ff, 62 and [72]ff; and see Piché, 'Figures, Spaces and Procedural Proportionality' at 155. C. Piché, 'La proportionnalité procédural: une perspective comparative' 40(2009–10) *RDUS* 551, 565ff. It should be noted, however, that the *Marcotte* decision, on a close reading, does not clearly articulate the difference between collective and individual proportionality. The distinction appears to be one Piché draws from the decision. Contrast with *L (a child)* EWCA Civ 1778 at [12], being the first English endorsement of the terms.

[109] See also *Matic v. Trottier* (2010) QCCS 1466 at [61]ff.

through which substantive justice was to be done where questions of compliance, non-compliance and amendment were concerned.

In all but one area, the post-1999 Court of Appeal failed to take that approach. In general, as the *Worldwide Corporation* to *Finken* authorities show, it went no further than to articulate the need to take account of the impact decisions had on the administration of justice generally or on other court users.[110] The one exception to this, and it is one that was confined to a specific area of civil procedure, was the approach taken to relief from the consequences of default that arose from a failure to serve a claim form within the requisite time limits. The interesting aspect of the line of authority that developed around this was that there was, as in the Victorian period, consistency in judicial personnel: the then deputy Head of Civil Justice, Dyson LJ, was a constant feature of the Court of Appeal that heard the cases. It is a line of authority that Lord Neuberger MR endorsed as demonstrating the approach to be taken to questions of relief from sanctions once the Jackson Reforms were introduced, although he did not, as has been suggested, endorse the view that the practical test articulated in those decisions was to be applied more generally.[111] It is also one that has been relied on in the justification of the post-Jackson attempt to introduce such a stricter approach to non-compliance in order to ensure that the approach articulated by Lord Dyson MR, which was discussed earlier, is implemented.[112]

The initial decision in this line of authority was *Hashtroodi v. Hancock*, in which the Court of Appeal refused to apply the rules relating to extensions of time to serve a claim form under CPR r. 7.6(2) in circumstances where the failure to comply was caused by inaction on the part of the legal representative.[113] In reaching its decision, the court explained how it had to exercise its discretion consistently with the overriding objective. It recognised that the purposive provision that implemented the new theory of justice governed the issue. It then noted how one of the Woolf Reforms' aims was to secure greater party discipline, i.e. rule compliance, in order to reduce litigation delay. Applying the overriding

---

[110] See Chapter 6.
[111] See S. Sime and D. French, *Blackstone's Guide to The Civil Justice Reforms 2013* (Oxford University Press) at 77–8. The approach articulated by Lord Neuberger MR was ultimately and indirectly, by reference to Sime and French's work, cited approvingly in *Mitchell v. News Group Newspapers Ltd* [2013] EWCA Civ 1537 at [42]–[43].
[112] *Venulum Property Investments Ltd v. Space Architecture Ltd & Others* [2013] EWHC 1242 (TCC) at [50]–[51].
[113] [2004] 1 WLR 3206.

objective was the means by which that was to be achieved.[114] It then justified refusing the application, because to do otherwise would denude the rule governing the specific procedural time limit in question of its intended normative value.[115] The appeal was dismissed, even though the court acknowledged that by doing so the claimant would be denied the opportunity of proceeding to trial and would merely be left with the option of bringing a professional negligence action against his solicitors.[116] It was not only dismissed despite a fair trial still being possible, but also in circumstances where the defendant had incurred no prejudice by the default. The *Tildesley* test was no longer relevant. The rationale behind the decision and the fact that it gave less weight to the need to secure substantive justice than would have been the case under the RSC was the need, as the court identified, to ensure that the previous lack of procedural discipline evident did not reassert itself under the CPR. In this, the court adopted the approach specified by Woolf in *Biguzzi*, which required the court consistently with the overriding objective to ensure that the RSC's approach to procedural obligations, a function of its commitment to substantive justice, did not arise under the CPR.[117] If it had not done so, access to justice for all would, as a substantive aim, have been undermined. Absent litigant discipline, it is not possible for the justice system to fulfil that wider policy objective. The interest of individual justice in particular cases, and in that particular case, therefore needed to be subject to the wider needs of distributive justice required by the theory of justice articulated within the overriding objective. In the words of the High Court of Australia, it adopted an approach that might suggest injustice was done in the particular case, but when properly looked at in the wider context, was justice.

The Court of Appeal subsequently affirmed the *Hashtroodi* approach in two of a number of appeals that were heard together and reported under the name of the lead case: *Collier* v. *Williams*.[118] In *Leeson* v. *Marsden* and *Glass* v. *Surrendran* the claimant's solicitors failed to serve the claim form in time.[119] In both cases the Court of Appeal emphasised that *Hashtroodi* was of general application and that if it were not and extensions of time were granted in such situations, the procedural rules would lose their normative value.[120] In so far as the *Leeson* appeal was concerned, the Court's approach was in stark contrast with that taken by

---

[114] Ibid. at [18]–[21].   [115] Ibid. at [31].   [116] Ibid. at [34].
[117] [1999] 1 WLR 1926 at 1933.   [118] [2006] 1 WLR 1945.
[119] [2006] 1 WLR 1945 at [130] and [150].   [120] Ibid. at [131].

the district judge at first instance, who had granted an extension of time to serve the claim form. In doing so, he critically referred to the Court of Appeal's approach in *Hashtroodi* to rule-compliance as a 'technical' one. Echoing Bowen LJ's statement from *Cropper*, he rejected such an approach and held that *Hashtroodi* had wrongly elevated procedure over substance. He thus took the same approach as Millett LJ and Lord Carswell: securing substantive justice could not be rendered subject to mere managerial considerations. The Court of Appeal rejected this stance. It emphasised how placing greater weight than had been done previously on the importance of rule compliance was not simply to adopt a formalist approach to doing justice.[121] Rule-compliance and its enforcement served a wider purpose. It was justified because it furthered the overriding objective. Taking difficult decisions that had an adverse impact on individual litigants was an inevitable consequence of having to ensure that the justice system could operate effectively for the benefit of all court users. As the Court had previously stated in *Vinos* v. *Marks & Spencer Plc*, where a similar application was refused on the same basis, the overriding objective required rules to be complied with, not for any formalistic reason, but so as to ensure justice was achieved.[122] Justice in this case meant, as Peter Gibson LJ put it:

> Justice to the defendant and to the interests of other litigants may require that a claimant who ignores time limits prescribed by the rules forfeits the right to have his claim tried.[123]

It was the very point the Australian High Court would go on to make in *Aon*. The Court in *Hashtroodi* cited *Vinos* with approval.[124] The point was endorsed again in *Collier*. In assessing whether to give relief from the effects of non-compliance, the court had to ensure its decision was consistent with the need to secure effective access to justice for all. Only by doing so would the Woolf Reports' aim be fulfilled; a point it emphasised in *Collier* through applying the approach previously adopted in *Vinos* and *Hashtroodi*.[125]

The ultimate consequence of this strict approach, which clearly demonstrated no weakness of will on the court's part, was noted by the Court of Appeal in *Hoddinott & Others* v. *Persimmon Homes (Wessex) Ltd*.[126]

---

[121] Ibid.   [122] [2001] 3 All ER 784.   [123] Ibid. at [26].
[124] [2004] 1 WLR 3206 at [21].   [125] [2006] 1 WLR 1945 at [1].
[126] [2007] EWCA Civ 1203 at [59]; also see *Nelson & Hanley* v. *Clearsprings (Management) Ltd* [2007] 1 WLR 962; *Tombstone Ltd* v. *Raja* [2008] EWCA Civ 1444.

The message had got across to judges, lawyers and litigants. Applications for relief from the consequences of a failure to serve claims in time had declined significantly. They had, because claims were being served in time. The rules had gained a degree of normative force that they had never had under the RSC. As such, those claims that were now being prosecuted with greater alacrity, were better able to secure substantive justice at minimal cost and delay. Both had been reduced because lawyers were getting on with prosecuting cases expeditiously and litigants no longer had to deal with the unnecessary expense of making, and challenging, applications for relief from sanction. Moreover, the court's resources were no longer being diverted from other claims to deal with such applications. The stricter approach had both facilitated substantive justice and, through applying the various aspects of procedural justice required by the overriding objective, it was furthering the wider public interest by ensuring all court users could access a fair share of the court's resources. Individual and collective proportionality were being promoted because litigants were keeping to the litigation timetable set by the rules in order to secure those aspects of the overriding objective.

The problem, however, with this line of authority is that the approach taken in it was confined to applications for relief from the consequences of failure to serve process. It was not generalised, as the Victorian Court of Appeal ensured that the *Tildesley* test was generalised. If, for instance, its approach had been taken to an application for permission to amend or to relief from the consequences of other procedural default, such as to serve evidence on time, it may have been generalised in the same way. What it does, though, is demonstrate that the Court of Appeal, through developing a consistent line of authority over a sustained period of time – one not even approaching that needed in the 1870s – which explains its rationale and why it goes beyond the RSC's commitment to substantive justice and the practical approach to take in determining the issue, can change the approach to justice. It is possible to change the litigation culture and to do so consistently with the true nature of Woolf's new theory of justice.

If the Court of Appeal post-Jackson generalises this type of approach through developing a clear, consistent line of authority that sets out a general rule and the fact, as in *Aon*, that that general rule overturns the old approach while explaining why it does, it will achieve two things. It will finally put an end to the traditionalist interpretation of the overriding objective which, due to giving paramount weight to achieving substantive justice, is inconsistent with it. It will also put an end to the rejectionist view; although, given reliance on the UK Supreme Court's decision in

NML, it is going to have to be supported in this by that court just as the High Court of Australia was called on to finally put an end to the RSC's theory of justice there.[127] It will require concerted effort, but as the Victorian, Australian and the *Hashtroodi* authorities show, it can be done. If Woolf's theory of justice is to be properly implemented, their approach will have to be replicated in the post-Jackson era.

Following the introduction of the Jackson Reforms in April 2013 the Court of Appeal took what can only be seen as a first step to proper implementation. Following a number of equivocal High Court decisions,[128] in *Mitchell* v. *News Group Newspapers Ltd*,[FN] it endorsed the new theory of justice as had been explained by Lord Dyson MR in the 18th Implementation Lecture. The Court of Appeal had, what might be said to be, its *Aon* moment.[129] It may not have done so in as much detail as the High Court of Australia in that decision, but it made clear that the Woolf and Jackson Reforms, properly understood, rejected the idea that substantive justice in the individual case was paramount. Justice was now to be understood as only achievable through the application of both individual and collective proportionality.[130] Justice was not something that simply arose as between individual litigants. It went further. It encompassed the need to ensure that all litigants had effective access to the court's limited resources in order to seek the vindication of their rights. Robust case management and a strict approach to relief from sanctions for procedural non-compliance were the means to an end: to ensure that no single claim expended an individual or collectively disproportionate amount of resources.[131]

Mitchell is, however, no more than a starting point. As the court noted, it is one which was made in an environment where some judges did not accept Woolf's new theory, its meaning and its consequences for the conduct of individual litigation.[132] It is likely to be met with the same

---

[127] [2011] 2 AC 495.

[128] *Mitchell* v. *News Group Newspapers Ltd* [2013] EWCA Civ 1537 at [34]–[51].

[129] Ibid. at [47]ff.

[130] For instance, *Venulum Property Investments Ltd* v. *Space Architecture Ltd & Others* [2013] EWHC 1242 (TCC), *Fons HF* v. *Corporal Ltd & Another* [2013] EWHC 1278 (Ch), *Ian Wyche* v. *Careforce Group Plc* [2013] EWHC 3282, *Raayan Al Iraq Co. Ltd* v. *Trans Victory Marine Inc* [2013] EWHC 2696 (Comm).

[131] Subsequently endorsed and applied by *Durrant* v. *Chief Constable of Avon & Somerset Constabulary*]2013] EWCA Civ 1624, *Thevarajah* v. *Riordan* [EWCA] Civ 14.

[132] *Mitchell* v. *News Group Newspapers Ltd* [2013] EWCA Civ 1537 at [38], endorsing Dyson, *The Application of the Amendments to the Civil Procedure Rules* at [25]–[27].

resistance, equivocation and rejection as the Court of Appeal's previous attempts to give effect to Woolf's new theory suffered from 1999. Hence the need, stressed earlier, for the Court of Appeal to develop a clear, consistent line of authority, and one that builds on and reiterates *Mitchell*. If it does so, it will leave, and have to deal with, one final practical problem: how the new theory's commitment to proportionality, and specifically its approach to relief from sanctions, applications to amend, etc., is to be practically implemented.

7.5 Practical proportionality: a problem from Bentham

The fundamental problem for Bentham's theory of justice, as it was for his utilitarianism generally, was its inability to provide a workable basis on which to ascertain the aggregate utility value of any action. Requiring a judge to manage and decide cases according to the direct application of the felicific calculus was as unrealistic a suggestion as anyone can imagine.[133] Bentham realised, however, that the application of the felicific calculus was practically impossible; that theory could not be translated into practice. In order to deal with this, he attempted to resolve the difficulty by removing reference to the various elements of the calculus through finding a single common denominator for each of them. Rather than carry out a complex analysis of various open-textured concepts, each pleasure and pain was to be accorded a monetary value. Once that was done, in theory at least, it was a much more straightforward exercise to ascertain the total utility value of any one action. All that had to be done was a summation of financial value. Much, however, rested on the ability to attribute an initial financial value, which simply shifted the problem without resolving it. The problem simply became one of attributing initial utility values to pleasures and pains. As that could not be done, then it could not be done in order to secure a financial value for each action which could not then be used as a basis for aggregation. The theory was of no practical application due to the nature of its elements, whether the calculus was said to apply through an assessment of the utility value of each action by applying the calculus as it was originally conceived, or through the attempt to apply it so as to create a financial value for each action, which could then be used as the basis of aggregation.

---

[133] For a recent discussion, see A. Baujard, 'A Return to Bentham's Felicific Calculus: From moral welfarism to technical non-welfarism' 16(3) (2009) *European Journal of the History of Economic Thought* 431–53; see Chapter 3, n. 70.

Woolf's theory brought with it similar problems. Proportionality lay at the heart of it. It was the means by which substantive justice was to be tempered in order to ensure that no single claim utilised more than an equitable share of the justice system's resources. While there was no great difficulty in devising and effecting structural changes to the justice system consistently with it, the same was and is not true of its application to the CPR's operation. The practical application of proportionality proved elusive, just as the practical application of Bentham's theory was elusive. There was no real, if any, detailed consideration of how to apply collective proportionality effectively. References to CPR r. 1.1(2)(e) and the need to take account of the effect of decisions on other court users provided no real guidance to how it was to be applied in practice. Just as Bentham's theory suffered from an inability to ascribe realistic values to its elements and then determine how to use them to effectively calculate aggregate utility, Woolf's theory offered no real basis for a court to assess whether or to what extent individual decisions effected overall access to justice. It was as useless in this respect as Bentham's.

Where individual proportionality was concerned, the court's approach was worse. Guidance was given in *Lownds* v. *Home Office*. It was, however, disastrous.[134] It was structured so that, rather than adopt an approach that gave a real role to proportionality in the assessment of litigation costs, it simply permitted the approach to costs developed under the RSC to reappear. If proportionality had played a proper role, this ought not to have happened. Litigation costs ought to have been limited to what was proportionate to the value of the claim at hand, as required by CPR r. 1.1(2)(c), and the conduct of litigation would have been affected accordingly.[135] The *Lownds* test frustrated this. The reason why it did was explained in *Willis* v. *Nicholson*:

> One element in the present high cost of litigation is undoubtedly the expectations as to annual income of the professionals who conduct it. The costs system as it at present operates cannot do anything about that, because it assesses the proper charge for work on the basis of the market rates charged by the professions, rather than attempting the no doubt

---

[134] [2002] 1 WLR 2450 at [1]–[10] and [23]–[40]; previous guidance had been given by Lord Woolf in *Jefferson* v. *National Freight Carriers plc* [2001] EWCA Civ 2082; [2001] 2 Costs LR 313 at [39]–[41]; D. Neuberger, *Proportionate Cost* (15th Lecture in the Implementation Programme) (The Law Society, 29 May 2012) at [4] <http://www.judiciary.gov.uk/Resources/JCO/Documents/Speeches/proportionate-costs-fifteenth-lecture-30052012.pdf>.

[135] R. Jackson (December 2009) at 27ff.

difficult task of placing an objective value on the work. When the Civil
Procedure Rules replaced the Rules of the Supreme Court, and encouraged active intervention by the court and the application of public values
and not merely those values with which the parties were comfortable, it
was hoped that that practice might change; and that hope was reinforced
when this court said, in §2 of its judgment in *Lownds v Home Office
(Practice Note)* [2002] 1 WLR 2450:

> Proportionality played no part in the taxation of costs under the
> Rules of the Supreme Court. The only test was that of reasonable-
> ness. The problem with that test, standing on its own, was that it
> institutionalised, as reasonable, the level of costs which were gen-
> erally charged by the profession at the time when professional
> services were rendered. If a rate of charges was commonly adopted
> it was taken to be reasonable and so allowed on taxation even
> though the result was far from reasonable.

However, in the event nothing seems to have changed. That is because, as
explained in §29 of the same judgment, 'proportionality' is achieved by
determining whether it was necessary to incur any particular item of
costs. And then 'When an item of costs is necessarily incurred then a
reasonable amount for the item should normally be allowed': and the
reasonable amount per hour of the professional's time continues to be
determined by the market.[136]

By focusing the question on which costs were necessary and then reasonable to secure substantive justice, in practice, proportionality fell out
of consideration. Litigants understood that they were likely, and more
often than not, more than likely, to receive the same level of costs as they
would have received under the RSC, and they acted accordingly. Proportionality was the aim. The RSC's approach was the result. The court
focused on whether an item of cost was incurred because it was necessary
to secure substantive justice. If it was, the RSC's reasonableness test was
applied. No consideration was given as to whether pursuit of the item
necessary to secure substantive justice was proportionate, either individually or, for that matter, collectively. The position following the
Jackson Reforms is not significantly different. In both cases, the problem
that effected Bentham's theory remains unresolved for Woolf's, although
not unresolvable. Practical guidance can be given to transform nebulous
concepts into applicable normative principles.

The problem in so far as collective proportionality is concerned is that
no real consideration has yet been given regarding how to transform it

---

[136] [2007] EWCA Civ 199 at [18]–[19].

into a concrete principle, or principles, that can properly be applied in case and costs management. It remains a nebulous concept. The Jackson Reforms do not assist to any great degree in this regard, as they did not focus on the issue, but were confined to the problem of costs as between litigants.[137] The only real consideration of an issue that related to this aspect of proportionality was the reforms' discussion of the court's failure to manage cases effectively through effective use of sanctions for non-compliance.[138] Its recommendations in this regard focused on standard-ising case management directions, introducing targeted docketing of claims, fixing early trial windows, and ensuring that case management conferences were carried out more effectively.[139] Such reforms, like the introduction of case management itself, only provide the means by which improvements can be made to the operation of the justice system. They provide a more detailed framework for securing proportionality. The need to provide a means of ensuring they are used to implement collect-ive proportionality remains unfulfilled. As with the Woolf Reforms, providing the necessary mechanisms for successful reform is one thing; what is crucial is making sure that they are used as intended. The aim needs to be properly understood and capable of effective application.

The Jackson Reforms also, however, recommended revision of CPR r. 3.9, the provision that governed applications for relief from sanctions.[140] This reform was intended to give proper effect to the need to secure effective rule-compliance, and as such, eliminate the culture of non-compliance that the CPR's introduction had allowed to continue. In order to achieve greater rule-compliance and a more limited tolerance of default, and hence further the need to secure both individual and collective proportionality, the Jackson Reports recommended the rule be simplified and should emphasise just two conditions upon which appli-cations for relief should be considered: that in assessing such applications the court had to, first, give specific weight to the need to conduct litigation efficiently and at proportionate cost and, secondly, take account of the interests of justice in the particular case.[141] The first aspect was implemented, and subsequently mirrored by revisions that introduced

---

[137] Neuberger, *Proportionate Cost* at [8]–[11].   [138] R. Jackson (December 2009) at 386ff.
[139] Ibid. at 469, recommendations 81–84.
[140] Ibid. at 469, recommendation 86; also see *Khatib* v. *Ramco International* [2011] EWCA Civ 605; *Ryder Plc* v. *Dominic James Beever* [2012] EWCA Civ 1737; A. Higgins, 'The Costs of Case Management: what should be done post-Jackson' 29 (2010) *CJQ* 317.
[141] R. Jackson (December 2009) at 397.

the same wording in the Mark II overriding objective. If the second aspect of the recommendation had been implemented it would have been as disastrous in effect as *Lownds* had been. It would have focused relief from sanctions exclusively on the interests of the immediate litigants in the particular case. The interests of other court users that CPR r. 1.1(2)(e) required the court to consider would not simply have dropped from the picture; it would have been positively pushed out. The difficulty the court had pre-Jackson in focusing their attention on the effect of their decisions on other court users rather than simply considering the case in hand would have been resolved, albeit in the opposite way than it ought to have been. The proposed revision would have excluded the wider public interest from consideration. It would have focused the court's attention simply on the need to do justice in the immediate case, which would inevitably have led the court back to giving primacy to the need to secure substantive justice. It would, in practice, have codified the *Tildesley* test's focus on the need to secure the substantive merits in each case. It would consequently have done no more than reintroduce the problem of non-compliance.

If introduced as the Jackson Report intended, the revision to CPR r. 3.9 would have undone any positive effect calls for a stricter new approach to rule-compliance would have had in practice. It was, in fact, a recommendation that was entirely contrary to the spirit or intention of Woolf's new theory, as it gave no weight to the need to take account of justice to other court users, i.e. to the wider public interest in securing an equitable distribution of the justice system's resources across all court users. In the event, the Civil Procedure Rule Committee rejected this aspect of the recommendation. The rule as revised, rather than focusing on the interests of justice in the individual case, provided that the court had to consider the need to secure compliance with rules, practice directions and court orders.[142] A reform that would have undermined the operation of the rules and the overriding objective was enacted through a revision, so that it emphasised that compliance was the norm and would be treated as such when litigants sought to justify deviating from it.

By treating compliance as the norm, the post-Jackson version of r. 3.9 should, in principle, ensure each claim receives a fair share of the justice system's resources. Exhortation to take a stricter approach to compliance had in this way been replaced by a concrete reform which, as Zuckerman

---

[142] CPR r. 3.9(1)(b) (post-April 2013) (SI 262/2013).

has pointed out, due to the reference in the revised rule 3.9 to proportionate cost, leads the assessment of relief from sanctions back to a consideration of the overriding objective and its requirement to take account of the needs of other court users.[143] This is a positive step forward for the rules, as it reinforces the role that both aspects of proportionality have in case management. It does not, however, answer the fundamental problem regarding this aspect of proportionality. It does not answer the Bentham problem of how the court is effectively to take account of the needs of other court users. How is it to be given practical effect, so that effective rule compliance and a stricter approach to non-compliance can be taken? How, in other words, is it to be applied so that procedural rules and court orders designed to provide a reasonable and proportionate litigation timetable for each case, consistently with both aspects of proportionality, do not lose their normative force and collapse back into the RSC's substantive justice-based approach?

What is needed in order to deal with this issue is for a two-stage approach to be taken to questions of rule compliance and relief from sanctions so that collective proportionality can be accounted for effectively, and through that, no more than an equitable share of the justice system's resources are expended on each claim.[144] Where, for instance, there has been a failure to comply with a time limit, the first question the court should ask is if granting relief would result in the claim using more than proportionate resources as between it and other claims. The question of collective proportionality should have to be resolved first. It should, because individual justice, under the overriding objective, is limited by the need to secure distributive justice across all court users. This first stage of the test for relief should not, however, be taken as merely indicative of how the court should exercise its discretion, in the way that the *Lownds* test for proportionality in respect of costs had. If that were to be the case then, just as in *Lownds*, this aspect of proportionality would be given no more than lip service. The first test would have to be determinative if it was answered in the negative. In this way, a danger Zuckerman has identified as lying in the revised r. 3.9 could be averted. He noted how, through requiring the court to consider all the circumstances of the case as r. 3.9 does, in assessing whether it should grant relief the rule could allow applications to be determined on

---

[143] Zuckerman, 'The Revised CPR 3.9'.

[144] Also see Higgins, 'The Costs of Case Management', 333. Higgins also proposed a two-stage test, although it does not render this aspect the first question asked.

general and ill-defined grounds of justice... [which in] the absence of a clear standard [would allow] sympathy for a litigant ... as in the past [to] sway a court to forgive default, even if it disrupts the efficient determination of the case and even though it tends to undermine the binding force of case management directions.[145]

If that were to happen, the old road to toleration of default would have been taken, and with it, the effective and equitable distribution of the court's resources across all court users would continue to be frustrated. By focusing the primary question on the needs of other court users, as in *Hashtroodi* and *Hoddinott*, the need to secure their interests is not lost. It plays its proper role in determining the issue before the court. Only if the grant of relief was found not to breach collective proportionality would the court then go on to consider the question of individual proportionality along with the other elements of the overriding objective, i.e. efficiency, economy, expedition and substantive justice. Within this two-stage structure, which would take as its starting point the idea that compliance with reasonable and proportionate case management directions was the norm, the court would have to ask itself a number of practical questions viz.:[146]

Stage 1: Collective Proportionality – CPR r. 1.1(2)(e) and (f) and CPR r. 3.9(1)(b)

(1) The extent to which relief from sanctions would cause prejudice to other court users and the efficient use of court resources, 'that ... the just resolution of disputes is not limited to justice between the parties, but 'requires account to be taken of other litigants'.[147]

---

[145] Zuckerman 'The Revised CPR 3.9' at 137.

[146] Guidance on this respect, where a number of these questions were outlined, can be found in *Aon*. For a summary, see Lyons, 'Recasting the Landscape of Interlocutory Applications' at 557; and see *Mitchell* v. *News Group Newspapers Ltd* [2013] EWCA Civ 1537 at [38]–[39]. *Mitchell* did not, however, go as far as it needed to in making it absolutely clear that collective proportionality was the primary issue, albeit it did endorse Dyson, *The Application of the Amendments to the Civil Procedure Rules* at [27]. As such, it endorsed the point that collective proportionality was more important than individual proportionality, and hence ought to be considered first.

[147] *Mitchell* v. *News Group Newspapers Ltd* [2013[EWCA Civ 1537 at [41]: was the default, for instance, minor or trivial? In *Adlington* v. *ELS International Lawyers LLP* (2013, unreported) at [28]ff, relief was properly granted, following *Mitchell*, on, amongst other grounds, that the failure to comply with an unless order was, in the context of the litigation as a whole, trivial, where there had been a failure to serve seven out of 87 Particulars of Claim due to the claimants being unavailable to sign them in time for service.

To satisfy this aspect of the test, a litigant would have to show that the nature of the default was minimal in respect of the case management timetable set for its case. The greater the degree of amendment it required to that timetable, the greater the prejudice to other court users, i.e. the more collectively disproportionate it would be, as the case management timetable as originally set would have given concrete effect to equitable resource distribution.

(2) The need to secure public confidence in the justice system.

Public confidence rests on the ability to secure a fair distribution of resources across all litigants and the expeditious and efficient prosecution of claims in order to maximise the prospect that the court can carry out its constitutional role for the generality of the population. Both parties and the court under their duty to further the overriding objective are required to maintain confidence in the justice system, which includes complying with court rules, directions and order. Failure to do so on the part of a litigant is contrary to the interests of justice and, if public confidence is to be maintained in the court's ability to secure distributive justice and through it maintain the rule of law. The grant of relief should rest on cogent evidence, so that there was a clear case justifying the grant of the application. Relief from the consequences of non-compliance, amendments etc., as a consequence, should be granted in those exceptional circumstances where an applicant can demonstrate that there was a good reason that arose from circumstances beyond their control that gave rise to the situation occasioning the application.[148] Examples of such exceptional circumstances would be, for instance, illness, or other unforeseen circumstances.[149] Lawyer error would not amount to such circumstances.[150]

In order to satisfy Stage 1 of the test, an applicant would thus have to show that the default was no more than minimal in extent and arose from exceptional circumstances, such as those identified above. Rendering this stage a condition precedent to moving on to Stage 2 would ensure that the court could not lapse into finding that, because a trial on the merits was still possible, relief should be granted. It would

---

[148] *Mitchell v. News Group Newspapers Ltd* [2013] EWCA Civ 1537 at [41] and [43].

[149] Zuckerman, 'The Revised CPR 3.9' at 136; *Mitchell v. News Group Newspapers Ltd* [2013] EWCA Civ 1537 at [41].

[150] *Hashtroodi v. Hancock* [2004] 1 WLR 3206 at [35]; *Mitchell v. News Group Newspapers Ltd* [2013] EWCA Civ 1537 at [41].

thus stop substantive justice implicitly becoming the predominant factor in the assessment of relief, as was the case under the RSC and under the traditionalist approach to the overriding objective. This would not deny the role that substantive justice plays in the overriding objective; it would simply ensure that it was properly treated as one aspect of the wider concept of justice that Woolf's new theory had introduced.

Stage 2: Individual Proportionality – CPR r. 1.1(2)(c), CPR r. 3.9(1)(a) and CPR r. 44.3(5)

(1) Whether the delay and cost engendered by the circumstances giving rise to the application or from the application if granted was or would be disproportionate as between the parties in terms of the efficient and economical prosecution of the claim.
(2) Whether any prejudice caused to the respondent could be compensated by an award of costs, subject to the qualification that such indemnification did not render costs disproportionate contrary to CPR r. 44.3(5). Costs are no longer a panacea between the parties.
(3) The nature and importance of the application in terms of the duty to secure substantive justice.

In this regard it would have to be shown that the claim could not proceed to a trial and judgment absent the grant of relief. It would not be enough to show that the grant of relief, for instance, to permit evidence to be admitted, would increase the prospect that the court would be able to determine the claim on its substantive merits. It would have to be shown that absent the evidence, it would not be possible for the court to determine the claim at all.

To satisfy these elements, the applicant would have to demonstrate that if granted the application would not render litigation cost disproportionate as between the parties. As such, it could only exceptionally be justified if it required the trial date to be moved, as the trial date would ordinarily set the limit in time by which a claim could be prepared at reasonable and proportionate expense in order to be determined with reasonable expedition. Where, for instance, the application concerned a question arising from a failure to comply with obligations concerning evidence, e.g. exchange of evidence, it would have to be borne in mind that it is not the court's duty to arrive at a decision based on all potentially available evidence, but simply to adjudicate upon all the evidence that is properly before it.[151] Refusing to

---

[151] See Chapter 5, n. 22.

permit evidence to be led where there has been a breach of procedural rules is, in the light of the overriding objective and its commitment to proportionate justice, within the ambit of that general principle. It is, just as the limitations on evidence provided by the creation of the procedural case tracks and court control of evidence are, within its ambit.

If an approach such as this were applied to applications for relief from sanctions, to amend process or otherwise to permit a deviation from the provisions of case and cost management directions, for practical purposes the Bentham problem can be sidestepped. In particular, by focusing the test on the fact that the case management timetable itself sets out what a proportionate distribution of resources is in each particular case a template is given for assessing the nature of any deviation from it: the greater the deviation, the greater the departure from individual and collective proportionality and the lesser the prospect that relief should be granted. A practical test on these lines would give a clear rather than a 'coded' message to courts and litigants on how proportionality is to be applied in practice.[152] It would render it less of a 'chameleon' principle apt to change its colours, in the way that equity was said to vary like the size of each Lord Chancellor's foot.[153] Most importantly, it would frame the test for relief or amendment in a way that is comparable with the approach taken in *Tildesley*. It is relatively straightforward and provides a clear set of principles to apply. It also makes clear that the court must give primary weight to the need to secure equitable access to justice for all court users. It emphasises the paramountcy of distributive justice over individual justice, and that the latter is only achieved through the former. It does so, just as *Tildesley* emphasised that substantive justice under the RSC was superior to common law formalism.

Assuming the courts are able to develop and apply this test, and the *Mitchell* decision emphasising the central importance of wider public interests and highlighting the practical adverse consequences to litigants outside the immediate set of proceedings before the court and to the court itself only develops it and the idea of collective proportionality to a limited extent,[154] the Bentham problem regarding the application of

---

[152] Zuckerman, 'The Revised CPR 3.9' at 137; it would properly take the courts beyond the approach taken by, for instance, the High Court in *Venulum Property Investments Ltd* v. *Space Architecture Ltd & Others* [2013] EWHC 1242 (TCC), which does little more than apply the pre-Jackson CPR r. 3.9 test, while adding to it the requirement that a stricter approach to relief had to be taken.

[153] See n. 1 above; *Table Talk of John Selden* (ed. Pollock) (1927) at 43.

[154] *Mitchell* v. *News Group Newspapers Ltd* [2013] EWCA Civ 1537 at [39].

individual proportionality would remain. It is a problem of application that does not simply arise where a litigant wishes to depart in some way from the case management timetable. It is one that must be factored into that timetable in the first instance. The approach to this problem taken by the Jackson Reforms was to introduce a new procedural rule that would replace the *Lownds* test. It would not do so entirely retrospectively, as that test had done, as it was applied when costs were being assessed at the end of a claim. It was to guide the operation of costs management and cost budgeting.[155] Claims were to be managed prospectively by the court, and litigants, so that no more than individually proportionate costs would be authorised as potentially recoverable at the conclusion of the claim. In this way, a new culture of individual proportionality was to be embedded in the management of claims, rather than simply forming the backdrop to a retrospective consideration carried out post-judgment of what had been done during the course of the proceedings. The new proportionate costs rule was to achieve this by explaining what CPR r. 1.1(2)(c) and its reference to proportionality meant.[156] It specifically provided that costs would be proportionate if they bore a reasonable relationship to: the sums in issue in the proceedings; the value of any monetary relief sought; the complexity of the litigation; any additional work generated by the paying party's conduct; and any wider factors arising from the proceedings, such as reputation or public importance.[157] Without evident irony, it has been suggested that this new rule is simple and needs no explanation as to how it is meant to operate.[158] Its suggested simplicity was also said to promote certainty and avoid satellite litigation.[159] Lord Neuberger MR was not so sanguine on these points. While he took the view that it would be invidious to give guidance prior to the new rule coming into force, he fully anticipated that it would give

---

[155] Neuberger, *Proportionate Cost*; V. Ramsey, *Cost Management – a Necessary part of litigation culture* (16th Lecture in the Implementation Programme) (The Law Society, 29 May 2012) <http://www.judiciary.gov.uk/Resources/JCO/Documents/Speeches/costs-management-sixteenth-implementation-lecture-300512.pdf>.

[156] CPR r. 1.1(2)(c) and CPR r. 44.3(5) (post-April 2013); R. Jackson (December 2009) at 27–40.

[157] CPR r. 44.3(5) (post-April 2013).

[158] R. Jackson, *Technical Aspects of Implementation* (3rd Lecture in the Implementation Programme) (31 October 2011) (Civil Justice Council Conference) at [2.1] <http://www.judiciary.gov.uk/Resources/JCO/Documents/Speeches/lj-jackson-third-lecture-implementation-programme-31102011.pdf>.

[159] Ibid. at [2.3].

rise to satellite litigation.[160] It is difficult to see how the new rule can properly be defined as simple, not least because properly simple concepts do not give rise to the prospect of detailed satellite litigation concerning their meaning and application as Lord Neuberger MR envisaged. This should be particularly obvious given that just like the overriding objective itself, the proportionate costs rule sets out a number of open-textured concepts, without any suggestion as to how they might be applied in any particular case, how they might relate to each other, or how they might relate to the other aspects of the overriding objective's requirements. Proportionality is only one aspect of the overriding objective, after all. Moreover, as Zuckerman has rightly pointed out, the factors in the new rule provide no real basis to assess proportionality in any event as, just like the *Lownds* test, they present an opportunity for the litigants and their lawyers to influence in their favour issues of value, complexity and whatever wider issues they might be able to render plausible.[161] Even where they do not attempt to take advantage of the nature of the test, the absence of guidance renders it difficult for litigants, and courts conducting case and cost management, to reasonably assess the relative weight and merits of the factors as they apply to a particular claim. It is a recipe for detailed, hard-fought, time-consuming and expensive procedural applications and cost management hearings where the litigants contest each of the elements of the new rule. It is a recipe for individual and collective disproportionality.

If the new proportionate costs rule is to work and not itself to become a source of both forms of disproportionately, guidance will either have to be given or it will have to be truly simplified to remove its open-textured nature. There is no reason in principle that guidance could not be formulated. The Civil Justice Council, for instance, prepared partial guidance prior to the introduction of the Jackson Reforms.[162] Examples given to flesh out the aspects of the rule were, for instance, that wider issues under CPR r. 44.3(5)(e) might include whether the claim is a test case, whether it involves issues of foreign law or multiple parties. There is no reason why such guidance could not be fully developed in order to

---

[160] Neuberger, *Proportionate Cost*, at [15].

[161] A. Zuckerman, 'The Jackson Final Report – Plastering over the Cracks to Shore Up a Dysfunctional System' 3 (2010) *CJQ* 263, 275.

[162] Civil Justice Council, *Report of the Civil Justice Council Working Party on Technical Aspects of Jackson Implementation* (October 2011) at 31–2 <http://www.judiciary.gov.uk/JCO%2fDocuments%2fCJC%2fCJC±Working±Group±on±Technical±Aspects±of±Jackson±Implementation.pdf>.

render the rule more concrete and capable of consistent, practical application. The alternate approach, and one that commends itself on grounds of simplicity, is one that revises the rule so that, as a general rule, it links individual proportionality to the value of the claim.[163] Litigants would then know from the outset the maximum recoverable costs, should their claim succeed: i.e. a claim for £50,000 would provide for a maximum £15,000 recoverability from the paying party.[164] Bentham's solution to his problem of ascribing value would thus be applied straightforwardly to the proportionate cost rule. It would be applied through what would in essence be a fixed recoverable cost regime. This would not stop litigants expending more than the limit. They would, as under CPR r. 44.3(5) as it stands at the present time, do so in the knowledge that it would be irrecoverable from the paying party. Equally, the court would be in a better position to carry out its assessment at the first case management conference of whether and to what extent the directions sought bore a reasonable relationship to the level of proportionate costs applicable to the claim. It would then be in a better position to carry out its costs budgeting and costs management role efficiently and economically. In this, it would beneficially go beyond the position under the present rule, which will of necessity engender detailed time-consuming discussion of the proper approach to take to managing the specific claim. The rule would have been given practical utility and be capable of consistent application. What cannot properly be done, however, is for the rule to remain as it is on the face of the CPR, bereft of the ability to be applied simply, straightforwardly and, if it is ultimately to play a proper role to secure collective proportionality, consistently across all claims.

7.6 Conclusion

It is one thing to introduce a new theory of justice. It is another thing entirely to ensure it can be and is implemented. The Woolf Reforms succeeded in doing the former. They were unable to secure the latter. The Jackson Reforms were a second attempt to secure effective implementation. In this regard, to a certain extent they were limited, as their predominant focus was one aspect of the new theory of justice – the application of individual proportionality. If the Woolf Reforms are

---

[163] Zuckerman, 'The Revised CPR 3.9'; J. Sorabji, 'Prospects for Proportionality: Jackson Implementation' 32 (2012) CJQ 213, 227.
[164] Zuckerman, 'The Jackson Final Report'.

ultimately to succeed in transforming English litigation culture, it will be necessary, post-Jackson, for the courts to tackle four issues concerning the new theory of justice. They will have to ensure that it is properly understood; that attempts to reject it are overturned; that its consequences for case and costs management are properly understood and implemented; and that the concepts of individual and collective proportionality are rendered capable of practical application. In doing so, lessons will have to be learnt from the process of law reform carried out in the nineteenth century, as well as from the manner in which Woolf-related reforms in other jurisdictions have been implemented successfully. Most importantly, perhaps, it will require concerted, long-term effort on the part of the judiciary to implement the reforms properly. A heavy duty lies on them to do so if, as the Woolf Reforms intended, they are to secure a justice system that can, within limited resources, secure effective access to justice and through it, vindication of rights and the rule of law, for the generality of court users rather than the few. If the issues raised in this chapter are dealt with as suggested, and specifically if the approach taken by the Court of Appeal in *Mitchell* forms the starting point of a consistent line of authority that is then developed in the way described above, there is a prospect that the new theory may be implemented successfully and that the courts will operate consistently with the aim of securing proportionate justice. If not, the likelihood is that the problems will remain unresolved, case management will slip back, as it did post-1999, into the habits that were the inevitable consequence of the RSC's theory of justice, cost management will be ineffective for the same reason, as it will be applied with the predominant aim being to secure substantive justice, and consequently, litigation will continue to be carried out at disproportionate cost both to litigants and the State. The consequence of that will be an inability to secure the equitable provision of justice to all court users, which will ultimately undermine public confidence in the courts and the rule of law.

Conclusion

the public interest in the due administration of justice necessarily extends to ensuring that the Court's processes are used fairly by State and citizen alike. And the due administration of justice is a continuous process, not confined to the determination of the particular case. It follows that in exercising its inherent jurisdiction the Court is protecting its ability to function as a Court of law in the future as in the case before it.[1]

In 1980, in *Moevao* v. *Department of Labour,* New Zealand's Court of Appeal considered the public interest in the administration of justice. In doing so, it identified a feature of it that is often, unconsciously, overlooked: that it is a continuous process, which goes beyond the interests of the litigants in any one particular case. To carry out its constitutional duty properly, a court dealing with one claim must consider the effect of its decisions on other claims. The traditional, RSC, theory of justice focused predominantly on the needs of individual litigants. Justice was done if substantive justice in the individual case was achieved. The collective benefit to society that arose from public confidence in the courts and securing the rule of law was believed to arise as a consequence of this. This theory was, however, flawed. Due to focusing predominantly on the need to secure justice in the individual case, it produced the perverse situation where the rules of court, which were intended if applied properly to secure substantive justice, could not achieve that end.

The Woolf Reforms accepted that the traditional theory was flawed, and that by focusing exclusively on the need to secure justice in the individual case, the justice system was unable to provide a reasonable guarantee that that aim was achievable for the majority of litigants. It could not, because through denuding the rules of court of normative value, it gave rise to excessive amounts of procedural litigation, which in turn led to excess cost and delay. This undermined both the court's

---

[1] [1980] 1 NZLR 464 at 481.

ability to secure substantive justice in reasonable time and at reasonable cost to individual litigants, but because it resulted in the disproportionate use of the court's resources by some litigants, others were effectively denied an equitable opportunity to gain access to the courts. In order to overcome these problems, which had been endemic since the justice system was subject to fundamental reform in the 1870s, a new theory of justice was to be introduced. This new theory would reject the idea that achieving substantive justice in the individual case was the justice system's predominant policy aim. It was to be downgraded. This was in order to ensure that no single claim could utilise more than an equitable share of the justice system's resources. The administration of justice went beyond the needs of the individual case. Justice could in fact only properly be realised through rationing access to it, by ensuring that the court's resources were distributed fairly across all court users. In that way, the justice system could maximise the prospect that it could vindicate rights, maintain public confidence in the courts and in their ability to secure the rule of law. Rationing had a purpose. It was to ensure that individual justice was realised through providing effective distributive justice.

Woolf's new theory of justice, which the Jackson Reforms were required to find better ways to implement, achieved its purpose by placing a limit on substantive justice. It was to be balanced by a new, equal commitment to traditional concepts of procedural justice: econ-omy; efficiency; expedition; equality; and proportionality. The former two aspects of procedural justice were intended to ensure that substantive justice was achieved at minimal cost and in minimal time. They were thus a means by which the achievement of substantive justice was to be facilitated. In this, the new theory went no further than that which had been in place under the RSC. Woolf's new theory went beyond the traditional, RSC approach, through its commitment to equality and proportionality. They placed a limit on substantive justice, in the same way that for Bentham the reductive role played by justice's collateral ends placed a limit on it. Equality requires an equitable distribution of the court's resources across all court users: access to justice is a right that is held indivisibly by all citizens. Where the justice system necessarily has limited resources, if that right is to be realised, individual claims cannot be permitted an inequitable share of those resources. Focusing on the individual claim so that it consequently, even if unintentionally, obtains more than an equitable share of those resources, means they are not available to other court users who also need to gain access to the courts in order to vindicate their rights. Only through securing such an equitable distribution of resources can the court fulfil its duty of securing the rule of law. Proportionality is the means by which an equitable distribution of those resources is achieved. Individual claims are to be permitted to utilise a proportionate share of the justice system's resources: collective proportionality. Equally, in order to ensure that substantive justice is not obtained at a cost greater than the benefit to the individuals concerned, individuals are to be limited in the amount they can expend on prosecuting their claim: individual proportionality. This aspect of proportionality, if properly applied, would equally ensure, through limiting what is spent on claims, that collective proportionality could not be infringed. Through this, equality and proportionality place a break on the nature and amount of civil process that can be expended on individual claims. They reduce the time that can be spent on litigation. They provide the basis for limiting the amount of evidence that can be obtained. They place a break on the disclosure process, for instance. As such, they limit and reduce the court's ability to secure substantive justice. In some cases this arises because the court has less evidence before it on which to find true fact and apply it to right law. In other cases it arises because the court must refuse to permit a claim to go forward to trial and judgment. Such consequences would have been antipathetic to the RSC's theory of justice and its commitment to securing substantive justice. Under Woolf's new theory, such consequences are an inherent aspect of it. It is a theory of proportionate, not substantive, justice.

This book has explored the nature of that theory, and how it goes beyond the traditional RSC theory. It has done so by reference to a previous reform of a similar nature in the nineteenth century, one that was successful. It has also done so by reference to a theory of justice developed by Bentham; a theory to which Woolf's new theory is consistent, in that they both temper the commitment to substantive justice through adopting a wider policy aim to which it is rendered subordinate. If this new theory is to be successfully implemented, it will need to be properly understood. It will then need to be explained, accepted and applied as consistently over a long period of time just as the Victorians did when they implemented the RSC's theory of justice. The experience of the first decade of the Woolf Reforms' implementation saw the Court of Appeal fail to take the Victorian approach to implementation. If the Jackson Reforms, which mark a second attempt to implement that new theory, are to succeed, the Victorian approach to reform will have to be followed: in this regard, the Court of Appeal's approach in *Mitchell* v. *News Group Newspapers Ltd* is a starting point in the same way that *Tildesley* was in the nineteenth century and *Aon* was in Australia. More will be needed on the Court of Appeal's part following these two decisions if the reforms are to succeed as the 1870 reforms succeeded. If it fails to act with the clarity and consistency of its Victorian predecessor, the Court of Appeal will, as it did following the Woolf Reforms' implementation in 1999, fail to ensure that a new theory of justice will govern the operation of the civil justice system. If it fails in this way, there is little hope that the Woolf and Jackson Reforms will ultimately succeed in their aim of reducing litigation complexity, cost and delay whilst better securing justice for the many. They will fail and, for instance, case and cost management will fail to produce the intended benefits in that regard, because they will operate so as to secure substantive justice and not proportionate justice. The end sets the way in which the means operate. If the ends of justice are not understood to have changed, then the way in which the means to those ends operate will not change. It is only if the courts start to manage cases consistently with the new theory, and in doing so accept that it properly requires the denial of substantive justice in some cases and the reduction in the quality of justice in others, that they will be able to protect their ability to function as courts of law in all cases,[2] rather than only in some. Only then will the revolution in civil justice that the Woolf Reforms attempted to introduce, and the Jackson Reforms continued, be accepted and succeed. It remains an open question, though, whether they will or whether, as in the nineteenth century, at least three attempts will have to be made before that can happen.

[2] Ibid.

INDEX

Note: Court cases and documents are in italics.

009669542